GAME WARDEN

GAME WARDEN

On PATROL in LOUISIANA

JERALD HORST

LOUISIANA STATE UNIVERSITY PRESS
BATON ROUGE

Published by Louisiana State University Press
Copyright © 2010 by Louisiana State University Press
All rights reserved
Manufactured in Canada
First printing

Designer: Laura Roubique Gleason
Typefaces: Minion Pro text, News Gothic display
Printer and binder: Friesens Corporation

Library of Congress Cataloging-in-Publication Data
Horst, Jerald.
  Game warden : on patrol in Louisiana / Jerald Horst.
      p. cm.
  ISBN 978-0-8071-3704-8 (cloth : alk. paper) 1. Wildlife conservation—
Louisiana—Anecdotes. 2. Game wardens—Louisiana—Anecdotes.
3. Poaching—Louisiana—Prevention—Anecdotes. I. Title.
  SK401.H67 2010
  363.28—dc22

                    2010019743

Sea Grant
Louisiana State University

Published with support from the Louisiana Sea Grant College Program,
a part of the National Sea Grant College Program maintained by
the National Oceanic and Atmospheric Administration of the U.S.
Department of Commerce.

This book is dedicated to the memory of those Louisiana game wardens who have been killed in the line of duty:

Frank E. Fagot Jr. (1927)

Kenneth Dale Aycock (1991)

Ricky Dodge (1992)

Leon "Buddy" Henderson Jr. (1996)

John M. Garlington (2000)

Jim Robyn Bennet Matkin (2005)

CONTENTS

FOREWORD

About forty-five years ago a small boy and his grandfather were out for an early fall squirrel hunt when they were approached by a lone horseman. He rode up, dismounted, and spoke to my grandfather for a few minutes, then remounted and rode away.

I thought him quite a dashing figure and asked Papa who he was. "That was the game warden," he replied, and went on to explain a little about what this lone horseman did for a living. I was hooked then and there and knew what I would do when I grew up.

In 1977, after going to college and working in the private sector, I applied to the Department [Louisiana Department of Wildlife and Fisheries], was accepted, and was given a job with a law enforcement commission. I was stationed in Avoyelles Parish, near two newly purchased wildlife management areas.

Not long after beginning my career, it came to my attention that the Department owned a couple of horses. They were located at the Saline (now Dewey W. Wills) Wildlife Management Area. I requested that those mounts be assigned to me, got the approval, and brought them home.

That hunting season found me patrolling from horseback in some very remote backcountry. Quite a few wildlife offenders got a big surprise—along with a summons to court—in those days. Had the Good Lord called me up right then, I would have died a happy man.

As far as I am concerned, this is still the best job in the world. The demands are great, but so are the experiences, training, and opportunities offered to those fortunate chosen few who become wildlife enforcement agents. It is a way of life, and those who view it simply as a job or feel it is no different than any other police work won't stay with it very long. But in truth, resignations are rare and, unlike the majority of police officers in other fields of law enforcement, game wardens stay on the job far beyond the first date of eligibility for retirement. It is just too much fun to quit, *if* you are cut out for it.

When Jerald came to the office to propose this book, I knew it was something that needed doing. We have so many adventures, tragedies, fascinating cases, and funny stories that need to be told and recorded. Hunting and fishing, the deer camps in north Louisiana, the duck camps in the marsh, and the fishing camps on the coasts, rivers, and lakes are all so much of what makes Louisiana great.

The wildlife agent is such a part of the history, lore, and legend of the outdoors that a night will seldom go by without a "game warden story" being told around the campfire.

This book is our opportunity to capture those stories straight from the men who lived them. It is my sincere hope that in doing so we provide insight into why we love what we do and why wildlife officers are so dedicated to the protection of fish and wildlife.

Lieutenant Colonel Keith LaCaze
Assistant Chief of Law Enforcement
Louisiana Department of Wildlife and Fisheries

ACKNOWLEDGMENTS

I have many people to thank for their help with this book. First is Senior Agent Scott Dupre, a Louisiana Department of Wildlife and Fisheries game warden. It was during a discussion after he made a routine stop of me during waterfowl season that the seed was planted in my mind for this book.

The book also would not have happened without the blessing and cooperation of Colonel Winton Vidrine, Lieutenant Colonel Keith LaCaze, and Lieutenant Colonel Jeff Mayne, the three senior officers of the Enforcement Division of the Louisiana Department of Wildlife and Fisheries. I am grateful to all three men. Very special thanks are extended to Lieutenant Colonel LaCaze, because he shared my vision most closely and was my guiding light during the entire process, most especially in clearing the way for my time in the field with the division's game wardens.

I owe a great debt of gratitude to every game warden with whom I rode. I anticipated encountering a "green wall," similar to the fabled "blue wall" of other law enforcement agencies. Instead, I was greeted openly and warmly. I can honestly say that I have never met a finer group of people.

I am very grateful to Ginger Corkern, who worked diligently as my proofreader and critic. Thanks are also extended to my wife, Glenda, who provided invaluable assistance to me in hammering the manuscript into final shape and managing the images that I accumulated during the course of my work on the book.

Lastly, and strange as it may sound, I would like to extend a note of thanks to the Nikon Corporation. Clambering up and down the rocky sides of north Louisiana hills and jumping in and out of boats was rough on my cameras. I constantly had damaged equipment—shattered housings, busted lenses, and scrunched speedlights—in for repair or replacement. Nikon kept me working.

GAME WARDEN

Steve Baker, an early Terrebonne Parish game warden, displays a market hunter's shotgun that has been modified to hold ten shells. *Courtesy Gerald Adkins.*

INTRODUCTION

This book is my effort to tell the story of fish and wildlife enforcement in Louisiana through the actions and voices of those engaged in the mission. The work of fish and wildlife enforcement agents, not just in Louisiana but in the whole country, may be the least understood branch of law enforcement. Some view it as a second-tier job, with narrowly defined responsibilities limited to catching violators of fish and wildlife management laws. Others view the job as one created solely to interfere with their happiness while they enjoy the great outdoors or while they wrest their living from the waters of the state. This view may be jaundiced, but it is more prevalent than one might think.

Neither characterization is accurate. Enforcement agents of the modern Louisiana Department of Wildlife and Fisheries are fully empowered to enforce not only fish and wildlife laws, but also all other laws in the criminal code of the state of Louisiana, including, but not limited to, those dealing with violence, drugs, traffic, and littering. Additionally, Louisiana game wardens are empowered to enforce most federal fish and wildlife laws, and do so routinely in the waters of the United States offshore of Louisiana territorial waters.

The Enforcement Division of the Louisiana Department of Wildlife and Fisheries also carries significant responsibilities as the lead search-and-rescue agency in the state. This responsibility includes the charge to react in the case of natural disasters, such as hurricanes, an ever-present threat to the state.

Hunters and fishermen, both recreational and commercial, view game wardens with fascination, tinged with a modest dollop of fear. The fascination has much to do with the perception that game wardens work in stealth at all hours and under adverse weather conditions that outdoors people themselves recognize as challenging.

Fear—the fear of being caught—is the dominant emotion felt by the small percentage of those in the outdoors who deliberately violate fish and wildlife laws. The fear factor among law-abiding hunters and fishermen, on the other hand, has its genesis in the sneaking suspicion that somewhere out there an obscure or new regulation exists that they may inadvertently violate. Laws pertaining to hunting and fishing are complex and become ever more so each year.

Before 1908, the work of enforcing fish and wildlife laws in the state of Louisiana fell to people commonly called "conservation men." Not trained as law officers, the duties of these people included all the responsibilities associated with fish and wildlife conservation and management of the day.

In 1908, the Board of Commissioners for the Protection of Birds, Game and Fish was created and vested with the power to appoint game wardens. The importance of the "Warden Service" was evident from the controversy surrounding how its members were appointed. The large majority of parishes had only one such warden appointed to them.

Until the last few decades, game wardens were relatively poorly equipped, with each agent having to supply his own vehicle and sidearm. Training and equipment have advanced light years when compared to what the force once had.

The story of this elite group of men and women was written during 2008 and 2009, while I rode with enforcement agents in the course of performing their duties from the piney woods of north Louisiana out to the blue waters of the Gulf of Mexico. Their stories are presented through my eyes and, except for the numerous quotes, my words. I was an outsider looking in.

1

BREAKING ME IN

On the road north to the Region 2 LDWF Enforcement office, I struggle to get my mind around the magnitude of the challenge to which I have committed myself. I know there is a story here, particularly if told from behind the badge. The public, especially those who fish and hunt, is fascinated by the work of game wardens. But how will I be received? Is there an invisible wall in law enforcement that I can't penetrate? Am I good enough to tell the story?

My apprehension isn't eased by the weather. It is brooding—one of those misty, nasty, drizzling days that characterize what winter is like in Louisiana.

I feel a little more at ease after meeting Captain Alan Bankston, who is in charge of the region. My concerns must be apparent because, with a big grin, he encourages me to "just dive in there." After he lays out what plans he has for me, riding along with his enforcement agents over the next four days, he introduces me to Senior Agent Scott Jeansonne.

We jump in Jeansonne's massive three-quarter-ton, four-wheel-drive Dodge Ram pickup truck. Jeansonne looks like what a law enforcement officer should look like, fairly tall and muscular with a perfectly shaved head. But he packs a big grin.

As we roll out, heading toward Union Parish, I look around me in amazement. I feel like I am in a rolling arsenal. On his gun belt, Jeansonne carries as his sidearm a .45 caliber Sig Sauer semi-automatic pistol. Within ready reach is a 12-gauge Remington 870 police shotgun. Also at arm's length is a .223 caliber Sig Sauer semi-automatic assault rifle. All are loaded.

Besides the tools of deadly force, each agent is equipped, I learn, with Freeze Plus pepper spray, an expandable metal baton, handcuffs, a police flashlight, a GPS unit, binoculars, a Leatherman multi-tool, a digital camera, body armor, an inflatable life jacket, hip boots, and in some cases night vision optics.

A .45 caliber Sig Sauer is the standard game warden sidearm.

Sig Sauer assault rifles were added to game wardens' arsenals during the Hurricane Katrina emergency.

Jeansonne's truck carries no shortage of communication equipment. Front and center is the LDWF-issued police radio, which provides contact with the department's dispatch office. Each agent also carries a portable version of the same radio. Many agents also carry special police radios issued by the sheriff's offices in the parishes they work in. In some cases, though, their most used communications tools are their personal cell phones. And sometimes all of them are in use at once.

A variety of communications equipment is found in the typical truck.

Jeansonne has six years' experience in the department, the first three of which were in New Orleans, a long way from Tioga, where he grew up as one of six brothers. Becoming a game warden was a natural choice for him, as he claims that growing up, hunting and fishing were all he knew and the college degree he got from the University of Louisiana at Monroe was in criminology.

By 3 p.m. we are near Union Parish, Jeansonne's turf. He says that we will hit some spots where "knuckleheads" that like to violate game laws like to hunt. The first stop is near Bayou de Loutre, where hunters may be tempted to shoot wood ducks as they come in to their roosting spots after legal hunting hours.

The red gravel road on the way into the spot he wants to set up on is absolutely littered with deer skeletons. Jeansonne has to weave his truck around the picked-over rib cages and skulls. It looks like a graveyard.

Catching my concerned look, he explains that these are hunter discards and an almost routine way of doing business in the area, even though it isn't legal. "The hunters think that if they put the animals' carcasses or guts where they hunt, they will attract coyotes and run the deer out." So they dump them on a remote public road.

Jeansonne stands outside the truck during a break in the drizzle and listens patiently. Nothing. Not a shot. After 4 p.m., he gets a little antsy and wants to try another duck roosting spot, Little Corney Brake, part of a creek system that feeds Lake D'Arbonne.

On the way, the misting rain returns. Then Jeansonne's Union Parish Sheriff's Office police radio crackles to life. The dispatcher alerts Jeansonne to be on the lookout for a maroon truck that is pulling a trailer with an ATV on board. A complainant reported that the truck's occupants shot a deer off the road, a violation.

Jeansonne spins his truck around and heads south. He and the deputy are in constant radio contact, trying to hem the truck in. At 5 p.m. the dep-

The road looked like a deer graveyard.

Scott Jeansonne stands outside of his truck to better hear gunshots.

uty has the truck stopped. Jeansonne pulls up shortly after, with the blue light bar on his truck lit up.

They question the forty-year-old man, who has his three-year-old daughter in tow. His story is that he filled his deer feeder and spotted some deer on the way home. He turned his truck around to show the girl the deer.

Jeansonne smells the rifle to see if it has been recently fired. After a few more questions he and the deputy tell the man that he is free to go and wish him well.

Back in the truck, Jeansonne explains that half the calls they get are without basis. "Some are folks just trying to do well. But you never know when you will get that good call that will make a big case."

As he cruises the smaller roads, he periodically flicks on his alley lights, spotlights that illuminate the fields and woods alongside the road. What he is looking for are deer "to set up on." If he finds deer, he will pull into an obscure spot from which he can watch the area and wait for someone who may shoot at them with the assistance of a spotlight.

"You need to find a place to set up pretty quickly," he says. "If you ride around too much, violators may see you, plus you can't hear shots well while the vehicle is rolling."

He picks a spot where, the previous night, a hunter who had finished his hunt had seen someone from the road shining a spotlight over the area. In the light mist Jeansonne rolls his truck windows down to hear better, and then moves to stand outside the truck so as not to miss a sound.

The mist turns into a rather serious fog. Jeansonne gets back into the truck and grumps that foggy nights are bad for shining activity. Fog reduces visibility and also muffles the sound of gunshots.

Cars pass on the road constantly, but nothing suspicious occurs. "Lots of folks around here just ride around all night without a gun," he says. "Then when they see a deer they want, they go home and get a gun."

In the inky blackness he muses, "Someone, somewhere in Union Parish, is shooting a deer. That's a fact."

He goes on, "My only allies are the public and the sheriff's office. Game wardens are pretty much lone rangers. We work alone except in boats, when we try to pair up."

At 8:30 p.m. he says, "Let's go see new scenery, move to a different spot." We move to an area near the city limits of Monroe. He flicks his alley light on often, still looking for deer. He picks a spot that he calls "a hotspot for shining," and backs well down a small gravel road.

After patiently sitting and listening for an hour or so, Jeansonne says, almost apologetically, "It's pretty quiet up here Monday through Thursday. Friday, lots of them go drinking. They hunt Saturday, then go to church on Sunday." Today is a Thursday.

Shortly after 10 p.m. a white pickup truck pulls onto the small road we are on and catches us in his headlights. "We're busted," sighs Jeansonne, who starts his truck for another move.

The fog becomes thicker and thicker, until Jeansonne finally calls it a night. My head is spinning with information as the hunt quietly ends.

2

THAT MAN IN THE DARK

Day One: The Boogeyman

Sergeant Wayne Parker lives in Lake Providence, about as far northeast as one can get and still be in Louisiana. Originally from a farm family, Parker still loves farming, and being outdoors, but he decided early in his life that he couldn't depend on farming.

He went to college at the University of Louisiana–Monroe, got his degree in criminal justice, and began looking for a job where he could be outdoors as the seasons changed. At twenty-five he found it, as a wildlife agent for the Enforcement Division of the Louisiana Department of Wildlife and Fisheries.

Now thirty-six and assigned to East Carroll Parish, Parker works that parish as well as West Carroll, Morehouse, and Richland parishes. Today, our patrol is to start in Richland Parish.

The patrol begins with a bang. As I follow him on I-20 to a secure drop-off point for my vehicle, an erratically driven out-of-state vehicle slams itself between our trucks and tailgates Parker, leaving less than half a vehicle length between them. For a while, it doesn't pass.

When it does, Parker flicks on the blue lights on the big black Dodge Ram and pulls the mud-splattered vehicle to the shoulder. Few know that Louisiana game wardens are trained and fully empowered to write traffic tickets. However, Parker lets the contrite driver go with a stern warning.

Once I'm in his truck, Parker explains the day's plans. Starting in the early afternoon we will cruise the roads looking for deer, geese, or other wildlife visible from the road. If we find such wildlife, we'll set up in a hidden spot to put the area under surveillance for road shooters.

Parker explains that we will stay away from deer hunting areas in the early and mid-afternoon to avoid alerting potential violators of our presence. Only after the hunters go to their stands at 3:00 or 3:30 p.m. will we check likely vehicles to decide which one to set up on.

Parker explains that at the height of hunting season he will often have a choice of many vehicles to target. To pick the one most likely to violate, he says he tries to "get in the mind" of the vehicle's owner.

"I will usually go for a young guy with offensive bumper stickers and a sloppy truck. Where the truck is located and whether the hunter has made an attempt to hide it is also considered."

What he says he would rather not do is sneak up on someone in the hunting stand. "That's a good way to get accidentally shot. At very least you mess up the hunt for a legitimate hunter. I prefer to let them come to me."

After checking the hunter when he returns to his vehicle, we will place under surveillance another area where illegal night hunters are likely to misbehave. That is the plan, if everything goes according to plan.

Parker studies a detailed map of the area, planning where to be by sunset, the end of legal shooting time. Agents, he explains, have different methods of working, but the need is always there to work aggressively.

Richland Parish is mostly flat, rural farmland. Some areas are too low to farm and have flooded timber. But most of what isn't being actively farmed is enrolled in CRP, the Conservation Reserve Program, which pays farmers to let farmland lie fallow—ideal habitat for wildlife as the land grows up in vegetation.

Richland Parish is also, after days of constant rain, a sea of mud. The fields are muddy, the woods are muddy, and the roads are muddy. The truck is seldom out of four-wheel-drive mode.

As Parker crawls along the sloppy roads, his head never stops moving. He is constantly surveying his surroundings for anything out of the ordinary. Periodically he stops the truck and listens intently for gunshots.

As he hunts, he talks about his job. "I am always aware of litter and DWI. If I see a garbage bag, I put my gloves on and look in it." What he is looking for is an envelope or a prescription medicine bottle with a name on it.

Parker goes on talking about his job. "A lot of judgment is called for in this job. Not everything is as black and white as it seems. But that doesn't mean everything is gray," he quickly adds.

"The most rewarding thing about this job," he says passionately, "is the satisfaction of apprehending violators, especially career outlaws. Career violators are a problem because they teach their 'students,' who admire them, to violate."

Parker stops frequently to listen for shots. And his binoculars seem to

Wayne Parker patrols through a sea of mud after days of constant rain.

always be in his hands. He turns off a nearly impassable road and onto a smaller, even worse one. The big truck seems to be swimming as much as rolling.

At a slightly better spot on the road, he halts the vehicle behind a hunter clad in orange who is unloading his gear into a dual-wheel wheelbarrow. Parker had seen the man's SUV traveling on the road ahead of us before we got there. Parker greets him openly and the hunter approaches the officer's truck window. The man seems friendly, although he seems to have a slight speech impediment. He repeatedly mentions his involvement with a prominent youth organization.

The conversation seems innocent enough, with Parker asking questions that don't seem to be going anywhere in particular. Spying a "for sale" sign on the vehicle's windshield, Parker asks if he can look at the vehicle, which has all its doors open. At that point, I suspect Parker isn't interested in buying a very used sport-utility vehicle. But the hunter doesn't.

Lying exposed on the backseat is a half-empty fifth of vodka. That, coupled with the slurred speech, gives Parker cause to ask him if he has been drinking. "A couple," the hunter squirms in reply.

"Where are the empties?" Parker asks. The man thinks a bit, then replies that he threw them out on the road. Case closed—or not.

Scrutinizing the man's face and behavior closely, Parker asks him if he really didn't have more than a couple of drinks. The subject volunteers that in addition to drinking he had been taking prescription medicine because of depression.

When Parker asks him to take a field sobriety test, the man freely agrees. Asked to repeat a portion of the alphabet, he concentrates intensely and gets it out. The other parts of the field sobriety test—the horizontal nystagmus test, the walk and turn test, and the one leg stand test—he fails completely. In fact, he is only saved from falling flat by Parker's catching him at one point. Things get tense. Parker tells him that more is going on than what he is admitting.

"Where is it?" Parker asks firmly, to which the man replies, "What?" Parker looks him in the eye and says, "You know what."

"It's in the pouch on the passenger door," he says resignedly. "What is it?" asks Parker. "Marijuana," is his reply. Parker asks for permission to search the vehicle, which is given. The officer then retrieves a snap-lid plastic container holding marijuana and also finds a bong.

The subject then refuses further cooperation and Parker arrests and handcuffs him, then calls another wildlife agent for transport. Agent Josh Estis quickly arrives and the subject is assisted into Estis's truck.

The two vehicles proceed to the Richland Parish jail, where the man is

The hunter's marijuana and a bong were found in his vehicle.

When the hunter refuses further cooperation, Parker is left with no choice but arrest him.

booked with driving while intoxicated, simple possession of marijuana, and simple littering. At the jail, the subject states that he will not take a Breathalyzer test. Parker slowly and carefully explains the consequences of refusing to take the Breathalyzer test. The subject repeatedly refuses to blow.

The lengthy arrest aborts the evening's plan to set up on deer hunters, so the two game wardens and I share supper at a truck stop near Rayville before splitting to set up for night hunters.

As we eat, Parker talks about night hunting activity. "Night hunting is busy Thursday through Sunday. Thursday night at 11 p.m. seems to be a peak—probably with folks that have plans for the weekend. I've made more night hunting cases that night than any other night," he says. "On Fridays, activity picks up after high school football games. Then, Sunday at 10 p.m. is another peak." Parker has it down to a science.

After we leave the restaurant and while fueling the big truck up, he carefully cleans the windows—twice. Then, with his pocketknife, he scrapes the day's mud off his outside mirrors. He wants a completely unobstructed view for night surveillance.

When we near Hatche's Bend, where he plans to set up, he takes great pains to remain unobserved. He momentarily flicks the high beams on his headlights to obscure the vision of an on-coming driver just enough that the driver can't see the huge LDWF decals on the doors of his truck. Then he blacks out his tail and brake lights. When the other car disappears into the night he turns off his headlights and eases down a dirt track.

In the utter blackness of a moonless night, far from any city lights, Parker guides the truck down the trail as if he has radar in his head. I can see exactly nothing. On boggy terrain, he parks the lumbering behemoth and rolls the windows down. It's black, and it's quiet.

I have no bearings until a car's headlights passing on the road reveal that Parker has positioned himself to overlook a vast green field of wheat, a treat for hungry deer.

As we sit quietly in the cool, dark night, Parker explains to me in a low voice that this kind of work can be very rewarding when it pays off, but that a wildlife agent can spend long hours with nothing happening. "It can be monotonous—always thinking that you should be someplace else."

He is not just watching; he is listening. "A high-powered rifle shot can be heard for five miles," he explains.

After sitting quietly for two hours, Parker murmurs, "The wildlife agent is that man in the dark that no one knows is there."

He strikes up a conversation about wildlife law enforcement. "Like other police organizations, wildlife agents are a brotherhood. If others run down a wildlife agent, I will stand in defense of him until I learn different.

The wildlife agent is that man in the dark that no one knows is there.

"But," he chuckles, "there is a little bit of rivalry between us. We don't have ticket quotas, but no one wants a month with zero tickets."

Competitive pride will get game wardens to make extreme efforts. Parker has been known, when on a hot lead, to get another wildlife agent to drop him off in the middle of the night, then walk a mile on foot so as to remain unobserved while getting to a spot he wants to stake out. There, he will lie on a bed mat, covered with a wool blanket, and use night optics to watch an area until after daylight arrives. "I've had deer walk as close as ten steps from me when I do that," he says.

We sit two more hours. A car stops on the road, engine running and lights on. Parker is on high alert. The car begins moving. "I thought I would at least hear an aluminum can hit the road. I can hear a beer can hit the pavement a mile away."

A bemused Parker says that game wardens see all kinds of things when set up at night. It's quite common for couples seeking romance to park their vehicle in what they think is seclusion, quite near a game warden's truck.

We sit in the dead silence for two more hours. He catches my glance in the faint starlight and grins, "I'm the boogeyman."

Fewer vehicles pass and Parker calls it a night. To keep his presence undetected, he creeps the truck out without lights. Not until he is down the road do the lights come on and he becomes just another vehicle in the night.

Day Two: The Cell Phone Is Fast

Starting his patrol at midday, Parker is nosing around East Carroll, his home parish. Catching sight of several bed mattresses dumped off a rural public road, he stops but finds nothing to identify the dumper. "Talk about rewarding," he declares, "is to pull up on someone who just dumped. They have that 'almost free' look on their faces." Parker takes littering personally.

Next stop is a deer processing shed, where a sixteen-year-old hunter and his dad are proudly hovering over the son's nicely antlered buck. The processor's eight-year-old boy straddles the deer and holds the head up for display. The inquisitive youngster follows Parker to his truck, throwing a barrage of questions at him. Parker, who has nine- and six-year-old sons, patiently answers every one.

East Carroll Parish is almost perfectly level, rich agricultural land, formed by alluvial deposits of the Mississippi River. Much of the land is enrolled in the CRP program and is growing over with natural vegetation and trees. But most acreage is farmed, mainly for cotton and grain crops.

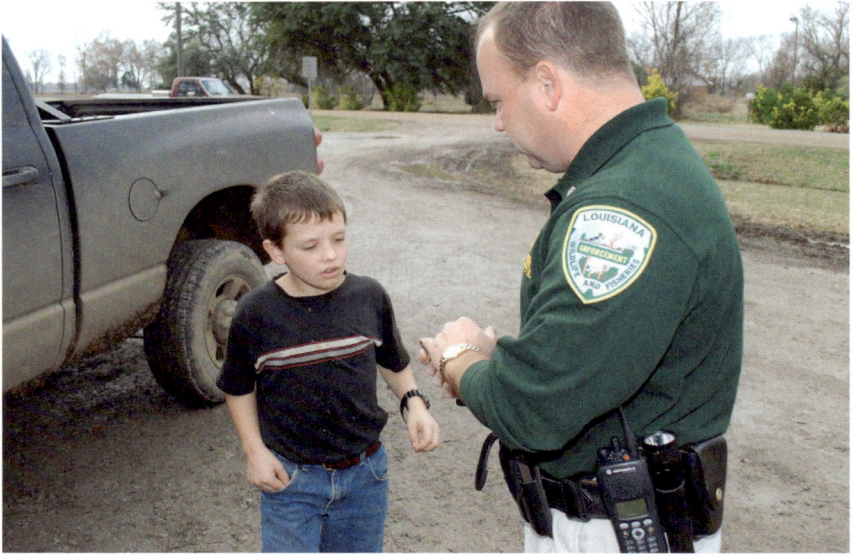

Like most game wardens, Parker makes time in his work to answer inquisitive kids' questions.

Like much of the delta lands of Louisiana and Mississippi, the parish displays a lot of poverty. As farms have gotten less in number and become much larger and more mechanized, jobs have disappeared. The country is flecked with deserted houses.

Yet the area has a serene beauty in the dead gray of the leafless stands of bottomland hardwood trees, mixed with the vast, windswept openness of the agricultural fields. Here and there, the gray is relieved by the vibrant bright green of wheat fields that thrive in Louisiana's winter weather.

On what he calls "enforcement patrol," Parker probes the nooks and crannies of the parish, places where outdoor activity is likely to occur. As he describes it, he will be targeting areas where "if there was no good to be had, they would be having it."

Part of any patrol, too, he explains, is scouting—looking for places to come back to. He looks across fields to see trucks, ATVs, and boats. He uses his binoculars constantly and misses very little.

The early part of the afternoon passes quietly, as Parker checks several hunters but finds no violations. Mid-afternoon finds him stopping at Bayou Macon Wildlife Management Area (WMA). Fellow agent Darren Bruce, who is pulling out of the WMA headquarters parking lot, informs Parker that he just heard a shot. Deer season is closed on the WMA, although it is still open on the surrounding private lands.

Parker slams his truck in reverse and guns it down the gravel road. He finds two hunters sighting a rifle on private land across the road from the WMA. When he asks if they have seen or heard any other activity, they reply that an ATV with two men had just previously entered the WMA. The use of an ATV on a WMA is illegal except on approved trails or to retrieve a harvested deer.

Parker quickly moves the truck down the road to (but not into) the cleared right-of-way that is the WMA's boundary. With his binoculars to his eyes, he spies a single hunter fleeing rapidly down the right-of-way on his ATV, repeatedly looking over his shoulder to see if he has been spotted.

After a brief conference, Bruce blocks the road exit from the WMA with his truck and Parker takes his own truck at breakneck speed in four-wheel drive down the route the hunter on the ATV took.

At the back boundary of the WMA, Parker locates the abandoned ATV, but the driver isn't to be found. Parker turns the fuel supply valve on the ATV off to prevent the driver from doubling back and fleeing, then goes into the woods after him.

He doesn't have to go far. The man is only a short way into the woods and watching us. He professes innocence of everything before Parker speaks more than a greeting.

Parker patiently explains to the man that his operation of an ATV on the wildlife management area is illegal. The hunter claims he doesn't know he is on the WMA, even though the right of way is marked with signs every hundred or so feet.

Parker asks the man why, if he wasn't worried about a violation, he was driving the ATV at high speed over the rough right-of-way and looking backward over his shoulder. The hunter offers no reply.

Parker retains the man's rifle and driver's license and follows him on his ATV back to Bruce's truck. Two agents search briefly for the other hunter where he was dropped off. Finding nothing, Parker drives to the hunters' vehicle to prevent the second hunter from circling through the woods and fleeing. Bruce, with the first hunter in tow, finally locates the second one sitting in the woods on nearby privately owned property, wearing no hunter's orange, another violation.

The first hunter is cited for the operation of an ATV on a WMA, having oversized tires on his ATV, hunting deer by illegal methods (rifle season is closed), and hunting from a permanent blind/reserving a hunting location

Wayne Parker (l) and Darren Bruce (r), like many other game wardens, use the tailgates of their trucks as impromptu rolling desks.

on a WMA. The second hunter is cited for hunting big game with no hunter's orange.

While he explains the citations to the men, Parker receives a citizen's complaint on his cell phone. The complainant identifies a hunter by name who has killed his sixth—and legally his last—deer under Louisiana's six deer season limit, but retained the last tag to kill another deer, rather than using it to tag the animal.

The man's home is reported as being a good distance away, so Parker starts quickly to try to get there before the man disposes of the evidence. Just before twilight he reaches his destination, a compound of poorly maintained trailers and ramshackle sheds that look as if they would fall apart with a sneeze. Every manner of debris litters the area, including junk cars and probably every discarded kitchen and washroom appliance the compound dwellers have ever owned. The larger items are liberally seasoned with kitchen refuse and fragments of clothes, and mud is everywhere. A couple of skinny dogs of highly mixed ancestry eye us dolefully.

The yard mills with people and all eyes are upon Parker's big truck when it stops. Two bare-chested men, who appear to be in their thirties, stare at the truck with lethal looks in their eyes. One of them exposes a mouthful of gold teeth, almost in a threat display, before both of them retreat into trailers. A gaggle of semi-feral children scrabble in the debris. Planted firmly in the yard and obviously in charge are two very large, well-fed women.

Into this steps Parker, his pressed uniform still neat at the end of a long day and with not a hair out of place.

The women tell him that the man he is seeking doesn't live here and give him directions to his house. Their directions take Parker through a maze of some of the worst roads he has traveled in two days. The axle-deep mud makes travel very slow.

Parker expects the man to be alerted, and isn't surprised when he pulls into the yard of his quarry and the man is standing outside waiting for him with his hunting license ready. With no reason for an oblique line of questioning, Parker explains the purpose of his visit.

The man grins broadly and points to the head of a buck deer hanging in the small barn where it can't be missed. Prominently displayed, the man's sixth and final tag is affixed to one of the spike's antlers.

The unfazed agent goes over the hunter's license and tag stubs, making sure that all is in order. With a cigarette dangling from his lips, the hunter assures Parker that he always obeys the law.

Before he leaves, Parker casually asks him if he had gotten a telephone call about his approach. "Yeah," he replies, grinning broadly, "a truck is fast, but the cell phone is faster."

In the increasing darkness, Parker mounts his truck like a steed, then heads back east—four-wheel drive engaged and throwing a blizzard of mud. His cell phone is in hand and both radios are crackling.

3

WHERE THE WHITE PERCH IS KING

Day One: The Net

The wizened, stooped old man sits at a table in the T-town service station and convenience store, halfway between Jonesville and Jena. He studies the game warden carefully before speaking. "Y'all been spending a lot of time up in the head of the lake," he twangs laconically.

Senior Agent Charlie Ferrington's head immediately spins 90 degrees to face the man. He answers in a friendly but banal way, but the man's comment clearly has caught Ferrington off guard.

Ferrington pays for his snack and hustles outside to meet two younger agents, twenty-five-year-old lanky and fair-skinned Lee Tarver and the darker-haired David Nelson, a veteran of the first Gulf War in Iraq and Kuwait. They are fueling their truck to follow Ferrington to the lake.

"They done figured out that we are in there," he blurts to his partners. "We made that one lead net case six days ago and already the word is out."

Turning to me, he explains that the people in this area form a small, tight-knit community. If they see the game wardens' trucks at one of the few boat landings in the area or if they see a strange boat on the water, they know something is up and they alert everyone else.

Ferrington disconcertingly fixes his brown eyes in an unblinking gaze on whomever he is talking to. Like others in the area, he speaks with a north Louisiana drawl, but much faster, almost fast enough to be Cajun. But he definitely isn't Cajun.

Although it's still dark, Ferrington is itching to get going. He wants to get into the area they will work before breaking day provides a lot of light.

In the truck he muses, "If we get to pop one more illegal white perch netter in there, we'll be lucky. They'll just shut down and pull their illegal nets until we go somewhere else. Then they'll go back to fishing. There are lots of legal commercial fishermen here, but these white perch netters are outlaws."

The two trucks are heading to French Fork Landing to launch their boats. "That's not the closest landing to where we are working," explains Ferrington, "but we would have to be stupid to launch at the closest landing. They would see our trucks and know we are in there for sure."

The area that the three men are working in east-central Louisiana is a tangled rete of lakes and bayous that, like the Chesapeake Bay, has been called an immense protein factory. For many decades, the waters of the area have been disgorging a seemingly inexhaustible supply of crappie, almost always locally called "white perch" or just "perch."

Although the entire system lies within the greater Mississippi River flood plain, most of the area's bayous and lakes were formed and are still influenced by the waters of the Red, Black, and Little rivers. Three lakes dominate the system, Larto, Saline, and Catahoula.

Larto Lake, Saline Lake, and their interconnecting and surrounding bayous, such as Cross Bayou, Long Branch, Saline Bayou, and Big Saline Bayou, are most commonly referred to as the Larto-Saline complex. The complex is arguably the most famous crappie/white perch fishing destination in Louisiana.

Catahoula Lake is largely man-made. Originally a low, treeless, swampy area nestled next to the hills of LaSalle Parish, it was used for years by local residents as a cattle pasture during the summer months, when river levels were low. Drainage from the area was blocked by a weir put in at Archie to hold water for ducks. A diversion canal was also constructed so the lake can be drained in early July each year to allow vegetation for waterfowl to grow. Management of the lake is still controversial. Duck hunters want the water kept shallow, fishermen want it deep, and some local residents feel cheated of their historical uses.

The rich waters of the Larto/Saline/Catahoula area produce prodigious quantities of white perch, a game fish, which cannot be sold like commercial fish can. For decades, an outlaw fishery using hoop nets, flag nets, and gill nets thrived and millions of pounds of white perch were shipped north to cities ranging from Memphis to Chicago. At the same time, the Saline-Larto complex produced world-class recreational fishing for white perch.

Several decades of relentless law enforcement have beaten down the large-scale poaching of white perch. But fishing for white perch to sell still goes on. Ferrington says, "It's ingrained in the people in this area." Today, the game wardens plan to watch closely (or "sit on," as they call it) an illegal white perch net they found earlier to try to catch its owner.

The game wardens launch their boats after reaching the landing and then hide their trucks in the woods. Their boats are modest, unmarked aluminum flat boats, similar to those used by many local fishermen. Obsessed with stealth, they slip jackets over their state-issued life vests, which are emblazoned with the LDWF logo.

The two boats skim the edge of Catahoula Lake, dodging the browning remnants of last season's duck blinds. At the northern end of the lake,

Charlie Ferrington (f) and LeRoy Tarver (r) check the illegal lead net to be sure that it has fish in it.

they guide their craft down narrow boat lanes, through a dense thicket of shrubby water elm and swamp privet trees.

It's cold and the skies are heavily overcast, typical February weather in Louisiana. Rain is predicted.

The game wardens slowly worm their two boats through the closely spaced trees. Suddenly they stop. I see nothing until one of them reaches into the water and hauls to the surface two hoop nets connected by a wall of nylon webbing called a lead.

After dropping the net back into place, Tarver, wearing neoprene chest waders, carefully lowers himself into the cold, chest-deep water. His job will be to watch the net from close by, hidden in a dense clump of water elm, with only his shoulders and ski mask-covered head protruding from the water. He is to keep Nelson and Ferrington apprised by radio of any activity at the net.

Ferrington reminds Tarver that the men who will run the net must not only remove the white perch from the net, they must also leave the location of the net with the fish in the boat for them to legally be in possession of the fish.

Nelson's role will be to hide himself in the brush nearby in the smaller

Tarver wades into the flooded forest to hide and wait for the illegal white perch netter.

of the two flatboats, a fifteen-footer with a twenty-five-horsepower motor. Ferrington cautions him not to bang anything around in his boat that will give his position away and to move in quickly to intercept the violator's boat upon Tarver's word.

Ferrington, in his larger and more awkward but faster boat, will be patrolling other areas of the lake. He will quickly move in should his boat be needed for a pursuit.

After the two agents are in position, Ferrington idles his boat away. He looks over his shoulder at the bubbles his motor leaves on the surface and shakes his head. "These bubble trails will bust you. A guy will see those and know someone was here. Unless it's windy or rainy, it takes an hour to an hour and a half before they disperse."

He explains why he likes to have one man in the water observing the net. "A good violator will sometimes try to get us to show ourselves by running up to the net but not taking the fish out before he leaves. If we stop him, we've blown our cover.

"Sometimes," he goes on, "a net is set where it is absolutely impossible to observe the net being run. Then, we may use a hole puncher to punch holes in the fins of the white perch in the net to mark them as having come from a net."

Ferrington explains that people from all walks of life fish nets for white perch to sell. "Lots of people with jobs do it for the thrill and the fun, but they can also make $300 to $500 a week to supplement their regular income.

"There aren't a lot of jobs here besides farming, oilfield work, and a little commercial fishing. In the hills of LaSalle Parish, the only real employer is the timber industry."

White perch, he explains, sell for a dollar to a dollar and a quarter a pound. That's far more than what the legal commercial fish species (catfish, gaspergou, and buffalo) fetch.

While the other two men watch the net, Ferrington plans to run to the diversion canal to check on fishing activity there. The look of the sky becomes forbidding, turning from slate gray to bruised blue to the south, the direction we are headed.

He cruises through a seemingly uncountable number of duck blinds in the lake. Some are huge and elaborate; others are modest. A lot of them still have dozens to hundreds of decoys around them, a month after the season ended. He catches me looking at the decoys and explains that some people leave them out year-round. "There are some lazy people up here," he drawls.

Interspersed with the duck blinds are oil wells set high on stilts over the lake.

Seeing a wall of rain sweep toward us, Ferrington ducks the boat into a large blind that, conveniently enough, is partially roofed. As we wait out the rain, I get a good look at my companion.

He is powerfully built, at five feet, eleven inches tall and 230 pounds. Sandy haired, fair-skinned, and freckled, he resembles nothing so much as a thirty-nine-year-old country boy.

With nothing to do but wait, we chat. "I was glad to get hired on," he says, nodding in emphasis. "I love this kind of work. I didn't get the job the first time I tried. It was ten years later that I tried again and was hired. I have loved to hunt and fish and the outdoors my whole life. I believe that if a man gets a job he loves, he will never work a day in his life."

The rain shows no signs of abating. We sit in silence for a while, each buried in his own thoughts, as the rain hammers the tin roofs of the two cubbies in the blind.

I break the silence and ask Ferrington about the parishes he works in. He describes the people of Concordia, Catahoula, and LaSalle parishes as "conservative southerners, most definitely church-going people."

According to Ferrington, the judicial systems of Concordia and Catahoula have traditionally been more lenient than LaSalle on white perch violations. "Family ties are strong, plus the fishery has historically been something that people turned to in hard times.

"Probably 98 percent of the people here are law-abiding. But, in general, people here don't view wildlife violations like other violations. 'It's just a few fish. Come on, the guy is just trying to get something to eat.' Some people have the opinion that God put the fish here for people. I guess the view is changing as animal rights groups become louder.

"But my job is to catch them. What the system does with them is beyond my control. It's a cat and mouse game."

The rain stops and Ferrington backs his boat out of the blind and continues the run to the control structure on the Catahoula Diversion Canal.

The gates are closed today, so no commercial fishermen are there dipping shad. Several groups of recreational fishermen are fishing. Ferrington politely checks their licenses and leaves. In the south end of the lake, he spies two commercial fishermen running gill nets and approaches them.

The commercial gill netters' boat is full of legally taken buffalo fish and carp.

The large fish well in the center of their boat is nearly brim-full of gourd head buffalo fish and carp.

As Ferrington's boat approaches them, the fisherman in the bow of the boat smiles and greets him. The older fisherman, who is seated near the outboard motor, just glares.

Ferrington obviously has a history with the man, whom he respectfully addresses as "Mr. Leon." Ferrington asks to check their commercial licenses.

Both fishermen produce their licenses. As Ferrington checks the licenses of the man in the front, they josh good-naturedly. When the second man's turn comes to have his licenses checked, he grumbles audibly, "I don't have no use for a game warden."

"Come on now, Mr. Leon," replies Ferrington. The man glares stonily at Ferrington and says with conviction, "I don't have no use for a game warden after what you done me."

"Mr. Leon," says Ferrington softly, "you know you weren't supposed to have them fish."

"I didn't want them thangs, no how," retorts the fisherman.

Ferrington returns his licenses with a smile. The fisherman locks his eyes on Ferrington's face and delivers his parting shot, "I hate a game warden."

Ferrington pulls his boat away from the commercial fishermen's boat and says by way of explanation that he recently caught the man with white perch in his boat that he had caught with a hoop net and hadn't returned to the water. "I've caught his nephew before, too," he adds.

At 9:30 a.m. sharp, Ferrington's cell phone rings. It's from the game wardens sitting on the net. He puts his cell phone away and cries jubilantly, "They are in there."

He immediately powers the boat up to full speed to run the length of the lake back to his teammates. Halfway up the lake he hits a pouring, flooding rainstorm.

Ferrington has a rain jacket on, but hasn't taken the time to slip on rain pants. He is getting soaked. The blinding rain makes it impossible for him to see. He tries navigating with his head down, peeping upward under his eyebrows.

Finally, he slows to a crawl and fishes his cell phone out from under his jacket. He has nine missed calls. The rain and motor noise had made it impossible to hear the rings.

Ferrington is amped up.

He tries calling Nelson repeatedly, but the soaking wet cell phone won't cooperate. He repeatedly tries to clear the phone by violently slinging the water out of it.

When he finally gets through to Nelson, the news is a letdown. The fishermen's boat passed so close to Tarver that water from its wake sloshed over the top of his waders, but they passed the net and went further up the lake, Nelson thinks to run another net. Then they left the area. Evidently, the net that the game wardens are sitting on isn't theirs.

Disappointed, Ferrington sits in the rain and contemplates his next move. He decides to slowly cruise the Big Bend area of the lake, looking for signs of another net. The entire area looks more like a drowned miniature woodland than a lake. Everywhere are knobbed, bushy water elms sticking their limbs ten to twelve feet out of the water. Under drab skies, it looks like a spooky, enchanted elfin forest. Narrow boat lanes run through the trees in no pattern. It's a maze.

Ferrington is looking for any visible netting or rope near the water's surface. A float may mark a lead net. Fresh scuff marks on trees may indicate a boat has moved through the area recently.

"We spend hours and hours hunting for nets," he says. "Some fishermen

In the spooky maze of flooded water elms, everything looks alike.

fish their nets completely blind [unmarked]. We find those by pulling metal drag hooks with our boats or we stumble over them.

"Sometimes we find nets when we see or hear fishermen going to run them while we are set up on another net. It's like trying to find a needle in a haystack.

"I've hidden in duck blinds and watched where boats go. You might not see them go directly to the net, but it narrows your search area from the whole lake to a spot the size of a couple of football fields. We get complaints from recreational fishermen that help us locate nets, too.

"Sometimes we do all that work and all we find is a trotline instead of a net. Experience is important. The more you look for nets the better you get at finding them. Nets are not just placed anywhere."

The first thing that game wardens do when they find a net set for white perch is check how many fish are in it, says Ferrington. If there are lots of fish in it, they start sitting on it immediately.

If only a few are in it, it indicates that the net has been recently run. They will check the fish in the net over a period of days to determine a catch and run pattern.

It's 1:15 p.m. and the cold, wet, and bedraggled-looking Ferrington is still searching for nets. Periodically he stops to listen for other boats running in the dense trees. "I like ketchin' 'em," he murmurs softly. "I wouldn't trade this job for any other one. Most of the time, I'm working by myself. Most of the time I'm trying to outsmart the other fella."

He stops during a lull in the rainstorms. The boat floats quietly in the middle of a big buffalo spawn. The amorous twenty- to thirty-pound fish are constantly splashing the water's surface during their courtship activities.

"There is kind of a little competition between you and the other agents to see who can be best. You get out of this job what you put in it. I get out and hustle to try to make things happen. Sometimes things do happen and sometimes they don't.

"The pay is good and we get all this fancy equipment. Up here, folks seem to like us. A lot of them would like to have our job.

"It's got drawbacks though. Doing the hurricane stuff doesn't really appeal to me. But the reward is helping people. It really makes you feel good to help someone."

His entire body is shaking in the clammy coldness. No mention of breaking for lunch is made.

Suddenly Ferrington's radio crackles to life. The voice on the other end is a hissing, static-charged whisper. "He's coming in!" Nelson is in cell phone contact with Tarver and relaying the message to Ferrington over the radio.

Ferrington slaps my leg in excitement and starts the boat motor. He idles toward the action. Even though his four-stroke engine isn't loud, he can't risk making too much noise.

"They are running it," the voice on the radio hisses.

Ferrington looks at me and says, "Everyone in the region is glued to the radio listening right now." Then he radios Nelson to be ready to take the boat down fast, adding that they probably have a big motor.

Ferrington's boat slowly but steadily moves toward the action. He is bent over the steering wheel listening, both to the radio and to hear another boat's motor.

Whether from the cold or the excitement, his chin is shaking violently. His hand is clenching the steering wheel so tightly that his knuckles are white. There is so much tension in the air, I can feel it snapping.

Ferrington thinks that he hears two boats, running, stopping, running again, then stopping again repeatedly.

Nelson relays a description of the man and the boat at the net, then tells Ferrington that the subject has dropped the net back into place without taking any fish out of it.

From the description, Ferrington deduces that the man is the same one

It is hard to tell if the shaking of Ferrington's body is due to excitement or the damp cold.

that he caught fishing nets for white perch six days ago. "I'll take him to jail this time; make him bond out. He didn't learn anything. Maybe he'll learn this time."

Nelson radios Ferrington that the man returned to the net, but seemed hesitant to run it. Then he left.

He radios Tarver and Nelson to sit tight. "If he doesn't run it today, we will check tomorrow to see if he ran the net at night."

Talking more to himself than anyone else, Ferrington spits out, "That's what aggravates me, when they think that they are smarter than me. If we don't catch him soon, he's going to move the nets."

At 4:00 p.m. Ferrington radios Nelson to pick up Tarver and meet him for the ride back to the landing. While we wait for them, the skies decide to quit messing around with mist and drizzle. A rainfall of truly biblical proportions envelops the boat. "Man, that's some big raindrops," says Ferrington in awe from under the hood of his rain jacket.

The rain takes an intermission just as the two boats reach the landing. After they retrieve their trucks from their hiding spots and load the boats on their trailers, the waterlogged but cheerful game wardens compare notes.

Tarver describes the man who checked the nets as a "ratty-looking" guy in his thirties with a little mustache and his hat on backward. The first time he approached the lead net, Tarver explains, he passed alongside it in the thick brush but wouldn't pick it up. He then ran his boat round and round and back and forth in the flooded brush, constantly looking in all directions. He smashed down smaller trees like a hunter trying to flush game. He shut his motor off several times and sat listening for another boat. But he didn't pay any attention to the sound of the other boat that arrived with him.

Tarver says that he had to move around the clump of water elm he was hiding behind several times to keep from being seen.

"He was hunting," said Tarver, "no smile, wide-eyed and mouth open. He was alert-looking. He was expecting to see or hear something."

After searching, Tarver says, the man returned to the lead and raised both hoop nets to see how many fish were in them. "Then," Tarver adds, "after checking the nets, he tore out of there, running over trees. When he got to the channel, he shut his motor off and listened for us."

"They know we are in here," summarized Ferrington. "They are scared to run their nets. What we heard, boats stopping and running, makes sense. He's checking for us. He's probably going to run them at night. We're fixin' to have to go on a night shift."

Day Two: Saline/Larto Patrol

The next day dawns still heavily overcast, but colder. More rain is a possibility. Ferrington is going on a boating safety and recreational fishing patrol in the Saline/Larto complex.

His ride today, borrowed from fellow agent Robbie Mayo, is a lot fancier than yesterday's. It's a big, comfortable, solid white, deep V-hulled boat with a big LDWF decal on its side. It's powered by a 150-horsepower outboard and has a big light bar bearing blue lights arching overhead.

Ferrington offers comment on the rig. "It's a real nice boat, but in my opinion it is a high-profile boat, a boat to be seen in. It lets people know their tax dollars are at work. My boat kind of blends in with the other fishermen's boats. They don't know that I'm the game warden until it's too late."

That the events of yesterday are still on his mind becomes obvious when he speaks up. "I've been married to my wife, Tammy, for eleven years and she can read me like a book.

"When I'm really trying to catch someone and they slip by, I'll beat up on myself about what I did—what other angle could I have used. I'm constantly rethinking every move, every little detail.

"Who saw me? How was I seen? Was it my foot prints, my four-wheeler tracks? Did he have a trail camera? Thousands of things run through my mind. What gave me away? Or was it just dumb luck on his part. Sometimes I feel that I can do everything right and just be unlucky.

"She can pick up on it by my mood change. If I catch someone, I'm on top of the world. Sometimes I work three weeks on a case and then lose it. She says I'm depressed," he chuckles.

"I guess that sometimes I do neglect her," he adds quietly. "But I definitely try not to neglect my three boys. It's easy to neglect your family."

The route to Lake Larto tracks Ferrington's big truck through vast, soggy agricultural fields that produce big crops of rice, cotton, corn, soy beans, and winter wheat.

Below Jonesville, parallel to the Black River, are more agricultural lands, flecked with loose gaggles of producing oil wells. What land isn't under the plow holds bottomland hardwood trees that shade dense growths of palmettos.

Nearer Larto Lake, hardwood forests almost take over from agriculture. "This land floods often," explains Ferrington as we near the lake. "When the Mississippi River is high, the waters of the Red and Black rivers back up because they have no place to go."

The community of Larto is set in the woods. The picturesque darklimbed, arthritically twisted oak trees of the area are festooned with gray Spanish moss.

"Larto is changing," declares Ferrington. "It used to have a bunch of poorer people who lived off of the land. They were territorial and wanted south Louisiana people to stay on the other side of the Red River—but all that has changed.

"A lot of people from the outside are building camps here. What used to be the poorest part of the parish is now where the building is going on." It isn't hard to see that elaborate elevated camps outnumber the modest older homes and aged house trailers.

"The people here were good people, just poor," says Ferrington. "This was an area of high illegal fish and wildlife activity, and some of it still goes on, but that's changing. The recreational value of the huge oxbow lake, flanked by the 60,000 acres of Dewey Wills Wildlife Management Area, is making this a recreational playground."

Ferrington launches his "high-profile boat" into the lake from a small, private launch. Before he leaves the launch, he fields a call from Tarver and Nelson, who are back on the white perch net.

They tell Ferrington that the fish are still in the net and that they have marked the fins of the fish with a hole puncher and returned them to the net. Ferrington instructs them to hide in their boat completely out of sight and intercept the violators after they run the net. "Be far enough away so that they can't hear waves slapping the side of your boat and be sure that they have taken the time to run the net."

After ending the call, Ferrington explains that Tarver isn't in the water with his waders because yesterday's waders were still wet inside and he had found a leak today in his spare set.

Even though a cold wind is blustering from the north, Ferrington starts checking recreational white perch fishermen immediately. A routine quickly develops. He greets them all with a friendly smile, asking, "How y'all doing? Ya having any luck?" He checks everyone's fishing licenses and life jackets and many boat registrations.

Boat after boat is in compliance. Boring work compared to trying to

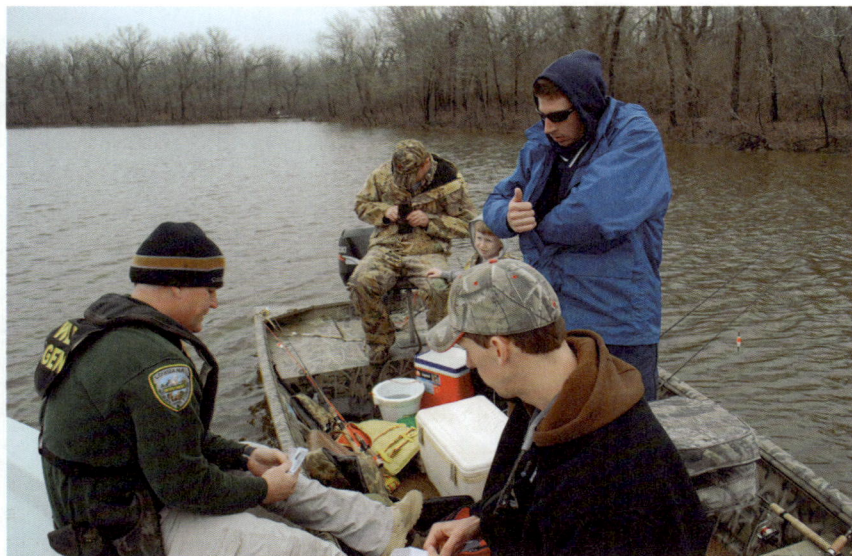

Ferrington checks recreational white perch fishermen for life jackets, fishing licenses, and boat registrations.

catch specific outlaws, but necessary nonetheless. Surprisingly, in spite of the strong, frigid, windy conditions, most fishermen are doing well.

With the exception of a handful of bass fishermen, everyone is fishing for white perch. The anglers are from all points in the state and as far away as Illinois.

"Saline/Larto is a big-time place for catching white perch in Louisiana," states Ferrington matter-of-factly. "I don't know any place better. In the spring, I regularly pull up to boats that are near their daily limits of fifty fish per person.

"And this place is heavily fished, legally and illegally. I don't believe you can fish it out, because the area floods with backwater regularly. In our seven-parish region, this is the best fishing."

Ferrington works his way down Saline Bayou to Saline Lake. Unlike Larto Lake, which is obviously an old river oxbow, Saline Lake has a sprawling reservoir shape and is speckled with cypress trees.

Fewer white perch fishermen are fishing in this lake, but all the ones Ferrington checks have fish in their ice chests. There is no shortage of bass fishermen in bass boats though. One pair of bass fishermen he checks explains that a bass tournament is being held today.

Big Saline Bayou, on the opposite end of the lake from where Ferrington entered, is postcard pretty, even without the lily pads that will fringe the shallows during summer.

The channel of the bayou is narrow, crooked, and twisting. As Ferrington routinely checks fishermen for licenses, life jackets, and registrations, bass boat after bass boat comes slaloming through the narrow channel, throwing huge rooster tails and barely keeping their grip on the water in the curves.

Figuring that he can slow them down a bit, Ferrington idles his big, de-caled boat to the edge of the channel. Not a chance. Bass boat after bass boat comes snarling up the crooked channel, passing within feet of the game warden's boat without even acknowledging its existence.

So he idles his boat into the middle of the channel. The next boat is a red metal flake monster carrying a single man. Ferrington waves for him to slow down, but the driver simply zigzags around his boat, only stopping seventy-five yards later.

The obviously indignant man pulls his ski mask off and demands to know what is wrong. He is in his seventies. Ferrington warns him that reckless operation of a boat is an offense, to which the man immediately replies, "Well, you are sitting in the channel."

Ferrington sighs, cautions him again, and waves him on. Then the game warden cranks his engine and silently heads back toward his launch site. "I really hate to write reckless operation tickets," he says. "They go on your automobile driving record."

He sits in silence as he works his boat back up the lake to his launch point. His mind is reworking yesterday's events. Finally, he pipes up, "If that guy doesn't run his nets soon, we will confiscate the net, because it is illegal where it is set. I don't want to be sitting on an egg that won't hatch."

4

ATCHAFALAYA FOG

Day One: The Kickenest-Ass Job in America

It has been cold for two weeks, sometimes almost bitterly cold. Yet this evening, on my way to the Lower Atchafalaya Basin, heavy clouds are rolling in from the south and the air is becoming noticeably warmer, almost by the minute. I know what that means in this area. Cold wintery weather immediately followed by hot weather and southerly winds means an almost certainty of fog on the near-maritime deltas of the Atchafalaya River, as well as the lower part of the Atchafalaya Basin.

I am going to meet Senior Agent Scott Dupre, and it doesn't look good. Dupre told me that he was planning to patrol the lower basin on the first day, then the Atchafalaya River delta on the second. But it is still clear. Maybe, just maybe. . . .

We leave in the dark the next morning, with the night air over land fuzzy with moisture. It isn't as bad as it could be. We cross our fingers about what we will find over the much colder waters of the river. The truck's headlights reveal that the land on each side of the road to the Myette Point Boat Launch is muddy, rutted, and desolate-looking, with its lush sugar cane crop having been sheared off within the last few weeks.

The launch is busy with hunters launching in the predawn darkness. Red, green, and white boat running lights sparkle brightly. And mercifully, the fog is not as bad as we feared.

Dupre explains as he readies the seventeen-foot aluminum V-hull boat for launching that today he plans to concentrate his efforts on and around the Attakapas Wildlife Management Area. It is the height of both waterfowl and deer seasons in the Lower Atchafalaya.

Deciding where to work on a day without any public complaints to respond to is challenging, he says. "You can only be in one place at a time and we have so much area. And there are very few of us. When I go to bed at night, I'm always thinking about where I want to go next. There are just so many hours in a day." Then he grins in the dim light of his truck's tail lights and adds, "Sometimes I don't want to quit."

He cranks up the big 150-horsepower Mercury OptiMax engine and backs the boat off the trailer. Soon he is picking his way through the patchy low-lying fog to an area called Raymond's Cove. There he sets up near enough to two groups of duck hunters to hear everything they do, although he is out of their sight. As the hunters throw out their decoys, Dupre talks in a hushed voice about his four-year-old career choice as a game warden.

Dupre says that while he grew up doing nothing but hunting and fishing, he knew very little about game wardens. Only twenty-eight years old, he had already pulled a four-year hitch in the navy and worked for a while as a helicopter mechanic before signing on as a wildlife agent. "My previous job was really good by most standards, but to me it was so boring that I couldn't see myself doing it the rest of my life," he explains.

A friend brought up the idea of being a game warden. "I ended up applying and he didn't," he laughs. He adds, "There is something to be said about loving your job and being happy to go to work. For one thing, it is good for your spousal relationship. But you have to be self-motivated to do this work. There is no one breathing down your neck. That all goes to loving your job. The pay is good, too."

He goes on, "Some things are different than I thought. It is a lot more involved. For example, I never thought of things like boat accident investigation. People look at you different, too. Some are afraid of us. Others are angry at us. The best part of my job is being outdoors every day and meeting people. The worst part is searching and recovering bodies."

Improving light shows Dupre to be of a slender athletic build, with closely cropped hair and a lean, angular face. He has a quick grin and speaks with a lilting Cajun accent.

We quietly sit in the thinning fog. The dank, fertile, fishy smell that only large rivers can provide penetrates my sinuses. The quiet is broken occasionally by the wings of waterfowl passing overhead.

Occasional gunshots echo through the fog, but the gunfire is sparse and sporadic from both groups that Dupre has set up on. One group decides to move early, after firing only once. At 8:45 Dupre begins to get restless and says, "Let's go see what we can find."

The big motor snarls to life and Dupre backs the boat from its lair to begin to prowl. First stop will be the duck hunters still set up near us. Hunkered down in crotch-deep water within a fallen treetop, the hunters im-

Scott Dupre checks two duck hunters who are using a fallen tree as a blind.

mediately begin digging for their licenses when they see Dupre approach. Everything checks out, so he moves toward an area where he heard some shooting earlier.

Weaving the boat through leaning willows, Dupre spots the three-man party moving very slowly in their boat outside their decoy spread. They greet him with friendly, if slightly apprehensive, smiles. He spots a partially cased rifle on the bottom of the boat, but checks their licenses and gun plugs first.

"Why do you have a rifle," queries Dupre. Deer season is now closed on the WMA.

"Oh, just to shoot a coon on the way in," replies the operator of the boat.

"May I see it," Dupre asks. When he pulls the bolt back on the .17 caliber rifle, he finds that the gun is loaded, an obvious violation of WMA rules, which prohibit loaded weapons in moving boats and vehicles on WMAs.

Right now, Dupre doesn't seem inclined to write them a ticket. Instead, he asks to see the five ducks that they have taken. He inspects them very closely, then holds up one with a shattered head. "This one looks like it was shot with a rifle." Without any further prompting, the boat operator admits that he used the rifle to shoot the duck, a scaup, which had lit on the water

Dupre checks each harvested duck for signs of being shot with something besides a shotgun.

far outside of shotgun range. "I'm going to have to issue you a citation," says Dupre.

Leaving this group, he zeroes in on Roger's Cove, where he also heard shooting earlier. He spies the hunters leaving the area after having picked up their decoys. He tries to take a shortcut to them through an area of tangled timber knocked down by Hurricane Gustav a few months earlier.

No dice. He gets hung up in the mass of mostly submerged treetops.

With the big motor roaring and water erupting from the stern like a geyser, Dupre tries to get the boat dislodged from the snarl.

Finally he stops and waves for the hunters—who are steadily quartering away from us—to wait. They turn their boat toward him just as he finally struggles lose from the grasp of the downed trees.

They claim no birds. Dupre looks the boat over and then checks their licenses. When he checks their guns for plugs to be sure that neither of them can hold more than three shells, he finds that one of the weapons is unplugged and will hold five. "I am going to issue you a citation for hunting with an unplugged shotgun," declares Dupre.

The gun's owner becomes argumentative and insists that Dupre is wrong. He demands to be handed the gun to try for himself whether it will hold more than three shells. Dupre obliges him. But the hunter isn't done. He aggressively complains that it isn't his fault that he was using a gun that he didn't know was unplugged. He insists that the ticket is unfair.

The driver of the boat asks if Dupre could just let his partner off with a warning. Dupre refuses and begins writing. "What color are your eyes," asks Dupre.

"Hazel, and right now my ass is red," he replies.

Dupre calmly says, "I'm sorry, sir; I understand. I am only doing my job."

But the hunter isn't through yet. In an aggressive tone he says, "People that are poaching—that is one thing. This is an honest mistake."

Refusing to take the bait, Dupre replies in a monotone. "I understand. Thank you for your cooperation."

That done, the young game warden moves to an area off the WMA, where deer season is still open. As he pulls through an intersecting waterway, he spots an orange-clad deer hunter floating in a boat. Dupre immediately tries to back up to remain unobserved, but it's obvious that he has been spotted. "Watch what he does, he will get on the radio," says Dupre.

As if on cue, a radio in the man's hand goes right to his mouth. "Working hunters who run deer dogs is hard. One spots you and then he gets on the radio and alerts everyone. The element of surprise is over, and so is any chance of catching someone in violation of the law," grumps Dupre.

Dupre pulls his boat up next to the hunter's boat, who talks his ear off about anything and everything, including everybody that the two men might know in common. Dupre asks if they have had any luck this morning. He answers that they have taken one three-point buck. Bidding the hunter goodbye, Dupre moves up the bayou.

He passes another orange-vested deer hunter passing in the opposite direction. Immediately, the hunter's hand raises a radio to his mouth. Dupre doesn't raise an eyebrow.

Stopping at a camp, Dupre gets another earful. Only this time it is complaints from a man about "those dog hunters that kill anything and everything.

"Just this morning, they shot a three-point buck swimming in the water. It's illegal to shoot a swimming deer you know," he says, looking at me. When he finishes with that topic, he complains bitterly about how useless it is to call the toll-free Operation Game Thief telephone number. Then he goes back to complaining about "the outlawing of deer." Dupre listens patiently and sympathetically.

On the way back in to the boat landing, Dupre stops other boats. All are hunters except for an older man and his grandson out to set out crawfish traps. At the landing, before he can load his boat, another boater hustles over to talk to him. He engages Dupre for maybe fifteen minutes.

As soon as Dupre gets the boat loaded, a man on an ATV asks to speak to him privately about a "known trouble-maker" with a stolen outboard motor, who is also a habitual night hunter. Another twenty minutes.

Dupre gets home late for his lunch, which his wife, Andrea, has patiently kept waiting for him. After eating and taking a nap, Dupre buckles on his gun belt and gets ready to go out on the second part of his split shift.

As he drives to the landing, he explains that an alert game warden always watches the hands of people he stops. "If they are drinking while operating a boat, the "beer shuffle" will give them away every time. The beer shuffle, he explains, is when the driver bends over slightly, with one hand going low to the deck. "What he is doing," says Dupre, "is putting his beer on the floor under his console.

"Then they will usually try to shove it further under the console with one foot. The ones to check are the ones too drunk to be coordinated and they knock the can over with their foot. When I confront them about the spilled beer they say something like 'Thash been der from a long time ago.'"

The other shuffle to watch for is the "rod and reel shuffle," he says. That one occurs when he pulls up on someone who is fishing without a license. "The ones without the license will always drop their rod like a hot potato and kind of shuffle their feet around, looking in another direction innocently."

Dupre launches the boat at the same ramp as this morning. After clearing the launch area, his boat darts out from Myette Point like an olive-drab missile. He plans to check out activity in the area that he was in this morning and then cross the Atchafalaya River to work on the other side of the Atchafalaya Basin.

Near Roger's Cove, Dupre encounters three friendly teenagers in an aluminum skiff. They tell him that they had been hunting, but haven't had any luck. After checking their life jackets, shotguns, ice chest, and the bow compartment of the boat, he asks them about the beer. About a case of full cans of beer, plus a bunch of empties, are scattered around the floor of the boat.

"Those are my dad's," answers one of the boys. Dupre asks where his father is. The boy replies that he is "at the camp." Dupre cautions them that a minor cannot legally be in possession of alcohol, but that he is going to let them go because none of it is iced. The youngsters are clearly sober.

Passing into Lake Fausse Pointe Cut, locally known as the G. A. Cut, Dupre sees a boat drifting with four men in it. The cowling is off of the motor and one of them is tinkering with the engine. Dupre sees that the boat is registered in Alabama, so he asks the occupants where they are from.

The man at the controls, a really, really big guy, replies that he is from Louisiana, but that he has purchased the boat from a friend in Alabama and is trying it out. He explains that he has applied for proper registration in Louisiana, but hasn't received it yet. Dupre picks up his radio, calls Dispatch, and asks them to check LDWF boat registration records for the application to verify that it has been made.

While waiting for Dispatch to reply, Dupre asks what is wrong with the boat and if they will need help. The big guy replies, smiling broadly, "It's just lazy. It's been sitting on the couch too long." Dispatch comes back that the registration application has been received and is being processed. As Dupre speaks on the radio, the man eyes him steadily.

Dupre wishes them a good day and prepares to leave. But before he can start his engine, the man, with his hands folded across his massive chest, says, "Can I say something?" Dupre nods his head, not knowing what to expect. "You must have the kickenest-ass job in America. I would trade my left nut for your job." Dupre can't help but grin ear to ear as he cranks up the engine.

Heading eastward, he crosses the Atchafalaya River and stabs the boat into a narrow crevasse that he says is a shortcut to Schwing Chute. The rapidly rising river's brown water is pouring through the narrow and crooked little channel that is barely twice as wide as the boat. On either side of us, in the lengthening evening shadows, loom the signature trees of much of the heavily sedimented areas of the basin: willow, sycamore, and cottonwood.

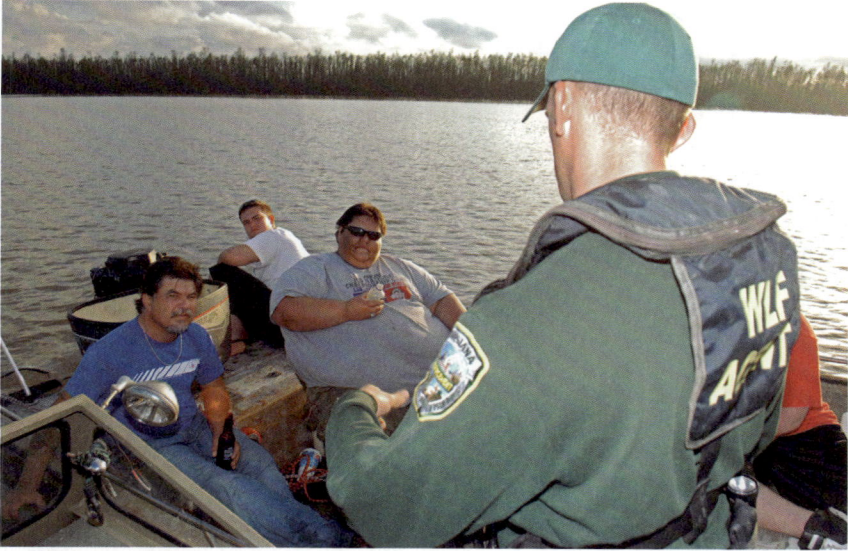

The big man tells Dupre that he would like to have his job.

In Schwing Chute he stops to check out a freshly placed trotline, probably for choupique, he says. A little ways down the waterway, he pulls up to a
man and a woman who have been hunting unsuccessfully for squirrels.

As darkness descends, Dupre parks the boat near the intersection of two
waterways and waits for the bad guys to come out and play. With no city
lights to obscure them, the stars of the heavens put on a spectacular display over the silently parked boat in the basin. First the Little Dipper, in its
cock-eyed position, becomes obvious. To the southwest, the crescent of the
setting quarter-moon hangs in the sky. The planet Venus, immediately beneath it, adds to the spectacular night sky.

In spite of it being a Friday night in the middle of hunting season, the
night is incredibly quiet. No gunshots and no motor noise mar the silence
until nearly 9 p.m. Then Dupre spots the reflection of a bright light banking
off of the overhanging layer of fog. He hustles to the top of the bank to get a
better view and confirms that it is a boat coming this way and shining both
banks of the bayou with a bright light. It could be illegal night hunters.

He moves his boat slightly to try to hide it behind some bushes overhanging the water. "I like the element of surprise," he explains. The light re-
flections become steadily brighter, but no gunshots are heard. Dupre hopes
that the boat will turn the other way at the intersection, so that he can slip

in behind it with his lights blacked out. If they do he will follow it to see what they are up to.

But no such luck. When they reach the intersection, they turn Dupre's way and throw their spotlight directly on his boat. He flicks on his blue light and identifies himself as Wildlife and Fisheries. The two middle-aged men say that they are frogging. And indeed, besides the spotlight and a boom box radio, they have nothing in the boat but some empty crawfish sacks to put the frogs in.

After they leave, Dupre resumes his watch. A dense fog drops on the boat like a wet blanket. So much moisture is in the air that gills would be more suitable for breathing than lungs

After a couple hours of fog-watch, Dupre turns on his GPS unit. With zero visibility, he will need it to trace his way back to the landing. He starts the engine, brings the boat up on a gentle plane, and pilots it solely by the little line on the screen of the GPS receiver. I get an involuntary knot in my throat.

I realize that he will have to navigate through the tortuous shortcut with no visual clues, then cross the treacherous Atchafalaya River to get back home. In my imagination I can see a giant log floating somewhere on the river, waiting for unsuspecting boaters

After what seems like a nerve-wracking eternity, the dim lights of the Myette Point Boat Launch appear. "I hate running in the fog," he says in a release of tension. Dupre quickly loads his boat on its trailer at the silent ramp. As a last item of work, he walks down the ramp to the water's edge and picks up a soggy slab of cardboard that once held a case of beer. He shakes his head silently, throws it in the bed of the big Dodge truck, and heads over the levee toward home.

Day Two: The Chase

The next day opens with the promise of more fog over water, although the visibility on land is manageable. Dupre's destination today is the Atchafalaya River delta, one the most fog-bound spots in the state. On his way to the boat launch, he stops at 6:30 a.m. at a convenience store in Centerville to buy a bag of ice.

As he walks into the store he is approached by an incredibly inebriated twenty-ish man with a wispy moustache and goatee. The man holds a beer can in a brown paper bag in his hand. Struggling to focus his eyes on Dupre, he asks, "Where ish you goin'? I need a ride. You goin' dat way?" he points. Swaying and staggering, he waits for Dupre to answer. "No," replies Dupre, "we are going the other way."

He persists. "Why ish everone goin' dat way? I need to go da udder way. Whas down dere?" Customers in the parking lot of the convenience store watch him and shake their heads. Obviously, he has pestered others for a ride.

Dupre brushes him off and enters the store. The clerk informs him that the drunk has been at the store since before daylight, drinking and bothering customers. Dupre retreats to the back of the store to call the St. Mary Parish Sheriff's Office.

While he does so, I step back out to the truck to retrieve my glasses. As I near the entrance to the store, the drunk accosts me again, minus the beer can, which he has discarded on the pavement. Staggering and swaying, he says, "I gotta have a ride." I reply that I can't offer one as I am riding with someone else. "Oh yeah, da wilelife guy, huh?" he stammers out. Following me to the entrance, he asks, "Wa do wilelife guys do?" As I open the door, I reply, "They catch bad guys."

He follows me through the door. "Wash a bad guy?" I point at Dupre standing in the checkout line and reply, "Ask him." Without batting an eye or smirking, Dupre answers, "People who are drunk in store lots at 6:30 in the morning."

Pulling himself as erect as he can while trying to keep from falling down, he defends his dignity with a lopsided grin, "I didnent come here for dis." Dupre, getting impatient with the drunk's persistence, asks, "What are you doing drunk in public?" When all he gets is a "huuh," Dupre repeats the question.

"I not dwunk," he replies and goes on. "I got kicked outta da house. I gotta get outta Dodge." Then, amazingly enough, the man goes back to questioning Dupre about a ride, followed by questions about why everybody seemed to be going the opposite direction from where he wants to go.

Dupre retreats to his vehicle, but stays on the store's parking lot to be sure that no trouble arises and that the man doesn't try to walk down the shoulderless Highway 317. The drunk continues to stop every customer walking in the door until a sheriff's deputy arrives. As Dupre pulls out of the lot, he chuckles and comments, "He was sure tore up, huh?"

Dupre heads south on Highway 317, through the Bayou Teche National Wildlife Refuge. Peering over his right shoulder, he spots a Chevy truck with its headlights on stopped inside the refuge. "Something might not be right," he murmurs. After turning the vehicle around, he unhooks his boat trailer at the entrance to the refuge and creeps down the dirt road.

As he nears the truck, a scoped rifle barrel creeps out of the driver's side window. Dupre flicks on the light bar on top of the truck, steps out of the vehicle, and loudly identifies himself as a game warden. Out steps a fifty-five-year-old man.

"Any luck?" asks Dupre.

"No" is the one-word reply.

"Whatcha hunting?" asks Dupre straight-faced.

"Nothing." Another one-word reply.

"You're dressed in all camo and have a loaded rifle pointed out of the window. That looks a lot like hunting."

The man points and says, "There are two squirrels in that tree and one in that one."

"So you're hunting," retorts Dupre.

"Just watching them through the rifle scope," the man replies.

"And why is the gun loaded," asks Dupre.

"Just in case I see a coyote," is the reply.

"Do you have the right to shoot coyotes on the refuge?" Dupre persists.

The reply is lengthy. "Well, we used to have this lease before they took it away from us for the refuge. We really took care of it and watching things. I come out here just to make sure that everything is alright." And he goes on some more.

After the man finishes his monologue, Dupre returns to the truck with the hunter's rifle and driver's license. He fruitlessly tries calling a refuge officer, then combs through the rules pamphlet for the refuge, but can't find a clear answer as to whether the man is in violation of refuge rules. He photographs the rifle and records the subject's contact information in his field notebook to turn over to the refuge officer later.

As we near the small remote boat launch at Burns Point, Dupre explains why, if given the choice, he will launch his boat at obscure launches not often used by outdoorsmen. "Have you ever heard of taking the road less taken?" he asks rhetorically. "Well, that's the one that the really good bad guys take, and I want to be there.

After launching, he zigzags through an intricate canal system and then into Horseshoe Bayou, which has to be one of the most crooked waterways in Louisiana. It has one hairpin turn after another as it meanders through a freshwater marsh. Willow trees are scattered in clumps along the bank.

Rouseau canes, elephant ears, cattails, and Louisiana iris whiz by as Dupre slaloms down the bayou.

Then, bam! We run into a solid wall of white where the bayou empties into Atchafalaya Bay. The bay and delta are socked in with fog. Dupre turns off the motor to wait and see if it will gradually get better. The only thing he sees besides the cottony white mass of fog is a wall of menacing black clouds approaching from the northeast, which isn't fogged in.

Deciding that he doesn't want to risk getting struck by lightning, he runs back up the bayou to an acquaintance's camp. As he runs, wicked forks of lightning flash in the sky. The storm is rapidly closing in. He reaches the camp not two minutes too soon. Sheets of rain, driven almost sideways by a powerful south wind, lash the camp. Ear-splitting thunder makes conversation difficult on the protected porch.

While waiting out the storm, Dispatch calls Dupre and advises him that they have received a report of a bear being killed by a vehicle on Highway 83 near Glencoe. Louisiana black bears are classified as an endangered species, and policy is to retrieve any dead bears reported, explains Dupre. Not only may the bears be useful to researchers, but retrieving them prevents the removal of body parts by the public. Any possession of body parts from an endangered species is illegal under federal law.

At the first break in the weather, Dupre jumps in his boat, dashes back to the landing, and loads it on its trailer. Then it starts to drizzle and get nasty. The paved roads are mud-covered because it is still sugar cane harvesting season. Cane trucks, wheels covered in mud, are constantly entering the highway to deliver their loads to cane mills.

For a big creature, black bears can be hard to see. Finally, after passing the hapless creature's body once, Dupre sees it sprawled in the ditch. In its death throes, its jaws had locked down on vines and twigs. It looks a lot bigger than the 150 pounds that Dupre estimates that it weighs. A slightly putrid smell is wafting from the body.

Dupre loads the animal's carcass into the bed of his truck and delivers it to the LDWF office in New Iberia. He carefully attaches an evidence tag and drags it into a walk-in freezer to join two of its kin already in residence.

As soon as Dupre washes his hands, another call comes in from Dispatch with a complaint that hunters are shooting from an airboat in the Cypremort Point area. This is immediately followed by a call on his cell phone from another complainant who tells him the same thing. He points his boat trailer-encumbered truck back southward toward the area he just left.

After reaching the point of the complaint, he walks quickly through a

The dead black bear is sprawled unceremoniously in a highway ditch when Dupre finds it.

wooded ridge and climbs a live oak tree to an unused deer stand. He leans out, listens, and watches. He hears nothing, but wants a better view. With simian agility, he scampers up another limb until he is high in the tree. Seeing nothing, he descends.

As he reaches the truck, his portable radio comes to life again. Dispatch reports that a boat has exploded in the Atchafalaya River and is adrift near Berwick. While trying to find out more about the explosion, he drives the truck further south and stops at a hunting camp that he has been keeping his eye on "for a while."

On the radio another game warden informs him that the boat is a shrimp boat and that the explosion was violent enough to throw pieces of the vessel on top of the old Highway 90 bridge between Berwick and Morgan City.

Three hunters are at the camp and receive Dupre cordially. He asks to look around and does so thoroughly. He finds no blood in their airboat, the cleaning area, or anywhere else. They tell Dupre that they hunt a lot for wild hogs, but haven't killed any in a few days.

After Dupre leaves the camp, he explains that he had no evidence of wrongdoing and because wild hogs are considered feral domestic animals and not wildlife, they may be taken from moving boats and vehicles.

Satisfied that he has done as much as he can with this complaint, he says, "Now maybe, finally, we can head towards the Atchafalaya delta."

On the ride to the boat launch, he says that he will have to catch up on some paperwork tomorrow. He goes on to explain that doing paperwork is a critical part of a game warden's job.

"Paperwork is a pain in the butt because it takes a lot of time, but it is the most important thing in making cases. If you don't dot your i's and cross your t's, you will lose in court. There is an old saying that if it isn't in the report, it didn't happen. Doing offense reports timely, while they are still fresh in your mind, is best. Having good field notes also helps."

Required paperwork isn't limited to offense reports, says Dupre. Game wardens also must complete vehicle logs and time sheets, which are due weekly, and a purchasing card log is required monthly.

This time launching the boat at the Cabot Launch in the Intracoastal Waterway, Dupre almost immediately begins stopping waterfowl hunters returning from the Wax Lake delta. He stops boat after boat after boat, gradually working his way down Wax Lake Outlet.

By the time he gets to the sign marking the entrance to the Atchafalaya Delta Wildlife Management Area, it is obvious that the fog has lifted over the bay. Some boats have no ducks, mostly because they gave up before the fog lifted. But some, who waited out the fog, have decent bags.

On the WMA, he sees a large fiberglass V-hull boat stranded where it ran up into a couple of inches of water. Dupre offers the three hunters help in pulling the boat off the mudflat, an offer they gladly accept. One hunter wades to the game warden's boat and grabs the end of Dupre's rope. From their brief conversation, the two seem to have met before.

With the 150-horsepower motor roaring and all three hunters pushing, their boat ever so slowly inches toward deeper water. Safely afloat, the men thank Dupre profusely.

Once he idles out of voice range, Dupre grins mischievously and says, "You see that fella I was talking to. Last year I was checking hunters at the campground and I walked around from the back of his tent and caught him with a joint in his hand. He said, 'Oh shit, the game warden,' and stuffed it inside the seat of his pants. It was still lit. It was really funny. I was laughing while I wrote his ticket out."

Back to the routine of checking boats. Every boat gets checked for life jackets, and since all of them admit that they have been hunting or have their kill in the open on the bow or deck, the hunters are checked for the re-

An important part of the game warden's job is identifying and counting every species of waterfowl that has been harvested by hunters.

quired licenses and stamps and their shotguns are checked for the presence of plugs. Their harvested birds are identified and counted.

Shortly before sunset, Dupre pulls the boat up to a sandbar near the mouth of Mallard Pass. While he waits, a towering wall of black clouds, belching rumbles of thunder, builds to the north. No more shooting is heard, so he decides to intercept and check a boat that hunted right up until the end of legal hours. The two Alabama hunters in the boat are in compliance, as far as the check goes. But then the check is interrupted by a volley of shots that rings out to the northeast; it is twenty minutes after legal shooting hours.

Breaking off the check, Dupre cranks his big engine and roars up the pass, into Main Pass, and then into Shortcut Pass. There, he stops to watch the spot that he thought the shots came from. Sure enough, silhouetted against the western horizon, several hunters are still set up and waiting for a shot. Meanwhile, the black wall of clouds is moving closer and the rolling booms of thunder are becoming louder.

Dupre wants to witness the men shooting so as to make a good case. But the birds don't want to cooperate. Nothing flies near the men. He waits. He waits some more.

In the last soft light that comes before dark, Dupre sees a trimmed-out boat throwing a huge rooster tail of spray running up Main Pass with no running lights. Deciding that a bird in the hand may be better than two in the bush, he backs his boat off the bank to give chase.

The boat is fast and Dupre struggles to close the gap. The chase is proceeding dead on into the black cloud mass, now being rent by visible lightning. Inch by precious inch he gains on the boat.

Strong winds ahead of the squall roughen the water and Dupre's boat begins bucking its way through the waves, throwing spray high in the air to the right and the left. When he's nearly on their tail, he picks up his Q-Beam spotlight and shines directly on the boat, highlighting two passengers. They ignore him. He flashes the light off and on repeatedly. They still ignore him. He mutters, "Why are they running?"

He puts the spotlight down until he can get even closer. It's completely dark now and the multiple lightning bolts snaking viciously downward around us are so close that they hiss and snap instead of thunder. The boat hits each wave with the force of a mailed fist. In my mind (I think), I smell sulphur and hear the seven trumpets of Revelation. Adrenaline is flooding my system

Then, just when it appears that he is getting so close that they will have to stop, the game warden's motor begins to sputter and spit. The fuel tank is empty. Dupre frantically works the switch to change tanks, but the motor has lost its prime. It alternately gasps and pukes, then jumps to life when it gets some fuel, then immediately chokes again. Dupre jumps onto the stern and pumps the primer bulb like a man possessed.

The boat is still visible in the lightning flashes. The long process of trying to catch up to them begins again. Then the motor completely shuts down. The crashing of the boat on the squall's waves has broken the bow fuel tank off its mounts and it has walked its way toward the stern, badly kinking the fuel line.

He runs to the bow, wedges the tank in place, re-primes the engine with fuel, and throws the throttle wide open again. But the runner has escaped into the storm, which is still increasing in violence.

With no clue as to which way the boat went at the intersection of the Intracoastal Waterway and Wax Lake Outlet, Dupre decides to run up the outlet to Calumet, where the most heavily used boat launch in the area is located. Still heading north, he weaves between the brightly lit tugboats plying the Intracoastal where it crosses Wax Lake Outlet.

Between the Intracoastal and the launch, a solid wall of rain descends on the boat. The lightning gets worse. When he gets to the launch, a boat is visible in the deluge. Its operator is waiting to power it on the trailer that his partner is backing down the launch ramp. The twelve-mile chase is over. Dupre erupts from his boat and strides down the slick wharf.

The security lights at the launch and the almost constant flashes of lightning reveal a lean, hawk-nosed man standing in a stiletto-shaped, high-performance aluminum hull. As Dupre nears, the man turns dark, glinting eyes on him. "In a hurry, huh?" is Dupre's questioning greeting.

He then asks him why he didn't stop when he flashed his light on him. "I wanted to beat the rain in," he replies. Dupre asks for and takes his driver's license, then allows him to load his boat on the trailer in the torrent.

The two men then retreat to an open-fronted boat shed for Dupre to write his ticket. As he is writing, his eye catches a medicine bottle protruding from the front pouch of the subject's neoprene waders. "What's that?" asks

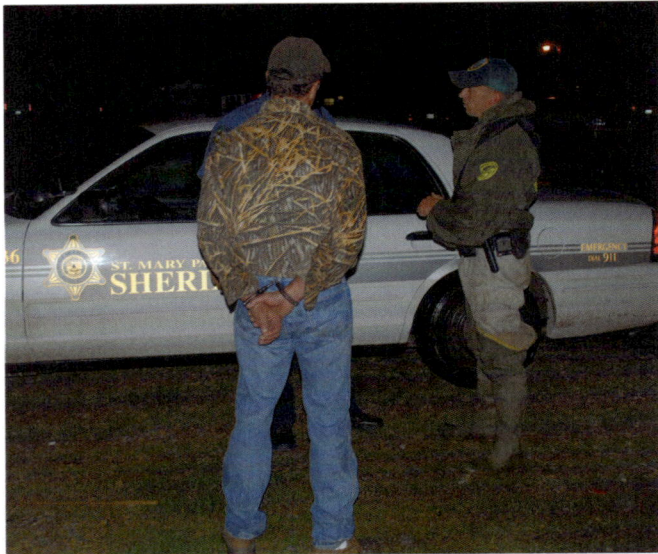

In the darkness after the storm, Dupre transfers custody of his prisoner to a St. Mary Parish sheriff's deputy. Even though his shift has ended, he must put his boat on its trailer and then go to the correctional facility where the man is detained to process the necessary paperwork before going home.

Dupre. Defensively, the subject partially turns and tucks the bottle deeper into the pouch. "Give it here," demands Dupre.

As the man hands it over, Dupre notes that the normally hard-to-remove label has been deliberately scraped off. Dupre again asks him what is in the bottle. "My diet pills," is the answer. Using the information imprinted on the pills and his cell phone, Dupre confirms that the pills are a Schedule III controlled substance, closely related to amphetamines, stimulants called speed, amp, or tweak by recreational drug users. Possession of controlled drugs that are not in a labeled bottle is illegal.

Dupre informs the subject that he is under arrest, allows him to remove his bulky waders, then handcuffs him. The squall passes to the south, and Dupre and the subject wait for a St. Mary Parish sheriff's deputy to provide transport to the Centerville Correctional Facility. Dupre informs the officer that he will come to lock-up to do the booking after taking his boat to the launch to load it up.

During the run back, Dupre sits silently as the adrenaline dissipates. But when he slows down to idle into Cabot, he looks over at me, grins, and says, "I love it, I love it, I love it."

5

THE DECOY

The trip west on I-20 beginning at the Mississippi state line provides me with a lesson in north Louisiana geography. After crossing the Mississippi River, some of Louisiana's most fertile soils, those of the Mississippi River flood plain, lay billiard-table flat for miles. Almost every acre is actively farmed, mostly in row crops.

After passing Bayou Macon, the road crosses over the almost unnoticeably elevated Macon Ridge, with its veneer of loessal soil deposits, then drops back to more bottomlands created by the Boeuf and Ouachita rivers.

Immediately past Ruston, the land rises noticeably into the Ouachita Hills, the beginning of north Louisiana hill country. This area was shaped by geological uplifting, unlike so much of the state, which is low and alluvial in nature. My destination today is in Bienville Parish, about a mile from 535-foot-high Driskill Mountain, the highest point in the state, and squarely astride the edge of the Nacogdoches Wold.

A wold is a hilly or rolling region, which certainly describes northwestern Louisiana. All of the area is strongly influenced by the Sabine Uplift, a great fold beneath the surface of the earth near the Louisiana-Texas state line.

I turn off the interstate into the beautiful little hill town of Arcadia. South of town, I meet with Bienville Parish wildlife agent Sergeant Patrick Staggs, a ten-year veteran. He informs me that tonight he will be working as part of a three-man team, along with Sergeant Michael Kelley and Senior Agent Jared McIver.

They have been receiving numerous complaints recently about night hunting taking place over a several parish area. The three men plan to set up a deer decoy tonight in one of the areas of complaint and see what happens. They have a lot of complaints to choose from.

Decoys are essentially just lifelike taxidermy mounts of wildlife, usually deer that are set up in areas of suspected illegal activity. They give violators an opportunity to break the law near where they can be observed by wildlife agents. Because of the potential danger of working at night in proximity to rifle fire, LDWF policy requires three agents to be present when a decoy is deployed.

Before Staggs meets the other two game wardens to set up the decoy, he gives some attention to another night hunting complaint in Claiborne Parish. It's still early, so on the way to this site he pokes around looking for outdoors activity. At the same time, he talks about his career and gives me a primer on the area.

A youthful thirty-four years old, Staggs is tall and lithe and packs a big, but shy, ear to ear smile. With his soft-spoken southern drawl, he seems a little reserved until he gets warmed up, then becomes an articulate talker.

Staggs says that while he hunted and fished "a bunch" growing up, he is not one of those who grew up always wanting to be a game warden. After accumulating 170 hours of credits in agri-business at Louisiana Tech and interning in a chip mill, he decided working in a paper mill was not his vision of what he wanted to do with the rest of his life. After a visit to a job fair in New Orleans, he set out on a game warden's career.

Patrick Staggs investigates the site of a night hunting complaint.

"I enjoy what I do," he says, "Most of the people that I deal with are good people. It's not fun having to write up ill-informed people, but it is fun to catch those who break wildlife laws deliberately. There are not many jobs where you don't end up dreading going to work. Here you can visit with your coworkers and smile."

It's just after dark, and spying what looks like the flash of a light, Staggs makes a sharp U-turn with his big truck and pulls into an oilfield site. "You never know what you will find at a place like this. It could be night hunting and it could be boyfriend/girlfriend stuff," he says diplomatically. The site is blank.

Back on the road, he goes on about being a game warden. "I really like the freedom to come and to go. It isn't like being stuck behind a cyclone fence or at an office desk. Here, no one is looking over your shoulder. Sometimes I go two weeks with everything quiet and then I get two days of non-stop activity and excitement."

At the spot that Staggs plans to watch, he pulls the blacked-out truck down a gravel road, then backs into a logging road. He lowers the truck's windows so that no gunshot escapes his attention, and waits. It is unseasonably warm and pleasant for January and a huge full moon beams overhead, through the tall, straight pine trees.

The complaint here, explains Staggs, is about hunters at a camp that sit in their deer stands during the day, go to the camp for supper, then hunt with lights from their ATVs in the early part of the night. "If we don't see or hear something fairly early, it probably won't be worth staying long," he says.

He talks about the country he works in and its people. "This is deer dog country, jacked up truck, Redneck country, with 10,000-acre hunting leases. I kind of dread dog season for deer, because of all the complaints that I know it will generate. Hunting deer with dogs will probably hang on longer here than any other place in Louisiana."

After apologizing for the bullet-perforated decoy's being "a little raggedy," he says that he gets a kick out of how people react to decoys. "I had a woman get out of a car and cautiously walk up to it. When she gets right up to it, she hollers to us in hiding, 'You ain't gonna fool nobody.' I thought to myself, 'It fooled you.'

"But people are harder to fool now than when it was new and a novelty. Still, working a decoy is a fun thing to do. When they were a new thing, I set one up in the daytime about seventy-five yards off a road. A truck passed by and turned around with a shooter riding in the bed of the truck with a shotgun. Boom! Boom! Boom! And then I stepped out in front of the truck.

The mounted deer decoy lies in the bed of Staggs's pickup truck.

All the guy wanted to know was 'Did I hit it? Can I go check?' The answer was 'no.'

"Sometimes people aren't too smart. I once pulled up in a person's yard and had the guy come out and say, 'Yeah, I did it,' and proceed to confess in detail to something entirely different than what I was there to talk to him about."

Staggs shakes his head and grins as he spins another story. "I had a complaint about a hunter who was supposedly not tagging his deer. I went to his house and he was in the process of skinning a deer that was tagged. I asked him how many he had taken this year and he replied that he had killed four deer so far. One of his friends standing nearby and watching him skin the deer told me that he had a lifetime hunting license and asked how he could get deer tags to go with the license.

"I told him that any Walmart can print them for him. Then I asked him how many deer he had killed this year. 'Two,' was his reply. So I started writing him up. He protested, 'Aw, man, you're gonna write me up for telling the truth? I'm just trying to do the right thing.' I asked him how many wildlife tickets he has had before. 'About nine,' he said. Like I said, sometimes people aren't too smart.

"One thing about this job," Staggs says with a little sadness in his voice, "is that you find out who your real friends are. Some people stop associating with you. You ain't a good ole boy anymore. Your real friends are your friends even if you have to write them up."

While sitting in the dark, Staggs hears the gravel crunch under the tires of the other game wardens' approaching blacked-out truck. They pull up next to Staggs and in the bright moonlight begin comparing notes on their alternatives. While they are talking, McIver fields a red-hot compliant on his cell phone.

A police officer in Webster Parish is on the other end and is loudly venting his spleen about a father and son who, among other nefarious activities, have been riding the remote roads of the hills at night on their ATVs, rampantly shooting any and all wildlife they encounter and leaving most of it unretrieved.

Earlier in the day the police officer had pulled into the approach to their home to get the license plate numbers from their vehicles, which he gives to the game wardens. The disturbed officer yells loudly enough that McIver holds the phone away from his ear. All three game wardens can plainly hear every word.

McIver thanks the caller and hangs up. All three agents are ready to

Jared McIver (in truck) and Mike Kelley (standing) plan with Staggs where to set up their deer decoy.

respond to this one. The two trucks set out for Webster Parish, winding through the hills and small towns of the area. After passing the stunning white-colonnaded courthouse in Homer, they zoom past Shongaloo and keep going.

As Staggs follows the other truck, he talks about how much he has learned from Mike Kelley, the older game warden in the other truck. "I came out of the academy hell-bent to write every ticket. I learned a lot about using judgment on ticket writing from Mike. He is really a good people person."

Near the area where they want to put out the decoy, the two trucks split up temporarily to scout. The other two game wardens call Staggs to tell him that a suspicious vehicle had passed them and is heading his way. "It might be a good one to follow," they say. Staggs positions his blacked-out truck down a side road and waits for them to pass.

They don't pass Staggs. Walker, in the other truck, calls Staggs and tells him that the vehicle has stopped and pulled off the road and now a person from the vehicle is going in the woods with a flashlight. McIver is going on foot to intercept him.

Twenty minutes later, the radio crackles again. The two occupants of the suspicious vehicle had a coon dog and were legally hunting for raccoons.

The three game wardens in their two trucks rendezvous in a spot where they will be able to keep close tabs on their decoy and yet keep their trucks hidden. They have chosen a spot not far down the road from the home of the alleged night hunters.

McIver puts the decoy in place. Now the waiting begins.

Magically, a barbeque pit materializes in the back of one of the trucks. The men are famished. None of them has eaten supper yet and it is almost 9 p.m. By just the light of the silvery moon they grill several varieties of deer sausage. These they eat on sliced white bread washed down with Dr. Peppers.

"This is a lot more effective than wasting time to stop and eat at a restaurant," says one of the men. "I've never made any wildlife cases in restaurants." The other two grunt and nod in agreement.

It is a beautiful night. The full moon is at its apogee and small clouds scud across its face. The wind sighs through the tall pine trees, and it's just cool enough to keep the mosquitoes at bay.

As they wait, the game wardens converse quietly about decoy work and catching night hunters in general. McIver says, "People from all walks of life and all professions shoot these decoys."

McIver preps the decoy with reflective eyes before carrying it to the roadside for set-up.

"And some from no professions," adds Staggs.

McIver goes on, "Teachers, coaches, a town constable, a grocery store manager, oilfield hands, sometimes you can even jack up a professional night hunter—one that goes almost every night."

Kelley looks at me and explains, "Professionals are those that do it like a sport, like legal day hunters do it—for the thrill."

Sitting in the moonlight, the three veterans discuss their experiences night hunting for night hunters and its rewards. "A high-powered rifle shot sounds so much louder at night than in the day."

"Yeah," agrees McIver, "sometimes you can see the fire from the muzzle."

"Hearing that shot in the dark is like shooting a big buck," says Kelley excitedly.

"Then," says Staggs, "we all throw the trucks into gear and there is gravel flying everywhere."

McIver pipes up, "It really is like shooting a big buck; you get the best of both worlds. You get the feeling of hunting big game and you get to catch illegal hunters."

The three men sit quietly on lawn chairs, their hunger sated with the deer sausage feast, and comment in low voices in expectation on each passing car—always waiting for the shot.

Kelley, the most experienced of the three, discourses more about the rewards of stalking night hunters. "Catching a night hunter is job satisfaction. You don't have much contact with people doing this—but when you do catch someone like this, they really need being caught. I'd rather do this than talk to two hundred people and write twenty little tickets."

He adds, "It's all part of the job. Sometimes you need to be seen and other times you need to be unseen and catch violators."

And so it goes. The hours ebb slowly in the swish of the wind through the pine boughs overhead and in the murmur of softly modulated voices. The official end of the shift for all three men is at midnight, but midnight comes and goes and they still are to be found lurking near their decoy.

Finally, at 1 a.m., they confer quietly and decide it is probably best to call it quits. Maybe the hunters were spooked by having seen the police officer turn into their lane earlier in the day. Maybe they just didn't want to come out tonight because the moon was too bright.

The decoy is retrieved and the two trucks head in different directions toward their lairs. The trip for Staggs, from northern Webster Parish back across Claiborne Parish to Bienville Parish, gives him a chance to talk about his love for the hills and to compare working as a game warden in this area to working in south Louisiana, which he has done several times.

"Rednecks operate different than the folks in south Louisiana do," he observes. "The funny thing is that when you stop someone or write them a ticket down there, they go to cussing and raising all kinds of hell. Then, the next thing—they offer you a Coke.

"If one of these rednecks in overalls starts cussing ya, you better be ready, because he's gonna grab you or you're gonna grab him. They mean it when they cuss.

"Their use of the F-word in south Louisiana is a literary miracle. It's a noun, a verb, an adjective, an adverb, a pronoun—the whole ball of wax."

Staggs has me laughing until my sides hurt.

"I love the hills," he says pensively. "When I head back from the flatlands and see that big pine tree in Lecompte, I know I am headed home."

The hour-long drive in the middle of the night is beautiful. The big truck rolls through the hills meeting no traffic. At 1:30 a.m. there is not a vehicle on the road but us. Even in the small towns, all the human inhabitants are asleep.

But the hills are alive with wildlife of all kinds, foxes, skunks, rabbits, and deer—lots and lots of deer, in singles, in pairs, in groups, and in what can only be described as herds. Staggs has to slow the truck repeatedly to keep from hitting them.

With the sight of all this wildlife, I comment half-questioning, "You guys must really have the folks in the hills behaving." Staggs chuckles and replies laconically, "I don't know about all that; I think the Good Lord provided us with enough for them and to have plenty left over for everyone."

As Staggs pulls close to my drop-off point, a flashy black- and white-striped skunk skitters away from the road, waving its tail high, warning us to keep our distance.

The area's wild creatures rule the night.

6

THE SMELL OF THE SWAMP

One of the first things one learns when riding with game wardens is that more often then not, most hunters and fishermen will begin dropping names of other game wardens when they are stopped. "Say, do you know . . . ?"

It's almost amusing. And if they don't know a game warden's name to float, they will go to sheriff's deputies or state troopers.

Everybody's name gets dropped, including Colonel Winton Vidrine's, Chief of the Enforcement Division of the Louisiana Department of Wildlife and Fisheries. But one name keeps cropping up more than others, especially in a six- or seven-parish area of south-central Louisiana.

Unlike with other names, when people ask a game warden if they know Dusty Rhodes, there is almost always an undercurrent in the question. Sometimes it is negative; sometimes it's positive. At times, one gets the impression that the questioner himself doesn't know Rhodes, but rather is asking obliquely if he really exists or is just a fable—like Bigfoot.

Today, I'm scheduled to ride circuit in the Atchafalaya Basin with Sergeant Rhodes and his partner, Senior Agent Jason Marks. I am running late for my rendezvous with the two agents at the Bayou Benoit Boat Landing. In Henderson, I run into road work and am detoured onto State Highway 3039, which has to be the crookedest road in Louisiana.

It baffles me why anyone, even a drunken sailor, would lay out a road with hairpin curves on a tabletop-flat landscape. To make matters worse, the detour signs disappear after they dump me off on the road.

I manage to get to the landing twenty minutes late. The game wardens are waiting in their boat, ready to go. I greet the two men and try to guess which one is Rhodes. One appears to be in his early fifties, is strongly built, and has his longish sandy blond hair cut in an almost pixie-style haircut. He is wearing a huge, toothy grin.

The other man is not as tall as the first, and much younger, perhaps in his late twenties. His dark hair is cut short, like that of most game wardens. His face is full-cheeked and he, too, wears a smile.

Neither man is six feet tall.

Hmm. Neither looks like what I pictured after hearing so much about Rhodes. I guess I was expecting someone who looked like James Arness, the rugged six-foot, seven-inch actor who starred in the TV western series *Gunsmoke*.

They introduce themselves. The dark-haired man is Marks. Rhodes is the blond guy with long hair. Rhodes doesn't look like a game warden. But then, perhaps that is why he worked so successfully undercover as a covert wildlife agent for five years.

Spring is a good time to be in the Atchafalaya Basin. The freshly leafed trees are wearing lime-green cloaks. They will only be this refreshing color for a few weeks before Louisiana's torrid summer sun will turn them somber dark green for the rest of the summer and into fall. The morning is chilly, but a bright sun in a brilliant blue sky promises to warm things up later in the day.

The men explain that they plan to take a big swing through the basin, down the G. A. Cut to Buffalo Cove, then through Gravenburg and the Phillips Canal, all the way up to the Crook Chene Cove area. At the latter spot, they want to investigate a complaint that they have received about a crawfish fisherman using wire crawfish traps constructed of square mesh rather than hexagonal mesh, as the law specifies. Square mesh traps retain smaller crawfish than hex mesh traps.

The boat pulls from the landing into the surging brown floodwaters being fed into the cut by the Atchafalaya River. Immediately, the smell of the Atchafalaya Basin in the spring penetrates me to my lungs. Nothing, but nothing, smells as good as the runoff from spring rains and snow melt from half of the United States surging through the trees of the swamp.

It smells like life. I inhale deeply.

The game wardens' boat passes the Sandy Cove Boat Landing. It is full of the well-used pickup trucks and homemade boat trailers of commercial fishermen. It's a weekday, so there are few of the fancy rigs driven by many recreational fishermen at the landing. Besides, recreational fishing is generally difficult in the muddy, brown floodwaters of spring.

Commercial fishing, they explain, is now mostly done for crawfish. Little market exists for finfish, like catfish, buffalo, and gaspergou. Crawfish season has been slow so far, but it is still very early April and a lot of fishing time remains.

Rhodes, a twenty-five-year veteran of the Louisiana Department of Wildlife and Fisheries, estimates that he spends 40 percent of his time within the guide levees of the basin. Marks, who has been with the department less than three years, spends even more time here, probably 70 percent.

Marks clearly enjoys being in the basin. "No way I could take a desk job," he says straight-faced. "While I was waiting for this job, I took a job in a jail. It depressed me so much that it almost caused a divorce." Outside of work, Marks is a dedicated hunter and fisherman.

Rhodes peeks out of a corner of his sunglasses and throws a stinger at Marks. "You know, I caught Jason's grandfather. He used an illegal weapon to take a deer during muzzle-loader season."

Marks replies, "He was a great outdoorsman. He lived to hunt and fish. He died of a heart attack in his boat while crawfishing nine years ago."

I give Marks a chance to get even when I ask about Rhodes's reputation. He says, "Everyone asks for Dusty when I check someone. I am sure that some who claim to know him don't, they just know of him."

Rhodes grins and interrupts to add that he has checked people who ask him if he knows Dusty Rhodes. He clearly gets a kick out of the notoriety.

Marks isn't done. "You know Dusty. Just about everyone agrees. If he

Both Dusty Rhodes (l) and Jason Marks (r) love to work in the vast Atchafalaya Basin.

wants you, he's like a dog; he's gonna get you. Yup, he is well known—a legend in his own mind." Marks lets out a huge belly laugh.

Rhodes grins and takes it.

Buffalo Cove is easily the most scenic part of the basin. The trees are almost all bald cypress, Louisiana's state tree. The gorgeous swamp is holding six more feet of water than it will after the spring flood passes. It's muddy at the surface, but the propeller wash from the 225-horsepower outboard turns up clearer, tea-colored water from beneath the muddy layer.

As they ease into Bayou Gravenburg, the immaculate twenty-two-foot Triton passes a large, waxed cardboard bait box hung on a tree stump. Rhodes jaw juts out and he says fiercely, "I can't stand litterers." Frozen fish to be used as crawfish bait are purchased in these boxes. A few fishermen still discard them in the swamp when they are empty, rather than bring them back in with them.

The bayou is utterly still at this time of the morning. All the crawfish fishermen are in the flooded woods running their crawfish traps.

As they ride, both men lament the collapse of waterfowl hunting for mallards in the basin. And without mallards, it seems, even hunting activity for wood ducks has declined.

Further on, they pass more bait boxes and some large paper bags that

Buffalo Cove may be the most classically beautiful part of the Atchafalaya Basin.

once held artificial crawfish bait. Rhodes shakes his head and mutters, "I know that the waxed boxes are biodegradable, but. . . ."

Marks finishes the sentence, "yeah, after two years."

Without seeing a soul to check, the two men pass into the Si Bon Canal, which they explain means "good" in French. Heading toward Crook Chene Cove, the boat crosses Gays Slough. Rhodes plows the boat carefully through big mats of water hyacinths, which can easily hide propeller-damaging logs. Snow white three-foot-tall egrets pulse through the cypress trees. Here and there, one stands on a log, beak at the ready to spear an unwary fish.

In the cove, Marks checks crawfish traps, looking for the offending square mesh ones. The location of each trap is marked by a strip of survey-or's tape tied to a tree limb. Each fisherman marks his traps with a different color of flagging tape.

Unable to find the traps, they conclude that the fisherman has picked them up. Back in the Si Bon, they begin to encounter boats of crawfish fish-ermen who have finished running their trap lines. They check everyone's licenses, life jackets, and boat registrations.

First up are two brothers with powerful Cajun accents, each in his own boat. Both are well into their sixties and pack big smiles, but brother number two is clearly very shy and happy to get on his way.

In mid- to late morning, commercial crawfish fishermen start returning from running their trap lines.

We sit quietly for a while. Brilliant sunflower-yellow male prothonotary warblers are flitting noisily everywhere. The tiny birds are staking out their breeding territories. A big, gaudy black and white pileated woodpecker calls from a nearby dead tree snag. Hawks mark their territories by screaming loudly and repeatedly. It is a riot of bird calls.

Next up is another aluminum skiff, the tool of the trade for Atchafalaya Basin crawfishing. This one holds a man and his three kids. While Marks joshes with the three youngsters, the man scrutinizes Rhodes and says, "You're the king of the game wardens." Rhodes grins but doesn't reply.

The crawfisherman knows Rhodes by reputation.

Everything checks out and as they are exchanging pleasantries another boat approaches. The driver wears a forced smile and has the look of a small boy trying to exit the kitchen after raiding the cookie jar.

As his boat squeezes by the two boats in the canal, he tries his best to ignore the game wardens, but at the same time sneaks glances at them out of the corner of his eye. He casually waves, but doesn't turn his face toward them.

After he is past the game wardens and thinks that he is home free, Rhodes hollers, "Hey," and crooks a finger at him to call him back. "Oh, you got me," he cries in anguish as he backs his boat up. "Oh man, I left my life jacket in my truck. Well, go ahead and write me."

Rhodes grins, reaches into a hatch in his boat, and fishes out a life jacket. "Which do you want?" he asks while waving the jacket in one hand and his ticket book in the other.

"I'll take the life jacket," is the grateful reply. He grabs it and straps it on. "Where should I leave it?" Rhodes tells him to leave it in the bed of his truck at the Bayou Benoit Landing.

"I wish that you had done that for me when you caught me running poule d'eaus," he says.

"That was different," Rhodes replies with a laugh.

The fisherman cranks up his motor, throws a level gaze at Rhodes, and says, "I owe you one. I might call you with some information sometime."

As he idles away, Rhodes explains that he had caught the man two years earlier on the last weekend of waterfowl season using boats to chase up coots to shoot in Sandy Cove. He and his partners had forty coots in their possession and another ninety-two untagged birds back at their camp. They openly admitted to rallying coots the day before as well.

When it seems no more boats will be coming their way, Marks and Rhodes start their engine and idle up the Si Bon toward the G. A. Cut. Before they get there, they pass a broadbanded water snake coiled up in a bush a couple of feet off of the water. Every basin fisherman's fear is a snake dropping out of a bush or tree into his boat. This one is lethargic from the low air temperatures and even cooler water and doesn't seem inclined to move.

When the men reach the G. A. Cut, they allow the boat to drift with the current while they eat their sandwiches. They repeatedly have to lay aside their lunch to perform safety checks on passing boats.

The couple in the second boat they stop has a small shih tzu lapdog. The woman holding the dog asks Rhodes to hold it while she helps search for their life jackets. Rhodes gingerly holds the nervous little creature, and it promptly proceeds to urinate in his boat. He grins. What else can he do?

As the two travel down the cut toward the northern end of the Attakapas Wildlife Management Area, Rhodes talks about how he has changed as a game warden. "It took a long time for me to get over having to write everyone up.

"But I realize that I can't let complacency set in; complacency will get you killed. I don't make a vehicle stop during hunting season without calling it in. You never know when you will meet that convicted felon who will do something.

"More game wardens are killed by making routine stops, doing something that they have always done and catching someone at the wrong time. I try not to be complacent, but I know that I am guilty of some of it."

They cruise into Crewboat Chute and then up the Atchafalaya River. The muddy brown river waters are roily and turbulent. Fearsome boils that look worse than they are break the surface of the great river.

We make a quick pass through the Amerada Hess oilfield canals. In the very back canal of the field they find a small tugboat and barge tied up near an oil well. Two men are fishing from the stern of the tug.

When the game wardens' boat pops out from behind the trees, the men drop their fishing rods like hot potatoes. "Oh yeah, we're going to check these guys," says Rhodes.

The father and son, both from Mississippi and both crewmen on the tugboat, have no fishing licenses. After the wardens write citations to the men, Marks explains to them how to purchase their licenses by telephone so that they can continue to fish.

From Amerada Hess, the men head upriver. Near where Jake's Bayou splits from the Atchafalaya River channel, a house seems to be planted in the center of the river. As the men close in on it, they find that it is a huge, derelict houseboat, abandoned to float free down the river. Its back is broken and the middle of the camp slumps precipitously.

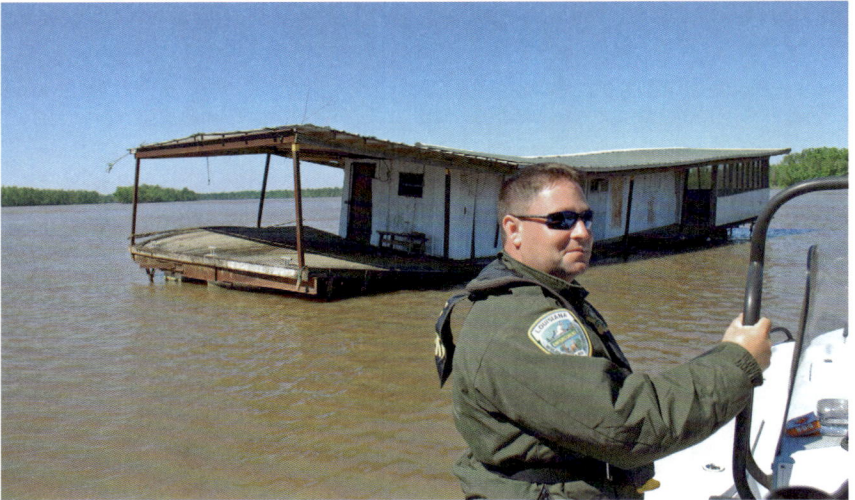

A huge derelict houseboat drifts down the middle of the Atchafalaya River channel at the mercy of currents and winds.

Obviously, the loose camp is a hazard to navigation. Marks enters the camp and, stepping carefully, inspects it to find some clue as to ownership. Everything that would have a name on it has been stripped.

Leaving the wreck behind, the men penetrate further north to the old Atchafalaya River–Whiskey Bay Pilot Channel split. They haven't seen another boat for hours. The only signs of human activity are the many water-accessible-only hunting and fishing camps, most of them, incongruously for a swamp, surrounded by a neatly mowed greensward.

"The basin is silting in," says Rhodes resignedly, adding, "It has shrunk and is more accessible for more people."

Marks adds, "The amount of camps has increased, there are more leases and even talk of high fences to control wildlife movements. Commercial fishing has dwindled. People used to be able to make a living fishing. The only thing feasible now to make money with is crawfish."

"The money is in crawfish," agrees Rhodes. "Catfish was fifty cents a pound twenty years ago and it still is—when they can sell them. Another problem in the basin is that people are preempting public lands," says Rhodes.

Marks nods his head in agreement and adds, "They make claims to land and then run the public off."

Recreational fishing has problems in the basin, too, according to the two game wardens. Marks points out that the basin has a lot more fishermen in it now and that people are complaining about there not being enough fish to catch.

"An increasing thing is bass boaters driving ninety miles per hour and thinking that they are right," notes Rhodes.

"Some of them seem to think that they own the water," adds Marks.

"Their first excuse when we stop one for reckless operation," says Rhodes, "is 'I am fishing in a tournament.' We will see more traffic and more boating accidents."

Rhodes changes the subject slightly. "Violations are down and compliance with laws is up though. People are changing. We don't have people surviving off of natural resources now. For example, until the 1980s people would hunt for coons from boats because coon hides were worth something.

"True market hunting is down, even lower than in the mid-1990s. Hunting is better because hunting clubs practice management."

While they are in a reflective mood, I ask them about the future. Marks says that he thinks that the basin will see more private camps and that he doesn't think it will pass into public ownership. Rhodes disagrees, saying he can see the U.S. Army Corps of Engineers buying more property for public use. He adds that he doesn't predict as much growth in private camps as Marks.

On the subject of trespass, specifically crawfish fishermen exercising the traditional practice of fishing over private lands that are flooded for months at a time, both men quietly groan, agreeing that the issue will likely remain as a "continued unenforceable nightmare." Both are happy that enforcement of the unpopular law is the responsibility of sheriffs' offices rather then theirs.

On recreational fishing, they agree that as long as the human population around the basin continues to grow, fishing pressure is likely to grow. In contrast, the future of commercial fishing has both men shaking their heads. They call it a "dying" activity. Even the commercial crawfish fishery is likely to dwindle, they agree, both because of the dominance of the crawfish farming industry and because of water level problems in the basin.

They diverge somewhat in their views of the future of hunting. Rhodes sees a way of life changing, with hunting becoming less important. Marks sees more pressure for trophy deer management coming. And he adds that if high fences are put in for management, it may ruin hunting in the basin.

As for the biggest challenge facing those that love the Atchafalaya Basin, Rhodes is succinct. "Because of siltation, the biggest challenge will be to keep the swamp a swamp."

Marks predicts that the biggest challenge lies in resolving the conflicts between the vision that the Corps of Engineers has for management of the basin and the views that the users of the basin have.

The men are quiet for the rest of the ride down the G. A. Cut. They are talked out. The setting sun throws long tree shadows across the waterway. The nip is coming back into the air.

At the landing, Rhodes looks in the bed of his pickup. Yup, the life jacket is there.

7

PEACE ON THE BAYOU

It's transition time, the period between the end of hunting season and the onset of wide-open summertime fishing and boating. Even commercial fishing activity is relatively slow this time of year. The peak of oystering is passed by March–early April, and shrimping and crabbing is not going full bore yet.

Still, game wardens patrol at all hours and 365 days a year. Today, Sergeant Mitch Darby and Senior Agent Jason Romero will be jumping off from Cypremort Point in Vermilion Bay to patrol the bayous, lakes, and marshes of the area.

We meet well before daylight at the Louisiana Department of Wildlife and Fisheries office just outside of New Iberia. Darby is five feet, five inches tall, 180 pounds, and all muscle. One look at his biceps convinces me that I would rather be shot by him than punched.

Sergeant Mitch Darby leads the day's patrol.

A love of the outdoors took Jason Romero to his job as a game warden.

73

The youthful Romero is taller, slender, and almost movie star handsome. He carries a dimple on his chin, and his deep olive complexion and black eyes give away the Spanish genes in his family history.

During the ride from New Iberia to Cypremort Point, the two men, both of whom hold associate degrees in law enforcement, talk about their paths to the Louisiana Department of Wildlife and Fisheries.

Only twenty-seven years old, Romero went to work for the department at age twenty-one. As a kid, a neighbor worked for the department's Fur and Refuge Division at Marsh Island and Romero was able to meet game wardens through him. He thought that it was a "cool job," largely because of working in the outdoors.

Darby's route to the job involved a stint as a deputy with the Iberia Parish Sheriff's Office. He liked law enforcement, but didn't like domestic dispute calls. Plus, he couldn't see himself sitting in a patrol car for twenty-five years. That, plus his love of the outdoors and a college job with the department's Fur and Refuge Division, convinced him to apply for a game warden's position.

Cypremort Point is an odd mixture of coastal resort and working waterfront. New condominiums and luxurious retreats are intermixed with camps managed under the benign neglect approach, and stacks of crab traps.

The boat the men are using today is spiffy, a twenty-seven-foot "justice hull" Whaler powered by two 250-horsepower four-stroke outboard motors. It is equipped with a push bumper, a huge bit in the cockpit big enough to handle a ship's hawser, and a boarding ramp projecting over the bow.

Once clear of the landing and in the open waters of Vermilion Bay, the residual winds from the cold front that passed the day before yesterday become evident. Through the drier air brought in by the front, the big, blue-tinged mounds of Avery and Weeks Islands rise out of the marsh to the northwest. Both are massive salt domes. We are headed in their direction, en route to Avery Canal.

A strong rising tide has water surging into the canal. It's muddy and doesn't look inviting. Avery Island looms much larger in front of us. The game wardens run through the area's canals and in the Intracoastal Waterway for a ways. They find only one boat fishing. The two men and a youngster in the boat have a solitary gaspergou as their catch.

The game wardens re-enter the bay and turn the boat south-southeast, heading for Southwest Pass, the deep channel between Marsh Island and the western shore of Vermilion Bay.

The wind has shifted from the northeast to the east and then to east-southeast and has picked up speed. The ride across the bay is brutal. Both men stand with half-bent knees to absorb the shock of the pounding they are getting. The bay's waters are muddy, both from the wind-induced waves churning up the bottom and from the high discharges from the Atchafalaya River.

As they near Marsh Island, they stop a commercial crab boat with its stern loaded with bright yellow traps. The crabbers are Asian. Although both are friendly, one can't speak English at all and communication with the other is difficult.

Darby and Romero inspect their crab catch for compliance with minimum size requirements. Darby reads the fishermen's license number to Romero, who checks that the number is the same as the ones on the traps' tags. All of the traps are equipped with the required escape rings to release small crabs.

Leaving the crabber, Darby pilots the boat through the pass into Gulf waters. Making a big arc around the island, they pass Diamond Reef and Shell Key. Not a boat is on the water.

Many of the commercial crabbers on the central Louisiana coast are of Asian heritage, and communicating with them is challenging for the game wardens.

They enter the interior of Marsh Island through Mound Bayou, then take a left into winding and scenic Oyster Bayou. Mottled ducks and late-migrating teal take flight ahead of the big Whaler, which rumbles down the tortuous bayou like an M-60 battle tank.

Birds are everywhere: brown pelicans, gulls and terns of several species, clouds of shore birds, showy egrets, grackles, blackbirds, stilts, and innumerable "LBJs" (little brown jobs), what biologists jokingly dub small nondescript birds such as sparrows. Marsh Island is a birder's paradise, but today human presence is at a minimum. There is lots to see, but little to check.

They pass through Oyster Lake, which Darby notes is a good redfish spot. But it is empty of boats. In Bird Island Bayou, they check a boat with three anglers but very little to show for their effort. At the "big dam," a weir on the bayou, several families are crabbing and doing well.

A police siren interrupts the quiet. It is Darby's personal cell phone, programmed to ring like a siren. On the other end is Sergeant Dusty Rhodes, who informs Darby that Lieutenant Donald Salpietra has been trying to get in touch with him on the radio.

Recreational crabbing with chicken parts is a popular activity on Marsh Island Wildlife Refuge.

Darby calls Salpietra on his phone. According to the lieutenant, a boater has called the U.S. Coast Guard for help after running fast aground on a mudflat in Oyster Lake. The men are puzzled. They had just passed through Oyster Lake and there were no boats in sight.

Darby calls the Coast Guard, which patches him through to the stranded boater. The boater, a redfish fisherman, tells Darby that he is on a large mud-flat too soft to walk on, a little south of Lake Ferme. He gives Darby his GPS coordinates.

The game wardens agree that they can't get their huge Whaler to where the man is stranded. The men go to the Marsh Island Wildlife Refuge head-quarters facility to see if the refuge personnel have a surface drive boat that can get into the nasty spot.

They don't, but they do have an airboat, which they launch for the rescue mission. A half-hour later, a profusely grateful and extremely muddy red-fish fisherman is alongside the Whaler. His boat is muddier than he is.

While we were waiting for the airboat to pull the fisherman off of the mudflat, Romero recalled a "Dusty story." A lot of stories seem to circu-late about Sergeant Dusty Rhodes, whose earlier call had set the rescue in motion.

According to Romero, he and Rhodes were investigating a complaint a couple of days before Christmas about a hunter who was spreading bait to attract ducks near Avery Island. They went back on Christmas Eve after-noon, when they thought that he might hunt the spot.

The hunter turned up, as they expected. He put out more bait and then got in his blind with his shotgun. After he picked up his downed birds, the game wardens walked up to the man and identified themselves as wildlife agents. Their appearance puzzled him, as he had been so busy calling ducks that he hadn't seen the game wardens approach.

He freely admitted that he both spread the bait and hunted over it. Then he gave the wardens a ride back to his camp on his ATV. While they were riding, he asked, "Man, have y'all ever heard of Dusty Rhodes?" Romero and Rhodes replied that they had indeed heard of Rhodes.

"Man, he must be eighty or ninety years old; he's a legend." Romero says the hunter then proceeded to tell them "Dusty stories," including the fa-mous one of Rhodes's capture by outlaws.

As the story goes, Rhodes was lured alone into the heart of the Atchafa-laya Basin by a false report of illegal activity. Once there, he was captured by the band of ruffians who set up the ambush. They stripped him naked, thrashed him to near unconsciousness, then tied him to a tree to spend the night in the mosquito-infested swamp.

Their lust for revenge not yet satisfied, the outlaws searched for his truck until they found it at a boat landing. They doused it in gasoline and set it on fire, burning it to a charred hulk.

After the hunter finished relating Dusty stories to the two men, Romero asked him, "See this guy right here? That's the famous Dusty Rhodes."

"His face almost fell off," says Romero. "He shook hands several times with Dusty, saying, 'I always wanted to meet Dusty Rhodes.' He completely forgot about getting a ticket. All his attention was focused on Dusty. Dusty was smiling ear to ear, like he always does."

With the stranded fisherman rescued and on his way, the men begin patrolling again, stopping at Belly Dam, another weir famous for its good crabbing. Two boats are there, but crab catches are slow, as the tide has slackened considerably.

Both officers are friendly as they check the crabbers. Romero moves with the fluid motion of a skilled outdoorsman. Darby's crooked grin is as contagious as a yawn.

Back in the boat, the game wardens comment on the lack of activity. "At this time of the year we have slow days more often than not," says Darby.

Romero laments, "Slow days are long days—days that you dread. This time of year we do a lot of equipment maintenance."

He goes on, "You actually need some slow days to regroup. You take advantage of it to explore new territories to work. I ride and look for deer stands and duck blinds. I mark them in my book to work next year."

Darby chimes back in. "Over the life of a career, you come to understand that not every day is packed with contacts. You have to learn to accept that. People that think about a game warden job should realize that it is not always action. There are slow times.

"It definitely doesn't discourage us. We don't evaluate our self-worth by the number of tickets that we write. Even slow days are better than being stuck in an office punching computer keys.

"The fresh air; the boat ride; the time with a friend. Jason is my friend. We did today for a job what most people pay to do on a weekend. Overall though, slow days are exceptional. They are less common than exciting days.

"Ninety percent of the time, I wouldn't trade my job for any. We have a good time when we work. I feel like we have contributed. It means just as much to have exposure on the water as it does to catch people."

Romero agrees. "Presence means everything. If we park a truck at a boat landing, we feel that we find less violations. With a high presence we are less likely to catch people over the limit, but we still have boats and life jackets to check."

"I have been in a boat checking someone," says Darby, "when they got a call from someone who tells them that the game warden is out. They saw his truck at the landing.

"The worst day at any time of the year is when you get pouring rain all day. No one is outdoors, even hunters, and you are stuck in your truck."

Romero sums up his view. "I am satisfied with today. I made some personal contacts; I got to interact with some kids; and I got a guy off a mudflat."

"Today was definitely not wasted," echoes Darby.

8

THE DESPERADO

Overnight, a strong cold front swept through and blew the damp, foggy weather out of north Louisiana, through south Louisiana, and into the Gulf of Mexico. In the morning's cold, dry air, the outlines of everything in sight are razor-edged.

It was the middle of the second split of duck season. Hunters had been doing relatively well in the flooded timber of Russell Sage Wildlife Management Area near Monroe, Louisiana. The 16,829-acre WMA is densely forested, with a high concentration of oak trees. About 2,400 acres of the area, called a "greentree reservoir," is flooded habitat for mallards and wood ducks, which feast on the abundant acorns.

The WMA is located adjacent to and immediately to the north of 10,989-acre Ouachita Wildlife Management Area, another WMA used by duck hunters. A 1,500-acre refuge for waterfowl is located within, and at the northern extremity of, the Ouachita WMA. No hunting of any type is allowed within the refuge.

Today, Senior Agent John Volentine and Sergeant Duane Taylor are planning to spend much of the day checking duck hunters on Russell Sage WMA for compliance. The rugged forty-four-year-old Taylor, a fourteen-year veteran enforcement agent, oozes the confidence that comes from experience in all types of situations. Volentine, although fresh-faced at twenty-seven years old, would be hard to peg as only having three years on the job as a game warden. He speaks and acts with the confidence of someone with far more experience.

Volentine, with his aluminum Go-Devil-powered boat, appears at the rendezvous point first, the headquarters building of the Ouachita WMA, right after daylight. Taylor arrives shortly after and the two men immediately begin a give-and-take banter that comes from comfortable partnership.

As the two men prepare their equipment, they explain that they don't want to get into the area during the early morning shooting flurry and ruin the hunt for the hunters. Also, much of the best hunting in flooded timber occurs after 10 a.m., so typically the hunters don't leave early.

As they prep, the talk drifts to their motivation for doing this job. They are remarkably similar. Both express a lifelong love of hunting and fishing, and the thought of having to work behind a desk indoors distresses them. "I had my heart set on this job a long time," says Taylor.

"Anytime someone can do what they love and get paid for it, it's a pretty good gig," adds Volentine.

Both men had experience with wildlife agents from their early years in the outdoors. "It's different," says Volentine, "being on this side of the badge. I'm still more used to being on the other side—being nervous about the approach of a game warden. I try to be considerate of hunters and fishermen. I still am one."

The slow-talking Taylor is more blunt. "I spent a lot of years running from this uniform. Then, when I got a little older, I decided that the outlawing I was doing was bad for the resource.

"I love the freedom of this job," he adds. "And the pay is good. But the hours are erratic. The one thing that gives me the reds is not being able to outsmart violators. It ticks me off if they are smarter than me."

"What P.O.'s me is when people blatantly break laws," chimes in Volentine. "The majority try to do right, but there are a few who downright test you. People will lie with the coldest, straightest face you ever see. It amazes me every day."

With their equipment ready, the two men head by truck to Russell Sage. As soon as we enter the WMA, an irate hunter flags the truck down and reports a small truck parked ahead with one window smashed, and two rifles and a spotlight in it.

At the truck, the two agents treat it as a crime scene as well as a possible wildlife violation. Glass fragments from the shattered window are strewn inside the truck and on the dirt road. They touch nothing with their bare hands, except the rifles, as they inspect the contents of the truck, which includes a large number of empty soft drink bottles and snack wrappers and bags. Whatever else the truck's occupants are, they aren't litterers.

Both rifles, a 7 mm and a .17 caliber, are locked and loaded. That, plus the high-powered spotlight on the seat, raises alarm bells about night hunting, especially on a WMA, where loaded weapons in a vehicle are prohibited.

Volentine calls LDWF Dispatch on his radio to get the identification of the owner of the truck by its plates, as well as POS (point of sale) information on what hunting and fishing licenses the owner has. While wait-

The scene at the truck puzzles the two game wardens. A window is smashed, but two expensive—and loaded—rifles are untouched in the vehicle.

John Volentine calls LDWF Dispatch to get information on the damaged truck's owner.

ing for Dispatch to reply, Taylor pokes his head through the window. He quickly withdraws it and asks Volentine, "How's your smeller? Do you smell marijuana?"

Volentine sticks his head in and sniffs. "Nah, it smells like rotten socks and Mountain Dew," he replies.

Working through Dispatch, the men manage to contact the truck owner's mother, who is asked to call her son by cell phone and alert him of the damage. Within thirty minutes two disgusted-looking young men come wading out of the flooded woods lugging duck hunting equipment on their shoulders.

After they drop their loads, the men, under close questioning, disavow having been night hunting with the spotlight, claiming they used it to locate the spot that they wanted to duck hunt. Their licenses are in order.

The men say they are sure that they know who broke the truck's window—some acquaintances they had a confrontation with the previous night. With permission, Taylor searches the vehicle, while Volentine writes a citation for possession of a loaded firearm in a vehicle on a WMA.

After they turn the damage investigation over to sheriff's deputies, the game wardens proceed to the parking area. There, in a friendly but professional mode, they check the take, equipment, and licenses of several groups of hunters who are leaving early.

Duane Taylor checks a handsome limit of ducks taken by hunters in the greentree reservoir.

Choosing to launch their boat in a secure area behind a locked gate, they find the mud challenging. Taylor, in the truck, maneuvers to back through a monstrous mud hole to launch the boat. With all four wheels clawing, the snorting truck slings gobs of mud thirty feet.

As the two men put their inflatable life vests on under their coats, Taylor remarks, "I'm glad that's your truck, not mine."

Concerned, Volentine reflexively asks, "It's burned up?"

"Nah," Taylor replies with a mischievous grin, "just muddy."

As Volentine gets the boat up on plane in the shallow water, I understand why they put their life vests on under their coats. Tree limbs and vines claw at my exposed life jacket. The black water, flecked with floating green duck-weed on either side of Hog Pen Trail, reflects the images of gray tree limbs and the blue sky like a mirror.

What they are looking for are openings in the tree canopy. Duck hunters usually pick openings as places to set up their decoy spreads. After checking the first set of hunters, they proceed deeper into the flooded forest. Periodically, they stop the boat and listen for the sounds of duck callers and shotgun blasts. These help locate the next set of hunters to check. The sight of the flashes of a spinning-wing decoy's wings through the trees allows them to zero in on the hunters' location.

When duck hunters are located, the two men rapidly close in on them to check for compliance with regulations.

The two men josh and tease each other good-naturedly. Their interactions with hunters are friendly as well. After identifying themselves to a pair of hunters, one hunter chirps, "I hope ya brought some ducks with ya." As the game wardens prepare to leave, his hunting partner asks, "Y'all wanna pick up our decoys for us?"

Grinning, Taylor replies, "That's just what I came out for."

While pausing to listen for more shots, Volentine's cell phone rings. After he hangs up, he explains to Taylor the nature of the call. A reliable informant has reported that a known wildlife violator has gone into the refuge part of Ouachita WMA on an ATV and shot a large buck deer. Additionally, he has posted a lookout with a cell phone on the road into the area to alert him of approaching game wardens.

Volentine and Taylor decide to move quickly in response. Instead of following the trail, they decide to cut diagonally across the flooded maze. Volentine gets out his GPS unit and turns it on. But he only has two hands and needs one to steer the boat and the other to hang onto the boat to keep from falling out. So he asks Taylor to guide him with the GPS.

Taylor objects, "I don't need that thing—go that way," he points. Volentine insists, and Taylor mutters, "That thing would make a good trotline weight if you could find a way to tie it on." Looking at me knowingly, he says, "You know GPS means "getchu partially stranded."

When the two get to where they launched the boat, Taylor leaves Volentine to pick up the boat and heads out in his truck to pick up his ATV to get into the refuge area overland rather than by road.

Before they separate, Volentine comments that the area is big and that they need more manpower. Taylor calls in two more agents, Stan House and Joe Gouedy from Lincoln Parish. But until they arrive, it's up to the two of them to hem in the violators.

While Volentine transports the boat to a safe storage spot, he explains that since hunting isn't allowed in the refuge area, it holds some really big deer—irresistible bait to an outlaw. And the reported violator is indeed an outlaw, having received at least seven wildlife citations in recent years.

As he moves into position, juggling contact with the other three agents on his cell phone and radio, he explains, "This is kinda like hunting, except you're hunting people. Fun, huh? If I catch this guy it will be like killing a ten-point buck!"

The man has at least a forty-five-minute head start on the agents, and Volentine knows it.

Taylor is moving in by ATV and then by foot from one side of the refuge.

Taylor (l) and Volentine (r) prepare themselves before separating to try to corner the deer hunter illegally hunting in the Ouachita WMA waterfowl refuge.

Volentine parks his truck and takes off on foot through the woods from the other side. He encounters a couple of weaponless youngsters practicing with their duck calls. They report hearing an ATV moving toward the north.

Volentine confers with Taylor by radio and then gallops back through the woods to his truck. "Arggah, I really wanna catch this guy." I can taste the adrenaline in the air of the truck.

As Volentine's truck proceeds down the road, Taylor, wearing his body armor and carrying his Sig Sauer assault rifle, charges out of the ditch in a combat crouch and hurls his body over the high sides of the truck and into its bed.

Less than a mile down the road, Taylor catapults his forty-four-year-old body out of the other side of the truck while it is still moving. Carrying the rifle at port arms, he blitzes across an opening and into the woods.

Volentine tries another approach to head off the exit of the violators. House and Gouedy are approaching. My throat constricts involuntarily, as if the noose that's being tightened is around my neck.

Just when it seems that the tension couldn't get worse, Taylor calls Volentine with the news that the bad guys may have slipped loose from their grasp and explains where he thinks they exited the refuge and WMA.

Volentine doubles around the WMA and finds the tracks where the ATV came out. He sighs dejectedly, "All that adrenaline and it just lets out like a busted balloon.

"We know who he is and what he did," says Volentine in a pained voice, "but there is no way you can bring anything to a court of law without good evidence. It would just ruin your credibility."

As he circles back by road to meet Taylor, Volentine passes the subject, with another passenger and a dog in his truck, going in the opposite direction. He manhandles the big Dodge Ram around and flicks on his blue lights. The truck pulls over.

A youngish man steps out of the vehicle, grinning. Volentine's approach is not aggressive and he presents the stop as an opportunity to exchange information. The driver acts excessively innocent, but never stops slyly smirking.

The verbal fencing between the two swordsmen begins. Thrust—parry—counterthrust—riposte. Volentine is hoping the subject will make an error; the man wants to know what Volentine knows. Neither makes a slip.

As Volentine bids the man goodbye and steps away from his truck, House and Gouedy's truck, lights flashing, pulls behind Volentine's. The three men stand on the road comparing notes and frustrations.

Then, a couple hundred yards up the road, an ATV with two adult men on it caroms out of a small side road in a cloud of dust and charges down the paved road straddling the center line. They seem to be doing their best to occupy both lanes of the highway at once with their unlicensed vehicle.

The game wardens, thwarted from their main objective, give chase. After a mile or so, the ATV swerves down a side road and makes a U-turn, coming face to face with two lit-up trucks full of armed men.

The riders straddle the ATV, mouths agape. As Volentine steps from his vehicle he, with a note of humor in his voice, says, "This isn't your lucky day. I wouldn't buy a lottery ticket if I was you." The two men chuckle, even when Volentine informs them that they will receive a ticket for operating the off-road vehicle on a highway.

Back at the Ouachita WMA headquarters, the three wardens compare notes with Taylor, who returns late from trudging through the flooded refuge. Taylor reports that he found the fresh tracks of two men and a dog, just what was in the truck Volentine had stopped. Taylor spins a stocking cap that belonged to one of them on one finger. The poachers had left in a hurry.

The game wardens ruefully consider the head start that the violators had on them. It was time enough to get out of the refuge, get cleaned up, and structure an alibi.

Then, with the aplomb of the veteran that he is, a relaxed Taylor says, "We'll get him. He'll make a mistake and we'll get him."

The ATV joyriders are stunned, after making a sharp U-turn, to be confronted by two truck-loads of game wardens. (Left to right, Joe Gouedy, John Volentine, and Stan House.)

9

A SPIDER IN A WEB

Day One: The Buck in the Ditch

It's the day after Christmas, and forty-four-year-old Sergeant Darryl Galloway's broad, smiling face greets me openly when I climb in his three-quarter-ton Dodge Ram pickup truck before daylight. Powerfully built, with an almost military carriage and a big, dark moustache, Galloway looks like the lawman he has been most of his adult life.

After a year with the Abita Springs, Louisiana Police Department, Galloway served in the army military police from 1983 to 1986. Following his military hitch, he went back to the Abita Springs Police Department, where he worked until 1988. From then until 1999 he was a St. Tammany Parish sheriff's deputy. In 1999, he was accepted by the Enforcement Division of the Louisiana Department of Wildlife and Fisheries, where he has been ever since—almost ten years.

"Game warden work has always intrigued me," he says. "It's a good people person job." He describes himself as "easy-going," but "a company man." "I take everything in stride; I don't waste time, but I don't need to be a fireball either."

Galloway explains that today he is working a split shift, four hours in the morning and eight hours from the late afternoon into the night. This morning he is heading to Ben's Creek Wildlife Management Area in Washington Parish, twenty miles or so from his home in Franklinton. It is the last day of doe season on the WMA and he wants to be there for the finale. Besides, someone has called Baton Rouge (LDWF Headquarters) and requested more enforcement presence on the WMA.

The truck enters Ben's Creek just as the very first faint light of day washes over the landscape. He blacks out his headlights, both to avoid being seen and to keep from disturbing hunters, then hides the lights of the radio and dash with homemade covers to protect his night vision. Slowly he creeps down the red dirt roads of the WMA. At unfamiliar vehicles, he stops and calls LDWF Dispatch with his radio to get a POS on what hunting privileges the vehicle owner has.

His intent is to get an early overview of hunting activity on the WMA and to check all the gates on the area to be sure that they are locked. With no other open roads out, all the exiting hunters will later have to pass his checkpoint before reaching the main gate.

He stops at what is obviously a grandfather-grandson duo. The man is wrestling with his rifle and frowning. The weapon is jammed. Galloway frees up the weapon and returns it to the man, along with a tip on keeping the rifle functional. He checks the man's licenses, speaks a few encouraging words to the young hunter, and leaves.

As it becomes light enough to see, Ben's Creek WMA shows up as piney woods on substantial rolling hills, with some hardwood trees in the small creek bottoms. The area is hunted primarily for deer and turkey, with some rabbit hunting after deer season is over, explains Galloway.

As he slowly creeps down the roads of the WMA, Galloway expresses no remorse about having to work during hunting season, saying that he doesn't hunt and fish as much as he used to because now he hunts people. He has a healthy sense of humor. His e-mail address includes the words "possum cop"—words considered derogatory by many game wardens. "That doesn't bother me," he says. "I've been called a water-Nazi and a fish-pig before. I don't mind some verbal venting, as long as it isn't physical or inciting."

He uses his binoculars constantly, calling them "the best tool we use." In the strengthening light, numerous hunters bedecked in hunter orange can be seen in tree stands, looking very much like colorful Christmas ornaments flecking the trees.

Galloway says that he is especially safety conscious during big game season. If he is on foot and he hears a whistle or deer bleat call, he says that he will drop to the ground. "When you hear that, the scope is on you." A hunter makes those sounds to try to get what he thinks is a deer to stop moving so he can make a clear shot, he explains.

As his truck passes through a low draw, he points out a tent-like ground blind and says, "He is in violation. There is no hunter orange on the blind." Going to the entrance to the blind, Galloway summons out the hunter, who is armed with a massive pistol, as well as a rifle. Galloway explains the problem to the hunter and issues him a warning citation. The hunter puts an orange vest on top of the blind as Galloway leaves.

Galloway fields a cell phone call from one of the younger agents under

Darryl Galloway considers binoculars to be a game warden's best tool.

his supervision seeking advice. He has been sitting on some possible wild-life violators and has just received a complaint through LDWF Dispatch about a crippled deer in someone's yard. Galloway directs him to complete his surveillance and then respond to the call. After hanging up with the agent, Galloway calls Dispatch and tells them that the agent will respond to the call later.

Each complaint, he explains to me, must be evaluated on its own. In the old days, night hunters would call in complaints to draw game wardens off from an area and then listen to police radio scanners to see if it was work-ing. That is a little more difficult to do now with police radios, plus agents often use cell phones to communicate with each other for just that reason.

Nothing misses his eye. A truck backed into a pull-off instead of pulled in could indicate someone trying to hide his license plate. The number of gun cases in a vehicle may indicate the number of hunters. Decals on the windows and bumper stickers, as well as how well the vehicle is kept up, can give some indication of the pride of the hunter and the likelihood of violation.

Galloway never slams the door on his truck when he steps out of it to check a vehicle, for the same reasons he turns his vehicle lights off. In fact, usually he leaves it hanging open. "That's so I can get back in quick—to use the radio, to get another weapon, or to leave. There is nothing wrong with a strategic retreat." This isn't his first go-round.

A pile of garbage someone has dumped on the WMA sets him off. "I can't take it—litter! I'll dig through it in a heartbeat to find something to identify the litterer. I can't do anything if you dump on your own land, but why take it to a WMA or public road?"

He doesn't stop, "I am super-sensitive about it. Litter gives us a black eye. Litter is like slapping us—police and society—in the face."

With his rounds of the WMA complete, Galloway sets up his truck at a choke point for hunters leaving the area after their hunt. Vehicle after vehicle stops, but none have deer. All are in compliance. Galloway calls everyone "Bubba" as he greets them with a smile. Finally, a truck with a young hunter and his father rolls up and the young man fairly bounds out of the truck. "I got a good one," he excitedly shouts. He can't wait to show his kill to the game warden.

After he relives the entire hunt for Galloway, the game warden congratulates the young man on his six-point buck and checks out his and his father's licenses. Soon, the first split of Galloway's shift ends. He starts his truck and turns it back toward Franklinton.

As he drives, he talks about his job, which he describes as "not just my job, but my career." He adds, "I don't wake up in the morning and dread going to work."

Three in the afternoon finds Galloway back on the road, looking for hunter activity—looking for someone "to sit on." He takes a tour through the Bogue Chitto State Park being developed in Washington Parish, where he has received a complaint about illegal wood duck shooting. Fresh tire tracks on the red clay roadbeds in the nascent park catch his attention. But this evening the park site is deserted.

Finding a truck parked in a likely hunting spot, he stops nearby and quietly waits for the hunters to come out of the woods. While he waits, he picks up the discussion on his job where he left off earlier.

"This job is less stressful than regular police work, but we see lots of guns. I would rather deal with someone that I know has a gun than with someone I don't know has guns. Hunters' weapons are mostly not concealed. We are trained to see guns as a normal part of our operations and we see them constantly."

Galloway goes on, "My wife, Phyllis, is definitely a police officer's wife. She's my Rock of Gibraltar. She puts up with my b.s. People call the house at all hours of the night and I keep strange hours. But it was worse when I worked in narcotics for the sheriff's office. The divorce rate in the field of law enforcement is unbelievably high."

Well after dark, the hunters come out to their vehicle. "How ya doin'? State game warden," greets Galloway. After Galloway checks them out and releases them, he is off to set up on a likely night hunting spot and eat his sandwich. It's well after dark.

Just as he turns off of Highway 16, he spots a truck farther up the road, parked on the wrong side and with its emergency flashers on. Galloway immediately wheels his truck around and quickly pulls up on the other vehicle. It's dark and nothing is moving in his truck's lights. He shines his police flashlight and a strange scene reveals itself.

In the pitch dark, a middle-aged man is rolling around in the bottom of the ditch, holding on to the antlers of a good-sized nine-point buck with one hand and trying to stab it with a knife held in the other hand. With the help of Galloway's light he manages to get enough control of the animal to stand on its antlers.

Then he sees that the holder of the light is a game warden. Not sure of the legality of his situation, he folds up the knife and stuffs it into his pocket with a bloody hand. He explains to Galloway that the deer ran out in front his vehicle and he couldn't avoid hitting it. While its back is broken immediately ahead of its hindquarters, it still has plenty of fire in its front half, and success in subduing it was projecting to be a close run thing in the dark.

Galloway confirms that its back is indeed broken.

"Can I finish it off? I've got a hunting license," queries the man. Galloway assents and the unfortunate creature is dispatched with an incision to the heart. While the animal expires, the driver cleans his knife, which he says he just got for Christmas a couple of days before. Galloway helps him load the animal in the bed of his truck and gets back under way.

Near where he wants to set up for night surveillance, he blacks out his truck lights and creeps near a pipeline right-of-way. As soon as he is within sight of it, he spies another vehicle on the right-of-way. They move, then stop, then maneuver the vehicle as if using its lights to shine the area, move again and repeat the process.

Galloway begins to stalk them in his blacked-out truck. The right-of-way runs over very steep hills that are heavily rutted, and none of the ruts can be seen in the complete darkness.

The occupants of the other vehicle are completely unaware of Galloway's presence, even though he has been following them closely. As they approach

Galloway admires the buck in the ditch after the truck's driver dispatches the fatally crippled animal.

the bottom of a gully, their lights light up another vehicle stuck in the mud in its lowest part. Galloway watches them for a few minutes until he is completely sure that their intent isn't to night hunt, then turns on the lights on his truck. The two men jump in surprise. Questioning reveals that the trespassers are here just to pull out their other vehicle. After a stern lecture, Galloway takes their names.

Leaving the two, Galloway passes a pile of garbage, which gives him cause to vent his spleen again, "Litter burns my butt." Even in the dark I see the glint in his eye.

On a small, rural road, Galloway catches a glimpse of what he thinks is a small LED light in an overgrown field, one perfect for shining rabbits. As he stops, he says that he thinks that the shiner has seen him. He turns the radio up full blast, opens the door, and makes violent vomiting sounds. Closing the door, he drives over the hill. "I don't know if that fooled him, but if he is any good he probably won't turn his light back on.

On the other side of the hill, he blacks out his truck, creeps back over the hill, and parks in an old silage pit. After an hour he moves to another spot that he says overlooks a vast field of green rye grass. I see nothing; the truck is blacked out. "This is a good one," he says. "I made several cases here."

He backs the truck into an ambush spot in the brush with only the front end exposed. Then he covers even that with a couple dozen green pine boughs that he stashed here three weeks ago. He gets in the truck and finally settles down to his sandwich.

"I love night work," he says between bites. "That's when good outlaws come out. So much goes on at night. You see things that you never see in the daytime."

I see nothing but blackness.

"You gotta have patience," he instructs. "I am like a spider sitting in a web. Sooner or later some poor fool will come along. . . ." We begin our wait. Time drags slowly.

I yawn. Catching me, he says that it is only 9:16 p.m. "Welcome to my world, heh, heh, heh," he laughs sinisterly.

Probably seeking to keep me awake as much as to educate me, Galloway says an hour later, "After you sit here so long and that night hunter turns up. . . . Oh man! That adrenaline dump! It's the best feeling you can have with your clothes on."

Still nothing is kicking. It has been gently raining for an hour. At 11 p.m., the rain stops and Galloway gets out and removes the pine camouflage from the truck, carefully stacking it for use again. "Let's go see what we can find," he says. We don't have to look for long.

On Highway 25, the ever-observant Galloway sees the brake lights of a truck that has passed him come on and the truck begin to make a U-turn in the road. Galloway goes around a curve to hide his maneuver and does the same. After the truck passes Galloway it repeats its turn, and after Galloway goes around the curve he does likewise. And then it happens again.

"He's a stopped son-of-a-gun," he says as he closes the gap between the two vehicles and flicks the blue lights on. A fairly scared, clean-cut seventeen-year-old male steps out, obviously shaken. Inside the truck is his girlfriend. The young man quickly admits that he saw a deer on the first pass and thought about shooting it. The high-powered, scoped rifle in the truck is unloaded.

Galloway turns him loose with a warning to be more careful. Back in his truck, Galloway explains that he didn't think that he had a good case. "I'm not gonna take a half-ass case to court."

So the night ends. Tomorrow will be a new day.

Day Two: Lost and Found

The next day, Galloway is again working a split shift, similar to the one he worked the day before. As daylight breaks, he heads to the state park site that he scouted the day before. "I am exited about catching this guy," he says, referring to the wood duck hunter. "No hunting is allowed on state park lands, even on those not open for business yet. I don't want to get there too early; we need to give him time to get set up and started hunting."

But to no avail. The shooter isn't cooperating today. It had rained the night before and the clay roadbed is a clean slate—except for a set of tire tracks that indicates a vehicle probed almost every corner of the park last night.

Even more interesting, at each building site or clearing, the driver had performed what Galloway called "turn-ins," using the headlights to shine for deer. He explains, "Lots of night hunters now use their vehicle's head- lights to spot deer because they feel that if they are stopped, possession of a headlight would be a nail in their coffin."

The more turn-ins he finds, the more excited he becomes, at one point rubbing his hands in anticipation and wearing a big smile on his face. "I'll be back here tonight," he proclaims.

Galloway jogs the big truck back over to Ben's Creek WMA to work there the rest of the morning's shift. He checks numerous hunters, all but a pair of which are in compliance. For those two, a retired minister and his son, he writes warning tickets. The father isn't wearing hunter orange and the son doesn't have a WMA permit. As he writes the tickets, the wind sighs mournfully through the pine trees and over the open clear cuts on the roll- ing hills, presaging coming bad weather.

Near the end of his shift, while slowly patrolling the dirt roads of the WMA, Galloway spies a truck at the top of the hill ahead of him. Allow- ing his own truck to roll backward to hide it as much as possible, the game warden watches as the two men intently scan the open area to the left of the road.

As the truck goes over the hill and disappears, Galloway charges after them and then stops right before the crest of the hill the hunters were just on. He cranes his neck and watches. As he expects, the hunters' truck stops on top of the next hill. "They are looking for a deer to shoot, and if they see one they are going to shoot it out of the truck," he says. "That's a violation because they can't have loaded guns in a vehicle on a WMA."

The scenario repeats itself on the next pair of hills, and then again on the next. As they descend the last hill, he says that he is going to stop them and floors the accelerator, blowing over the hill, blue lights flashing, right up on to the rear bumper of the other truck. The driver throws his hands up in dismay. Slamming his shifter into park, Galloway jumps from the vehicle and charges up to the driver's side, shouting his identification several times.

Galloway asks for their hunting licenses and identification as he moves to the passenger-side door. A lever-action rifle lay there with the action open and unfired rounds littering the floor and seat.

While looking over their licenses, he says, "You know you can't have loaded weapons in a vehicle on a WMA. The passenger replies defiantly, "It's unloaded."

Galloway toughens up, fixes a level gaze on each in turn and issues a warning not to lie to him or it can become hard on them. "I heard you jacking shells from the rifle as I came up to your truck, so don't lie to me." Reluctantly, the two admit to having had a loaded weapon in the vehicle with the intent of shooting a deer.

As Galloway writes their tickets, he eases the tension by engaging them

The illegal road hunters had jacked all the shells from their rifle before Galloway got to the truck.

in small talk, and after they sign their tickets they part on almost friendly terms.

At 4 p.m., the beginning of the afternoon shift, Galloway explains that he wants to follow up on a really good tip in the eastern part of Washington Parish. An ex-wife has reported her former-husband and his friends to Galloway for deer hunting without hunter orange, hunting without licenses, shooting late, and "shooting anything that moves."

"Some of our best tips come from scorned women," he laughs. "They know their ex-husbands very well and will roll on them in a heartbeat. They will tell it all."

While moving eastward, Galloway talks about his relationship with the Washington Parish Sheriff's Office. "We work very well with the sheriff's office. In fact, we get 90 percent of our complaints through them. We have a great rapport. They are our back-up a lot of times. When we need help, they come lickity-split. We back them up, too."

As we pass over a small road in a remote area of the parish, Galloway groans audibly. It isn't hard to guess why; a huge pile of mattresses was dumped off the road. "I hate that! When there is nothing going on, I will drive to these areas and go through garbage with rubber gloves looking for an address on an envelope." But right now he is on a mission.

At 5 p.m. he eases onto the property of the reported violators. Everyone that is hunting should be in the woods right now, lessening his chance of being seen. He parks the truck on the entrance road, where it will be difficult to spot from the hunting camp, but from where he can observe what is going on. We sit quietly, listening to the sound of the wind moaning through the scrubby pines growing on the nutrient-poor sand left behind by an abandoned gravel mining operation.

At 5:20 p.m., shooting starts in the distance. First a few shots, then more and more. Someone in the distance is shooting a wood duck roost after legal shooting hours, but Galloway doesn't want to abandon the stake-out here.

Then a truck with its lights on approaches us from behind. "We've been burned," he mutters. When the truck nears, he says, "Watch how I handle this."

He gets out of his truck and introduces himself to the driver, who identifies himself as the very man Galloway is looking for. "I am trying to locate that shooting over there," he points. "Can you give me directions how to get there from here?"

After he listens to the man's helpful directions, Galloway pulls out on the road to move toward the shooting. "Well, that's it for them today," he says, "but I'll be back. Now I want those roost shooters." He calls Senior Agent Robert Larsen, another game warden on duty in the area, to help him triangulate on the shooting. Both trucks set up on a gate from where the game wardens expect duck hunters will exit.

Two sets of headlights bounce through the trees just at twilight. A flash of adrenaline surges through my veins. But they are just deer hunters. The two game wardens quickly abandon them and set off in a great arc to encircle the area of the shooting.

Larson goes down one road and as Galloway is preparing to go down another, a small truck pulls out of it. The blue lights come on. As Galloway steps out of the truck, the hunter, with his hands up in the air in disgust, complains to him about the roost shooters' activities ruining his evening deer hunt.

Galloway quickly jumps back in the truck and pulls out on the road with the gravel flying. Time is an enemy now. Then, when he charges up another road, he runs up behind a pickup truck with three hunters and two pirogues. "There they are," he says as he activates the light bar on top of the truck.

As Galloway checks licenses and plugs in the shotguns, Larsen joins the group and searches the vehicle and the hunters' bags while keeping an eye on their retriever, a pit bull. Only three wood ducks are in their possession. Considering the amount of shooting heard, this group is either the world's worst shots or an entirely innocent trio.

Galloway asks if they have heard any other shots, without mentioning the late shooting. All three claim to have heard nothing, which seems amazing considering the fusillade heard by everyone else. Since Galloway has not seen who made the illegal hours shots, he has no case and bids them a good day.

It's dark as Galloway's truck coasts westward through the hills, their houses still festooned in colorful Christmas lights. All is well.

A call about a lost hunter on the Pearl River WMA comes in. Galloway directs Larsen and another agent on duty to handle it. He has an appointment with the maker of the tire tracks in Bogue Chitto State Park.

Then another call comes in. A hunter is lost between Enon and Franklinton, between Highway 16 and the Bogue Chitto River. Galloway must respond. The area is a very small strip and heavily incised with small roads from the highway to the river. Galloway asks for more details from the sheriff's office. He is told that the man is fifty-one years old and in poor health. He has been missing since 10:30 a.m.

These duck hunters have perhaps the oddest of retrieving dogs, a pit bulldog.

"It don't sound good," he says to me. "If he had a health problem in the woods, we will never find him in the dark." By 7 p.m., both radios and his cell phone are going off like popcorn.

Following directions to where the man and his worried family have been camping, Galloway arrives to find three sheriff's office cars already there. Galloway interviews the family members. They reveal that the man is unfamiliar with the area, has a bad hip, and was carrying a shotgun when he left to hunt for "whatever."

Galloway guides his vehicle down a lane to a riverside camp just down from where the family is. The brush is incredibly dense. Galloway shouts and flashes his lights. He walks a ways into the brush and returns with a worried look.

As he gets ready to move to another road, his sheriff's radio comes to life. The lieutenant on duty tells Galloway to call off the search. They have found the man. "Where?" inquires Galloway. "In our jail," is the reply. Galloway is both relieved and amused.

As the three sheriff's office patrol cars and Galloway's truck converge on the campsite almost simultaneously, Galloway laughs heartily, "I love this job! It's the best job in the world."

The family is assembled to get the news, and they are relieved that he was found alive. They are unfazed by the fact that he is in jail and don't even inquire why. As the group breaks up, the deputies and Galloway assemble to one side to discuss what has happened.

The man had indeed gotten lost earlier in the day. He walked out to the highway and hitchhiked a ride into town. He went to a service station and asked to use a telephone. The attendant saw that he had a large pistol concealed in his coat and called the sheriff's office. In the meantime, the man walked to a convenience store, which was where the deputies found him.

They asked for the concealed pistol, which he produced. Upon running the serial numbers, the gun came back as stolen. They took him into custody and searched him. They found pills on "every part of his body" according to one deputy and not a single one was in a bottle. He was arrested and booked with a variety of charges, including possession of three kinds of Schedule II narcotics, one of which was methadone.

Galloway decides that he is going to go to lock-up to find where the missing shotgun is and to write him some tickets. "There is no way a guy like this has his required licenses," he says.

At the jail, an emaciated, very old-looking man, who is shaking violently, is brought out of the holding cell for Galloway to talk to. Galloway asks him what he was hunting for. He replies that he wasn't hunting. Galloway warns him not to lie to him and tells him that his wife told him that he had a shotgun. The man repeats that he wasn't hunting.

Galloway repeats what his wife had said and tells him that he knows the sheriff's deputies found buckshot in his possession when he was arrested. He admits to having a shotgun, but says that he wasn't hunting. "Don't give me that," Galloway snorts. The parrying goes on a few more rounds until the shaking man finally admits that he was indeed hunting.

Galloway then asks where the shotgun is. The hunter plays dumb again. "What shotgun?" Still trying to be patient, Galloway asks the man if he would like to be responsible for a child finding the gun and killing himself or other children. To this approach the man responds. He describes where he stashed it under some bushes along a road.

Amazingly, in a process like finding a needle in a haystack in the dark, Galloway finds the shotgun, which he brings to the sheriff's office. As he enjoys Christmas leftovers with the deputies, Galloway writes tickets to present to the man for hunting without a basic hunting license and without a big game license. Not until after 9:30 p.m. does he break away from the sheriff's office to go to the park. He wants this night hunter badly.

Since he can't enter unobserved, he enters the raw, unfinished park with

Galloway perseveres and finds the loaded shotgun that the lost man had hidden.

his radio blaring and the windows down, hoping to sound like a carload of partying teenagers.

Then he stops and blacks out. "Now the waiting game begins," he proclaims with satisfaction. In the deep blackness of a moonless night, when even the faint light of the stars is missing because of the heavy cloud cover, time passes slowly.

But he never nods off or dozes. At midnight, when his shift is supposed to end, he is still there. At 2 a.m. the cold front hits with a spurt of rain. The big truck shudders from the blast of icy wind. Still he doesn't leave. Not until 4 a.m. does the spider in the web retreat. There will be another night.

10

TURKEY BAIT

Day One: Cat and Mouse

Turkey season. It kind of hangs out there all by itself in the spring, two months after deer and duck hunting seasons end. Wildlife enforcement agents run themselves ragged during those seasons and welcome a change of pace during February and early March. But those agents who love to work hunting seasons are raring to go back to working hunters by the time turkey season rolls around at the end of March.

Lieutenant Eric Stokes is one of those. "Time passes slowly for me in June, July, and August. A lot of fishermen couldn't violate fishing limit laws even if they tried," he says, although he allows that there are lots of things for game wardens to do in almost any season.

"To me, there is no routine in this job," he says. "It is real diverse. In one day I could be working on turkey baiting in the morning, and then follow up a complaint about game fish snagging in the evening."

Stokes is a big guy, six foot three and 235 pounds. He has strong facial features and a deeply tanned complexion. Except for blue eyes that he can fix on you with unblinking intensity, and his shaved head, he looks uncannily like Iron Eyes Cody, the Italian-American actor who portrayed the crying Indian in the 1971 anti-litter commercial by Keep America Beautiful.

Stokes's whole life has been focused around the Louisiana Department of Wildlife and Fisheries. His father was a Freshwater Fisheries Division biologist. Stokes worked as a wildlife specialist for the department for seven years before moving to the Enforcement Division over thirty-three years ago.

"I've always liked law enforcement, even since I was young," he explains. Growing up in Glenmore, in Rapides Parish, he played cowboys a lot when he was a kid, adding, "Oh yeah, I was always the sheriff.

"It wasn't an overriding passion for hunting and fishing that brought me

Lieutenant Eric Stokes's face is tanned from a lifetime spent working outdoors.

to this job. I got to meet game wardens and know something about the job because my father worked for the department."

He goes on, "I like to match wits with people who are really trying to get away with something. They rely on thinking that they know your routine. I was blessed with great patience. I like to be there when they don't expect it. Hunting season flies by because I am busy."

March is a neurotic month. The old adage says that the month comes in like a lion and goes out like a lamb, but it is usually a mixture of the two all the way through. Now the month is almost over and the lion is still roaring.

It has been raining and forbiddingly brooding for days. Finally, on the Friday night before the first day of turkey season, a cold front, accompanied by a powerful lightning storm, blows through Rapides Parish, where I am spending the night.

When Stokes picks me up at 4:15 a.m., an unflagging north wind is whipping through the tall pine trees, one of the worst weather conditions for turkey hunters. We are heading north to a spot near Iatt Lake in Grant Parish, he informs me, to set up on two spots close together that have been baited with grain.

Working with Stokes will be Sergeants Marcus Constance and Travis Burnett. They have eighteen and twenty-two years of experience, respectively, as wildlife enforcement agents. This is an experienced crew. Stokes informs me that two other game wardens in his district, Senior Agents Kevin Hill and Adam O'Neal are going to work a baited spot in Rapides Parish.

In the darkness, with his face illuminated only by the dash lights of his truck, Stokes explains that game wardens in the central part of the state work a lot of turkey and dove baiting cases. "Using bait makes it too easy to kill turkeys," he says. "A turkey is like a chicken; they feed in the day and roost at night. They will visit a bait site every day. Baiting for deer doesn't hurt because they feed at night.

"Baiting cases are fun to work," he says with a steely grin visible even in the darkness. "The hunter has no clue that you are watching him. But baiting cases are a lot of work, too."

For two to three weeks before turkey season starts, game wardens scour the woods, mostly on private property, looking for bait. Most of the scouting is footwork, although some illegal baiting is located by complaints to the department.

The more walking a game warden does, the more likely he is to find bait. Baiting, he says, was a big problem about ten years ago, but it has tapered off the last two or three years.

When game wardens find a baited spot, they photograph it and then periodically check it for activity. Searching for and checking on bait also requires some stealth. Game wardens must be careful not to leave footprints or ATV tracks as they search. If a violator finds tracks, it is likely to spook him and waste all of the game warden's work.

We cross the Red River in the dark and rumble into the piney hills. Everything is wet from the recent bout of bad weather and it is cool—downright nippy. Stokes has the truck's windows up and the heater on.

The five game wardens working turkey bait this morning rendezvous at the Region 3 office in Pineville at 5:00 a.m. After the normal banter that takes place between law enforcement officers, they split up.

Hill and O'Neal leave in one truck. Constance and Burnett pile in Stokes's truck. The plan is for Stokes to hide at one bait site and Burnett to set up on the other. Constance is to hide the truck and stay with it, in case it is needed quickly for pursuit.

During the ride, Burnett worries about the strong winds. He hopes that it doesn't make the turkeys sit on a tree limb all morning. Stokes seems more confident. "Just so long as the illegal hunters turn up, it doesn't matter if the turkeys do or not," he replies. All three men worry that the strong winds will cause the hunters they are looking for to just roll over in bed and wait for another day.

Five forty-five a.m. finds Stokes tip-toeing and hopscotching his way down an open, muddy pipeline right-of-way. He cautiously steps from grass clump to grass clump to avoid leaving any tell-tale footprints that will give his presence away. He quickly finds and inspects the bait site, on the edge of the clear right-of-way and near a deer stand, then evaporates into the woods nearby.

The dark woods smell fresh and green, like southern forests are supposed to smell in the spring. Stokes stoically sits cross-legged, in absolute silence, like a green-clad Buddha. The wind whispers assertively through the pine needles on the trees around him. Slowly dawn creeps in and Stokes unfolds himself to stand motionless.

It is well after daylight and the hunter should be in the woods if he is coming.

Suddenly, three vehicle doors slam and Stokes's head goes to alert like a predator's. He quietly creeps to the edge of the right-of-way. After a quick peek, he hustles back and retreats further into the woods to hide himself.

The progress of the hunters down the pipeline can be measured by the

Stokes shows infinite patience as he waits for dawn to break over the fresh spring woods.

owl hoots that they make periodically in an attempt to get a turkey to gobble. Stokes tenses as the hunters near.

Then they stop, still out of sight, about a hundred yards before they reach the bait. They hoot several times, then enter the woods on a logging trail on the opposite side of the right-of-way. They stop calling.

Stokes calls Constance on his radio and quietly instructs him to hide the game wardens' truck and go "sit on" the hunters' vehicle. Then he whispers to me that because the hunters are no longer calling, he suspects that they are set up within sight of the bait on the other side of the right-of-way. Hunters hunting over bait don't need to call to attract turkeys, he explains.

The minutes pass slowly. The suspense is palpable. The woods are silent except for the cawing of crows and the occasional squealing of wood ducks passing overhead to and from the lake.

An hour passes and Stokes stands stock-still. The man is indeed blessed with patience.

Then, coming from the opposite direction from which the men entered, he catches a glimpse of movement on the pipeline. It's them. He steps to the edge of the woods, greets them, and identifies himself.

He immediately alerts Constance by radio that he is in the presence of the hunters. He unloads their shotguns, checks them for plugs, and then inspects their hunting licenses.

Constance and Burnett arrive and Stokes begins to question the three hunters.

One says that he is a member of the hunting club that holds the lease for the property, but claims that all three of them are novice turkey hunters. His story is that they were running late this morning and decided to hunt this spot rather than near his own deer stand, even though the man that usually hunts it has a reputation for being "territorial."

Stokes informs them that they are subject to a citation for hunting over bait, as they had owl-hooted earlier that morning near the bait. The three game wardens question the unhappy men, looking closely for inconsistencies in their stories.

After huddling, the wardens decide that in all probability the three hunters had stumbled over the baited spot inadvertently and that they had no case. One of the hunters receives a citation for not having turkey tags in his possession, and then the three are released with the admonition not to discuss the morning's events with other hunters in the club.

After the hunters leave, the game wardens inspect the site closely. The baiter has set up an elaborate two-man ground blind and has expensive turkey decoys stowed behind the blind.

A close look at the bait spot reveals damage to the stems of shrubbery and small trees from shot fired from a shotgun shell. A few turkey feathers are also found, leading the game wardens to conclude that a turkey had already been taken over the bait, probably during the previous weekend, when turkey hunting was open for youths and handicapped hunters.

Later, over coffee and biscuits, the three men agree that with the investment that the baiter has made in equipment and preparation he will be back to hunt. That is, unless he saw the game wardens' vehicle parked where the right-of-way crosses the highway while the hunters were being questioned that morning.

After the discussion, Constance, whose shift is ending, bids the other two men good luck and leaves. Stokes and Burnett decide to work some Rapides Parish waterways for fishing and litter patrol.

Before the two men reach Bayou Rigolette, blue skies unfold, a welcome change from the previous four days of drabness and rain. After checking several bank fishermen there, they check the Red River boat landing. The winds are still blustering from the north and few boaters are on the water.

At Lake Buhlow, they check two bank fishermen for licenses. One blithely hands Burnett an expired North Carolina license, as if he fully expects it to pass muster. The other fisherman swears that he has a license and pulls a monstrous pile of dog-eared and raggedy papers from his auto's glove box. When none of these prove to be a fishing license, he makes a great show of dismantling the interior of his car.

Finally, Stokes tires of the charade and makes a POS to Dispatch in Baton Rouge. Neither man has purchased a license, this year or any other year. Two tickets!

As they drive away, Stokes says with a grin, "I'd like to have a quarter for every fishing license ticket that has been written on Lake Buhlow."

Burnett shakes his head and chuckles in agreement, "I don't know what it is about that lake."

From there they bounce through blooming dogwoods to Camp Beauregard Wildlife Management Area and then to Flagon Creek, which is in a stretch of cypress bottomlands in what is otherwise mixed pine and upland hardwood forest.

Few fishermen are out and the midday's activities yield only two tickets.

At 3:30 p.m., Burnett turns the truck north for another go at catching the turkey baiter. As the game wardens' truck slides by the right-of-way holding

Marcus Constance (l) and Travis Burnett (r) inspect and photograph the illegal bait.

The three game wardens (left to right, Travis Burnett, Eric Stokes, and Marcus Constance) inspect the illegal hunter's ground blind and turkey decoys.

the bait, Stokes's sharp eyes spy tractor tire tracks going down the right-of-way where there were none this morning.

Burnett turns the truck around, drops off Stokes, and waits with the truck in a secluded spot. After thirty minutes or so, Stokes calls for pickup, which Burnett promptly does. They drive back to the hiding spot to decide what their strategy will be.

Stokes tells Burnett that the hunter has taken a tractor down the pipeline and used a blade to try to scrape out and cover the bait, not just at the site that Stokes had watched that morning, but also at another baited spot that the game wardens hadn't known about. The two men agree that the hunter would not have bothered to try to scrape out the bait if he weren't planning to come back to hunt the spot.

Fixing Burnett with an ice water stare, Stokes says, "This guy wants to play cat and mouse with us. If it would have been me, I would have gotten my decoys and blind and got out of there. It will be so good to catch him."

Burnett almost imperceptibly grunts in agreement.

Stokes adds, "He either got tipped or he saw all the trucks there this morning. He lives nearby."

Stokes is undecided about whether to set up on the bait this evening. He picks up his cell phone and calls Constance, who has some enlightening news. He tells Stokes that he talked to one of the three hunters they checked this morning. The hunter told him that he ran into the owner of the blind and decoys, and that the owner had asked him if he had had trouble with game wardens this morning. The blind owner said that he hadn't hunted this morning because it was too windy.

The young hunter told Constance that he told the baiter that they had no serious trouble and were just checked for licenses and that one of them got a ticket for not having turkey tags. The baiter apparently told the hunter that he was going to go to his blind this evening. Constance believes his report.

That clinches it for Stokes and Burnett. Rather than creating more commotion this evening, they decide that they will set up to catch him the next morning, when the wind had abated. That settled, the men ease their big enforcement truck out of hiding and slip down the road, trying to clear the area as soon as possible.

In the failing light, Stokes drives silently a while before turning to me and sharing his thoughts. "What we are doing now is what I love. We are trying to out-figure his moves. We don't think that he is done; the challenge is being there when he is going to hunt.

"I think that he thinks that he has everything covered. No one said anything about bait, but to be safe he went and scraped it out. But he did a bad job of it and he still can't legally hunt the spot for a big part of the season."

With that said, he lapses into silence for the rest of the ride, obviously deep in thought.

Day Two: Day of the Mouse

Day two begins the same as day one did, at 4:15 a.m. It is cool and the night air is crisp and transparently devoid of humidity. Hopes are high and Stokes is in a talkative mood during the ride to Grant Parish.

"Turkey bait work takes a lot of time and effort. It seems to always involve a drop—where one game warden drops another off. You can't just park and go in.

"Turkey hunting over bait sounds serious, but the charge is a class 3 charge, less than possession of an illegally taken turkey, which is a class 4. Turkey hunting over bait is one of the few charges that I would increase if I could.

"There isn't much I would change though. We have come a long way in the last fifteen years, both in pay and in equipment. I've talked to people who ask what they would have to buy if they go to work as a Louisiana game warden. I tell them underwear, socks, and ink pens. Everything else the department supplies."

At Region 3 headquarters, Stokes meets Burnett and two younger agents from Avoyelles Parish, Sergeant Gabe Guidry and Senior Agent D. J. Anderson. Constance is off today. Burnett and Stokes ride together and Guidry and Anderson follow in another truck.

The game wardens hide their trucks in the same spot as yesterday and discuss whether to go in before the hunter arrives or wait until he gets in and then move in on him. They decide to wait, and so stand quietly in the dark waiting for daylight.

A half-hour after daylight, they still hear nothing, so they move ultra-quietly through the woods over rough and rocky terrain to the location of the blind. No hunter! Disappointed, but not out of the game, the four men wait for two hours—until it becomes obvious that the hunter won't show today.

Back at the convenience store over a cup of coffee, the two warriors remain positive. "I think that he will go back," says Stokes firmly. "We will

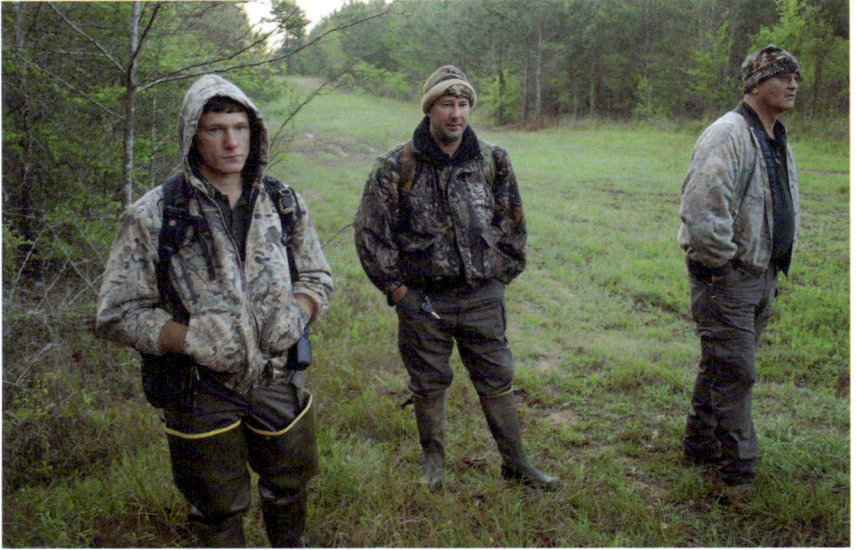

Stokes, with reinforcements Gabe Guidry (l) and D. J. Anderson (c), again draws a blank on the second day that he tries to catch the turkey baiter.

work the spot this week. If he is going to hunt it at all, he will hunt this week. If he wasn't going to hunt it, he would have gotten his decoys and gotten out of the area. We have a decent chance of catching him."

Burnett speaks up. "The weather got us the first day, and when he saw us there later in the morning it deterred him from hunting today. But I believe that he will hunt."

Agreeing with Stokes, he opines, "I think that we have a good chance of catching him this week or this weekend."

Heading south, the game wardens do some fish patrolling together before splitting up for the rest of their shift. At stop after stop fishermen are largely in compliance, until they near two men who, when they see the game wardens' truck, immediately back away from the fishing tackle laying on the bank, three rods and reels and two cane poles.

Neither man has a fishing license and both uncomfortably disavow using the rods and reels, claiming that they are for one of their daughters, who just happens to be away buying shiners. Having not seen either man with a rod and reel in his hands, the game wardens can only write them tickets for not having a cane pole license.

Both men readily admit that they received tickets for the same violation last year. While Burnett starts writing, Stokes calls LDWF Dispatch to check on what they said. Dispatch confirms that the men received the tickets and also tells him that the fines were never paid.

After they drive away, Burnett grumps, "I hate writing those tickets."

Stokes explains, "That's a five-dollar fine for this offense. The license only costs two dollars. But this is still a good job."

Burnett agrees.

Stokes sums up his feelings, "I've always felt that I was born to do this work. If the Good Lord took me back to eighteen years old and asked me what I wanted to do—I would tell him that I've already done what I want."

Epilogue

The next weekend of turkey season, Constance and Hill arrive on Saturday to find a truck parked where the pipeline right-of-way crosses the road. The hunter is not hunting near enough to the bait to be in violation of the law, and after a very short hunt they see him walk out while griping loudly on his cell phone. A vehicle driven by a woman meets him at his truck and picks him up. He does not come back to hunt.

On Sunday the agent assigned to check the baited spot calls in sick and Constance and Hill take his place at the last minute. Arriving late, at 7:20 a.m., the game wardens find a forty-seven-year-old hunter hunting from the deer stand box blind rather than the ground blind. Turkey hens are feeding on the bait.

The blind is only 115 yards from the bait. Hunting within 200 yards of bait is an offense. The game wardens approach the hunter, interview him, and get a written statement from him. He says that he thought that if he covered the bait and stayed a little ways away from it, he would be alright.

He claims to have covered the bait so that others wouldn't get caught. He admits to hunting during the youth/physically handicapped season, but denies killing a turkey, in spite of the presence of turkey feathers and shot damage to the tree saplings. He also claims to have only taken photographs from the ground blind.

He is charged with four counts of hunting turkeys over a baited area. The hunter, a bail bondsman, is very cooperative in accepting his ticket and tells the game wardens, "Y'all put people in jail and I get them out."

11

THE GLORIOUS FOURTH

It's a beautiful, glorious Fourth of July on the Amite River Diversion Canal in French Settlement. Expensive fiberglass boats, worthless as fishing platforms but great for being seen in, are cruising up and down the canal. The air resonates with music and everyone is dressed in bikinis and swim trunks. It feels like Margaritaville in the warm south Louisiana air.

But not everyone is playing. Men in uniform are converging on the Hilltop Inn Restaurant, which is perched on a mound that could only meet the definition of a hill in the swamps of Louisiana. The "hill" overlooks the diversion canal.

Many people celebrate the nation's birthday with parades, backyard barbeques, and picnics. Other places, they drink too much alcohol, get on the water in high-performance craft with no brakes or turn signals, and operate on an aquatic roadway with no center lines, street lights, or speed limits. If they survive a collision, they can't walk away—that is, unless they can walk on water.

The Fourth of July is a big workday for Louisiana Department of Wildlife and Fisheries game wardens. They carry the responsibility for water safety and accident investigation in the state, and they take their charge seriously.

Huddled in the restaurant planning the day's patrols are Sergeants Todd Lewis, Paul Stuckey, Will Roberts, and Ronnie Englehardt, and Senior Agent Randy Lanoux. An agent just out of the academy, Carl Armstrong, will be joining them. Overseeing the whole operation is Captain Len Yokum, the administrator for the region.

Englehardt and Stuckey will patrol the lower Amite River, Roberts and Lanoux will work Blind River, and Lewis will focus on the diversion canal. The group breaks up and the men walk down the hill toward their boats. Before anyone can get in a boat, a monstrous, rumbling, and snarling Fountain high-performance cigarette boat blows into the no-wake zone around the restaurant and boat launch. It is throwing a huge wave in the canal, which is only about one hundred yards wide.

"Holy crap," someone screams, and everyone scrambles for their patrol boats. Fortunately, Jesse Martin, a Livingston Parish Sheriff's River Patrol deputy is already in his boat on the water. He flicks his lights and siren on and the game wardens flag the boat operator to the wharf. The game wardens immediately start writing a citation for him.

I am riding with Roberts and Lanoux. The day promises to be hot enough to scorch a salamander, and both men have prepared for hot weather by wearing shorts.

Relatively tall and slender, youthful Will Roberts has been with the Louisiana Department of Wildlife and Fisheries since age twenty-two. Focused on becoming a game warden, he obtained a two-year degree in business technology solely to meet the minimum qualifications for the job.

Always a hunter and fisherman, Roberts says that he was attracted to the variety of the job. "You never know what you will deal with on this job. A guy threw a Styrofoam cup overboard and ran from us in a nineteen-minute pursuit. When we caught him, we had to fight him. He told me that he was part of the Mob and was going to bury me and my partner in the water with cinder blocks."

His enthusiasm carries him on. "What other job do they give you a four-wheel-drive truck, a four-wheeler, and a boat, and tell you to go to work? I wanted a job where you have the freedom to do things in the outdoors. I'd probably do this job for free.

"The hardest thing is being called for a boating accident with a fatality and it's a kid."

His partner, Randy Lanoux, has been with the department for less than three years. He went through the training academy at age forty-two with a bunch of twenty-year-olds, a challenge that he says wasn't easy.

A former bodybuilder, Lanoux sports a completely shaved head and a full brown moustache and looks the picture of a professional law enforcement officer. Before this job, he worked at the Louisiana Department of Corrections' Hunt Correctional Institute, where he achieved the impressive rank of lieutenant colonel.

After two years as an Orleans Parish Criminal Sheriff's Deputy, he moved on to work for a professional friend who was elected sheriff of Ascension Parish. There, he was in charge of the sheriff's water patrol, where he developed friendships with game wardens.

"I always wanted to be a game warden," he explains, "but for one reason or another, I just never came here. I had one chance in the 1980s, but back then the pay was too low and I would have had to move.

"When Hurricane Katrina hit, I did thirteen days straight in New Orleans. I always had a high opinion of game wardens, but after Katrina it was higher. I heard that there was an opening and I called.

"I love being outside and the freedom of the job. As a deputy you deal with the same people doing the same thing over and over, like domestic violence. Some people say that they don't like game wardens because they are sneaky. Well, you've got to be sneaky because they are doing something illegal.

"Doing game warden work is a lot like deer hunting, except the quarry is people. People know they are illegal and you've got to outsmart them. They think that they are smarter than you. It is fulfilling to catch someone who thinks that he is smarter than you.

"The worst thing is when you see things that can be avoided. I have never seen a boat wreck that couldn't have been avoided. I believe in what we do. In my time in the sheriff's office and here I have had to go to a lot of people's houses and tell them that their son or daughter won't be coming home. Accidents with kids are especially hard.

"I am tough on DWI, basic boating safety, and kids."

Roberts echoes him, "You can quote me on that, too!"

The Amite River Diversion Canal, where we are right now, was constructed between 1957 and 1964 through poorly drained wetlands. The purpose of the canal was to alleviate flooding by the Amite River by shunting some of its waters to Blind River and into Lake Maurepas.

Dredged material from construction of the 10.57-mile, 350-foot-wide canal was deposited on both sides, creating two strips of high ground in the otherwise swampy terrain. That's the way it remained for decades, a canal with spoil banks on each side of it through a cypress swamp.

Then the seemingly unquenchable desire for waterfront property overtook the area. The canal is now lined with upscale homes, jammed one beside the other. According to Roberts, lots sell for up to $200,000, and a $250,000 house is considered small. People will pay any price to live on the water.

Every home down the straight-as-an-arrow canal has boats, personal watercraft, or party barges in stalls or slings. Most of the boats are heavily powered and few have troll motors, which would mark them as fishing boats.

Some boaters abuse the easy access to the area's waterfront bars, some of which are accessible only by water.

Roberts explains that the Amite River, the diversion canal, Blind River, and some of Lake Maurepas have a high rate of boating DWI from April to September. He calls the straight, narrow, congested diversion canal "the interstate highway of the system."

"The number of boaters," he says, "along with ten bars located on the water, some accessible only by water, create a high-risk boating environment. So we have a zero tolerance for impairment—alcohol and drugs. We don't let you switch drivers, we don't let you call a cab. You are going to jail!"

In the background nodding his head in agreement is Lanoux, who adds, "From April to September our primary duty is boating safety. When we are working, we are in a boat somewhere."

It looks like they will be busy today. Boats are buzzing and swerving everywhere. Some are joyriding. Others are pulling tubers or water skiers.

Through the melee, the two men head for the intersection of the diversion canal and Blind River, a no-wake zone and also the location of the famous Blind River Bar. Not until they reach the lower fourth of the diversion canal does the boat break out of the waterfront subdivision and into a verdant green cypress swamp.

Today, they explain, Roberts will do most of the driving and Lanoux most of the checking. They will be checking life jackets, fire extinguishers, and boat registrations.

They start checking boats immediately. Most of the boaters are friendly, although one woman mildly complains about being stopped twice. "Why don't you give a card to wave after the first time we are stopped?" she asks.

Roberts patiently explains that they can't do that because conditions change. After the first stop, boaters may add people and not have enough life jackets or later drinking can impair the driver.

After the boat pulls away, Lanoux says, "The majority of people out here are glad we are here, but some resent us. People are in a recreational mode and get forgetful. But just by taking your eyes off of the water, in the time it takes for one heartbeat, your whole life can change.

"Will and I try not to inconvenience people. We do our check and let people go to have a good time. We treat people with respect until they make us disrespect them, and even then it's still business."

Roberts adds, "You treat them like you would want to be treated. You must be firm and assertive, but still treat them with respect. You must control the situation; stay one step ahead of the subject to prevent escalation."

Certain "red flags" catch the game wardens' attention. "Careless operation is one," says Roberts, "weaving and speeding. An expired registration may indicate someone not taking care of his equipment. Body mannerisms that indicate obvious intoxication are certainly red flags."

Will Roberts presents a t-shirt that says "I got caught wearing my life jacket" to a proud little girl boat passenger.

"Swapping drivers is another," adds Lanoux. "Sometimes they just try to ignore your presence. Having a crowded boat is another. You can't check everyone when things are real busy, so it is important to focus on where problems might be."

Today, everyone seems to want to wave to the game wardens. They cordially wave back to every boat. It seems tiring. "You have to wave back," grinned Lanoux, "or they will think that you are a snob."

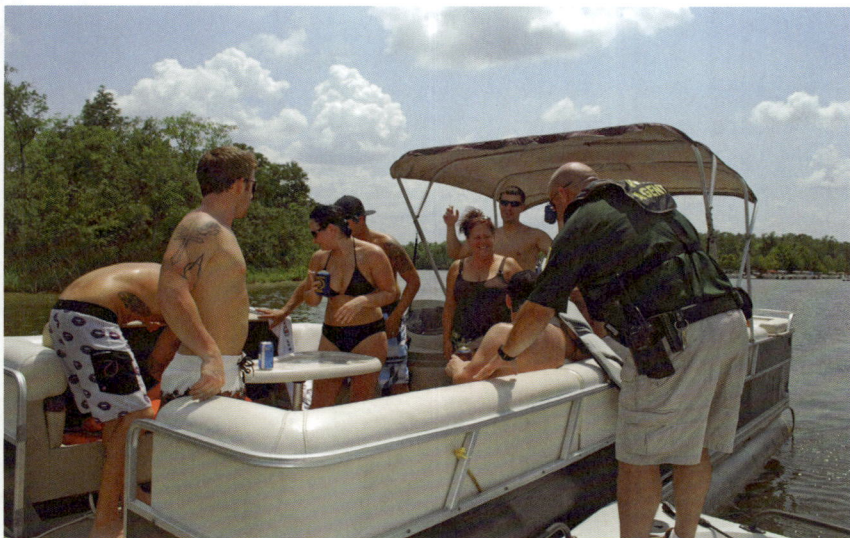

The game wardens are popular figures on this hot, sunny Fourth of July day.

Patrolling the same area in his own boat is the Livingston Parish River Patrol deputy, Jesse Martin.

They stop boat after boat. Most check out fine; a few have problems. One boat with a Mississippi registration has a Louisiana owner. He claims to have just purchased the boat this week. The game wardens call Dispatch to search Mississippi records to verify ownership and find out that the previous owner had put a 2009 Mississippi decal from another boat on top of an expired 2002 decal for this hull. Lanoux believes the boater's story, but cautions him to get his paperwork straight before letting him go.

Another boat with problems is an overloaded party barge with fourteen people aboard, two of whom are riding on the bow ahead of the rail, a practice called bow-riding. Lanoux explains to the operator that if he hits something, the bow-riders will go overboard and the boats propeller will "chop them up" before he can react.

He leaves no fudge room. "It's not going to break the bank, but you're going to get a ticket. You are the driver."

It's blistering hot. Not a breath of air stirs that might cool the men off. Beads of sweat the size of buckshot form on top of Lanoux's bald pate and run off in a shower.

Everywhere, there are people in boats out to be seen. It's a parade of bare red bellies, exposed flesh, and body art.

The two boats are joined by another one containing two Ascension Parish sheriff's deputies. Still, the officers can't keep up and most of the boats that pass miss getting checked.

They use their binoculars whenever they get a moment to check out the behavior of boat occupants before they get close enough to the game wardens to put on their game face. "The red boat just changed drivers. The people in the black and white boat just poured out all their alcohol."

The two men seem to be going full bore in mid-afternoon, but by 5 p.m. they accelerate their pace. Boatloads of people are returning from a party spot in Lake Maurepas called "the beach." For the most part, they are sunburned and happy. A few of the passengers are so drunk that they are passed out.

The drill is usually the same. Lanoux greets them with, "What's going on, guys?"

This is followed with "Everybody hold up a life jacket." Sometimes the scramble to find the jackets and get them to everyone is comical. Usually the count is right.

As the afternoon wears on, Lanoux finds reason to conduct more and more horizontal gaze nystagmus tests, but they all pass the sobriety checks. Most people are remarkably cooperative. Several times the officers are thanked for "keeping it safe out here." Most of the tickets that they do write are for expired or absent boat registrations.

The two men are experts at making boat stops. In spite of what are obviously novice boat operators at the helms of so many of the other boats, not a one ever gets bumped.

Person after person in boats being checked makes reference to *Party Heat,* and some almost treat the game wardens as stars. A few females out and out flirt with the photogenic Roberts, who is occasionally asked to pose for photos, much to Lanoux's amusement.

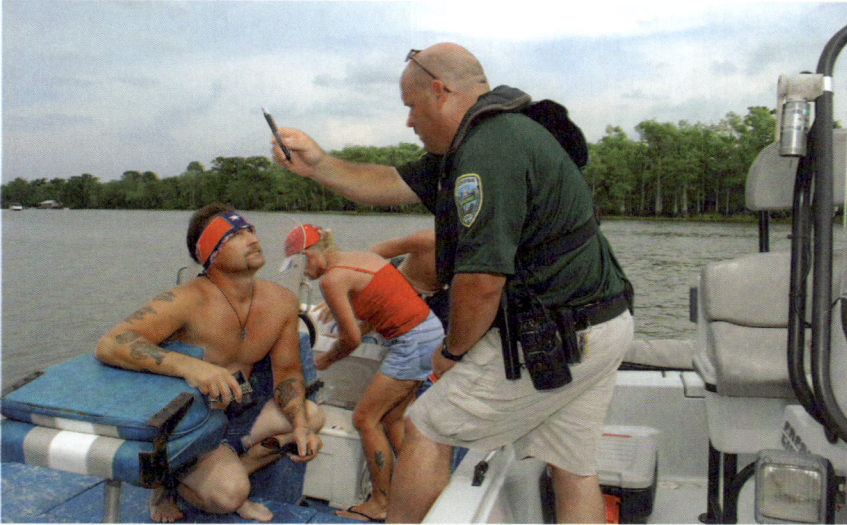

Most of the boaters are readily cooperative when Randy Lanoux administers the field sobriety test.

Roberts explains the references to *Party Heat*. "One summer, TruTV filmed with me and Randy a lot right in this area. It produced two thirty-minute shows called *Party Heat*. They filmed all over the state, but for some reason we ended up with half of the time.

"This year Randy won the department's DWI award, and I won it three years ago."

Lanoux reacts with passion, "Out of all the awards that I have ever won, and I have won a lot, that one means the most to me. There is a marked difference in accidents here in the last ten years. It is hard to find a DWI; it's not like it used to be. The agents in Region 7 have all contributed to this."

The two men are not always so serious. Lanoux complains about his size and his heat tolerance. "I went into the enforcement academy weighing 237 pounds and came out at 194."

Roberts jumps on the opening immediately. "It like to killed him. He shriveled up so much that his moustache covered his entire face." Lanoux chuckles good-naturedly.

Roberts isn't through with him yet. "Ask him if he has a license for that moustache." He pauses and adds, "We kid a lot out here when we aren't interacting with the public."

Lanoux nods and says, "A lot of the reason that I wanted to be a game warden is because of Will and the other guys."

"Yeah," Roberts agrees, "when Randy was with the sheriff's office we worked together a lot out here." It shows. Almost as if by code, the two men can communicate their intentions by a look or a glance.

At 6:30 p.m., boat traffic slows slightly and the two men run down Blind River toward Lake Maurepas. The ride is scenic, what a classic Louisiana cypress-tupelo swamp is supposed to look like. Rustic, waterside family camps are scattered liberally in the lush greenery.

Set at the mouth of Blind River, the men commence making stops again. An early stop involves a shapely woman in her twenties trying to catch a little of the waning sun by sitting on the stern rail of a huge cruiser, a ticketable offense. The operator is polite and convincing in his assertion that he was unaware of the woman's actions. The game wardens warn him and let him go.

The triple-digit heat eases its grip on the day, and evening shadows are beginning to extend across the river's waters. The men turn and run the boat back upriver, checking a few boats as they go. The two other patrol units in the area are processing DWIs, so Roberts and Lanoux plan to set up in the no-wake zone around the Hilltop Inn to be more centrally located for the whole area.

As their patrol boat nears the built-up area of the diversion canal, they also close the gap on the large cruiser that they checked earlier. And there she is, perched in all her bikini-clad glory back on the rail, accompanied by a male companion.

Roberts flicks his blue lights on. The man's eyes open wide and with a disgusted look he shouts to the boat's skipper up on the flying bridge. The woman eyes the game wardens with a look of utmost contempt, pouts her lips out, and flounces into the cabin. The bearded skipper looks down from the bridge in time to see her actions. His own disgusted look is classic.

The young woman comes back out of the cabin and Lanoux tells her that he, pointing at the skipper, is getting a ticket for what she did. She turns her head away and sits down with her back facing Lanoux. "Do you hear me, ma'am?" "Yes," she condescendingly snaps.

"Next time I see you do this, I'm taking you jail. Do you understand?" he adds.

"Yessir," is the reply. She still has her back to the game warden and her pouty face shows that she is not convinced.

The operator of the boat apologizes profusely and attempts to ease the tension by making small conversation while he waits for his citation. The woman never sneaks even a glance backward.

With light failing, Roberts and Lanoux tie their boat to the dock at the Hilltop Inn. Lewis is already there, having processed his DWI. The three men stand on the dock ready to inspect boats passing by in the narrow canal.

When the first boat passes, the driver not so subtly keeps his head turned toward the canal bank opposite the game wardens. Lanoux and Roberts exchange looks. "He is ignoring us," says Roberts.

Lanoux uses his booming voice to shout them over. Ten people, including two kids, are on the boat, but only seven life jackets are aboard. The driver's language is stumbling, as if the man in inebriated. Lanoux doesn't want to perform the horizontal gaze nystagmus test near the children, so he invites the operator up the bank, away from the boat. The man passes the test and then explains that he has a speaking disability. He still gets a ticket for the shortage of life jackets.

It's almost dark when the boat leaves. In no time, a fiberglass runabout flies into the no-wake zone. Roberts jumps from the wharf into his boat and flicks the boat's blue lights on.

The runabout immediately slows and pulls over, with the driver profusely apologizing, saying that in the darkness he didn't realize that the no wake zone was so close. Roberts asks for his life jackets and boat registration. The operator passes a horizontal gaze nystagmus test and the game wardens release him without a ticket.

"The no-wake signs are hard to see in the dark," explains Lanoux. "If he had been drunk he would have got a ticket."

"Oh yeah," chimes in Roberts, "if he had been drunk, he would have got it."

"We're not Nazis," says Lanoux with a grin.

The descent of full darkness is signaled by the beginning of a fireworks display from a nearby residence on the canal.

Next up is a party barge jammed full with sixteen people and with no front running lights. The blue lights come on again. The operator pulls over and asks what's wrong. "No lights," is the reply.

"Well, they were working the other day," retorts the man.

"Where are you going?" ask the game wardens.

The man replies that they are headed to a camp about a half-mile above the Blind River Bar. In a generous mood, the game wardens lend the man a flashlight and instruct one of the passengers to sit at the bow of the boat with the light on and let him go.

Boat after boat gets pulled over for no running lights. It seems to be almost standard operating procedure to not have functional lights here.

The beautiful fireworks display that commenced earlier is in full bloom and other homes have joined in the festivities with their own fireworks. The explosions of light sparkle over the water, and whoops and hollers fill the sensuously soft night air. Lewis leaves as his shift ends, and Englehardt, Stuckey, and Armstrong join Lanoux and Roberts.

By 9 p.m. boat traffic slows dramatically, but the fireworks continue unabated. Right at 10 p.m., the officers pull over another boat with no front running lights. The driver is surly and resentful and shows every bit of it. He passes his horizontal nystagmus gaze test, but is unhappy that it has been administered.

He stands silently, glaring, while his citation is written.

A half-hour later he returns with his bow lights lit up. "Hey," he shouts aggressively, "The light started working—you want your ticket back?"

"No," is Robert's simple one-word reply.

"Well, it's working," he comes back.

"It wasn't at the time of the ticket," says Roberts.

"Well, I hope that yours goes out," the man pops off, then throws his boat into a tight circle and juices the engine so that it throws a wake on the game wardens' boats.

"This is a no-wake zone," Roberts warns the man loudly.

"I know," he answers sarcastically. "That's why I'm not making a wake.

Roberts wearily lets the comment go unanswered.

It's late. The day has been hot and long. Boat traffic has quit. With their shifts ending, the four game wardens load their boats on their trailers, say goodbyes, and disappear into the night.

The fireworks are still snapping and popping.

12

THE DROWNING

Probably the most stressful and difficult part of the job of being a game warden is search and recovery of boating accident victims. Often, when they are called in, the hope is for a search and rescue—something with a happy ending. But after a period of time, it very often sinks in that what they are doing is no longer a search and rescue, but a search and recovery. Every game warden feels the eyes of anxious family members on him when he returns to the shore or boat launch during a search and recovery.

Even the toughest and most hardened man finds his emotions being ripped up by search and recoveries. The Coast Guard conducts rescues, but not recoveries. They often leave early. Depending on where the accident takes place, sheriff's office personnel may hang in on the search as long as do game wardens. But often the game warden is the last man searching. Some recoveries take days, but in rare cases the body is never found and the family never receives closure.

As a result of the trauma, most game wardens take their job as boating safety officers very seriously. Rare is the game warden who will not write a ticket for the absence of life jackets for the occupants of a boat. Taken just as seriously is the checking they do on the water for operating a boat while intoxicated. Some experts estimate that alcohol is involved in 30 to 35 percent of boating accidents, and the figure may be higher for serious accidents.

The Search

The telephone call comes at 7:50 a.m. on a Tuesday morning. It's Captain Len Yokum, administrator of Region 7 for the Enforcement Division of the Louisiana Department of Wildlife and Fisheries. "We have a dragging operation going on in the Tchefuncte River right now. I thought that you might want to know."

Forty-five minutes later, I meet Lieutenant Eddie Laviolette beneath the

I-12 bridge crossing over the Tchefuncte River. Three television station cam-era crews are already there and taping. Two newspaper reporters are taking notes from Laviolette and two St. Tammany Parish sheriff's deputies.

On the surface of the small river, three boats are dragging for the body. One belongs to the Department of Wildlife and Fisheries; the other two are from the Special Operations Division of the St Tammany Parish Sheriff's Office. The boats have been dragging the bottom of the river since 6:30 a.m.

The press stays a short time, then leaves.

Laviolette explains the situation to me. Sometime after midnight on Sunday, a thirty-year-old man left friends in a bar on the water to run his bass boat alone to the landing and put it on his trailer. A strong late-season cold front, with powerful north winds, blew through shortly before he left the bar.

He never made it to the landing, but no one missed him enough to be concerned on Monday. At 8 p.m. on Monday, a passer-by in a boat noticed the victim's boat wedged behind the wooden fender system under the bridge and notified authorities.

The boat's owner was nowhere to be found and a lot of blood was in the heavily damaged boat. Inspection of the bridge showed that the boat hit and caromed off of bridge pilings and the fender twice before striking the fender once more and lodging itself. It doesn't look good.

The victim's boat first hit a concrete piling that supports the I-12 bridge over the Tchefuncte River before bouncing into the bridge's heavy wooden fender system.

The fiberglass boat, now on its trailer, is shattered from its impact with the bridge.

Laviolette waves the game wardens' boat in to the bank so that I can join them. Operating the boat is Sergeant Chuck Strain, a twenty-two-year veteran of the department and two younger men, Senior Agents Robert Larsen and Rick Clark.

After picking me up, the game wardens lower their drag back overboard. The drag is a simple device, constructed of a short length of metal pipe, to which four large, wicked-looking treble fishing hooks are attached by chains. As its name implies, it is slowly dragged by boat on the water's bottom, with the intent being to snag the victim's clothing.

Strain has done this before, having investigated well over one hundred accidents in his career. He talks about recoveries as he operates the boat. "It's not easy to describe what it does to you. Different people handle death in different ways. My first time, I went home and sat on a sofa and didn't talk to anyone for four or five hours.

"You learn to handle it, but it's never easy. Some of these are senseless. If boaters would wear life jackets and engine cut-off lanyards, more people would survive. When it gets really bad is when you have to go to an accident involving a child, especially if it is the same age as yours.

"The thing I dread the most are the phone calls to the family."

"Whoa, whoa," call the two agents as the drag picks up something heavy.

A body drag is a simple but effective device made from a metal pipe from which four large treble hooks are suspended by chain. Most Department of Wildlife and Fisheries vehicles have one.

Strain stops the boat and the drag is retrieved by hand. It is a log. Such false alarms will happen repeatedly during the search.

Strain resumes my education. "These things have to be investigated thoroughly. An accident can lead to charges of negligent homicide or vehicular homicide if other victims besides the operator are involved.

"There is a lot more to accident investigations than just collisions and sinkings. For example, with fires the investigator must look at the boat's electrical system. And there is always the possibility of arson."

Time after time the two agents on the drag sing out that they have something. Each time it is debris of one sort or another. The men keep dragging relentlessly, up and down the river, back and forth. The search is confined to a couple hundred yards above and below the bridge. Drowning victims' bodies usually go straight down, explains Strain.

Another sheriff's office boat arrives. This one is big and powered by two huge V-8 outboard motors. The officers tie this boat off to the bridge, stern toward the bumpers. The huge engines are then revved up, creating powerful currents that will hopefully dislodge the body if it is next to or hung up on the fenders or the pilings, where a drag can't be used.

The process is repeated so that every nook in the bridge-fender system is swept. Still no body is produced.

On a pier on the east side of the river above the bridge sit a group of people in lawn chairs. They aren't idle oglers. They are family members. They sit in absolute silence, watching everything.

The trees along the river are leafing out in the vibrant green of springtime. They are harbingers of life, in the midst of which sober-faced men are searching for death.

Strain ponders whether divers will be called in. Both the Department of Wildlife and Fisheries and the St. Tammany Sheriff's Office have trained dive teams. Some places are too dangerous for divers to work though, explains Strain.

He says that he remembers a case in Pearl River where diving was judged too dangerous and the body didn't surface for three months. He casts an eye toward the family members and mumbles that he hopes that doesn't happen here.

At noon, the men take a break from their grim task. During the break, Laviolette says that he has done a lot of these searches. "When I started with the department in the late 1970s, they had just taken over responsibility for boating accidents from the Louisiana State Police. In 1986, there were thirty-four boating fatalities in St. Tammany Parish alone. That was almost all I did that year.

"Boats react differently in a crash than vehicles do. Most agents enjoy trying to figure out the puzzle of what happened after an accident. No two accidents are ever the same, so putting the pieces together is a challenge.

"If you don't like investigating boating accidents, you won't have a long career in the Louisiana Department of Wildlife and Fisheries. There is less and less hunting activity for us to work on and more on the water."

His outlook seems a little gloomy. "The atmosphere of common courtesy of thirty years ago on the water is gone. Speed is a factor in almost every case—by far. We have larger engines and faster boats.

"The largest engine I remember as a kid was a 105-horsepower Chrysler. . . ."

Strain interrupts him with a snort, "That's a flatboat engine now."

Laviolette nods and continues, "Now a lot of engines are 300 horsepower. The future appears to me to be more congested—more boats—with waterways the same size. Things could be safer if people took classes." He notes that Clark is a regular instructor of the department's boating safety classes.

Clark observes that usually only younger people, who are required by law to take the class in order to operate a boat, attend the classes. "Any adults there are typically parents of the kids taking the class. Older guys think that it won't happen to them. I see it all the time. They are the ones that it happens to."

The search team returns to the river. I hadn't noticed how noisy it was under the bridge this morning as I-12 traffic clunkety-clunked over the bridge, oblivious to what was going on beneath them.

The victim's family members are still there, sitting silently.

The game wardens start dragging again, scouring the river bottom. Soon a flatboat with three men who identify themselves as the victim's friends pull up below the investigation site and tie their boat to an overhanging tree limb. One of them identifies himself as the person who just helped the victim mount the motor on the boat. They will maintain their vigil until dark, sitting quietly and watching.

Their boat is joined by a second, and then a third.

Divers from the St. Tammany Parish Sheriff's Office arrive shortly after lunch. The men dive repeatedly, searching largely with their hands because of near-zero visibility at the bottom of the twenty-foot-deep river. Even with wetsuits, the 60 degree waters sap their ability to stay down longer than twenty minutes at a time.

The search team grows to include three divers from the St. Tammany Parish Sheriff's Office, but they find nothing in the cold water either.

As the game wardens continue to drag, the youngest agent in the boat, Robert Larsen, talks about how body recoveries affect him.

"I knew it was going to be part of the job and that I couldn't take it too personal. But I wasn't ready for it the first time. Nothing can prepare you for it. It helped being there with other agents that had been through it.

"I have been on ten or twelve body searches in my five years. The worst thing is seeing the reactions of the immediate family when we find the body. It is the worst part of a job that I enjoy very much."

As the afternoon stretches out, the men talk less, but still go about their task with determination. Drag, drag, drag. They drag until the lengthening shadows signal that dusk is near, then call it a day.

The family is still perched on the pier, watching and waiting.

The game wardens drag the hook across the bottom with their boat in reverse gear.

Epilogue

On Wednesday, three game wardens spend another twelve hours dragging for the body. Members of the sheriff's office dive team search for five hours, their diving again hampered by low water temperatures and almost no visibility. The victim's family watch all day.

Thursday, three game wardens continue the search. They are joined by St.

Tammany Parish deputies and a side-scan sonar team from the East Baton Rouge Sheriff's Office. Again the search is fruitless and again the family has kept an all-day vigil.

On Friday, three game wardens drag for the body for ten hours, again with no success. The family is on the pier watching the search periodically.

On Saturday, the search resumes. During the day, a private boat traveling through the area finds the body floating face down about fifty yards upstream of where the accident happened. On Friday a strong southeast wind had caused the current in the river to reverse itself, apparently dislodging the body from wherever it was.

The coroner rules that the death occurred due to blunt force trauma to the skull and drowning. The victim's blood alcohol level was within the legal range required to operate a boat.

The family was not present when the body was found.

INDELIBLE MEMORIES

We had to search for one of our agents, Ken Aycock, who drowned in the Ouachita River. When we snagged him the first thing that came out of the water was his shoulder patch. I'll never forget that. When his body was in the boat, the silence between the agents was hard to forget. It was eerie.

—Captain Alan Bankston

One search and recovery that sticks in my mind was six or seven years ago in the Tensas River. It was in the winter and the man was in his thirties. He must have lost control of his tiller handle while draining the boat through the plug hole while it was under way. The drain plug was still looped around the index finger of his left hand, which was clenched to his chest. The hand was purple because of the cold water.

—Sergeant Wayne Parker

Dane Thomas and I got called to Highway 51, off of Maurepas. A boat had hit a stump and there were injuries. They brought in a little girl about three years old while I was questioning people. She was curled up in a fetal position and the paramedics said that she was brain-dead. When they removed the mask I thought it was my daughter. Even Dane, who knew my family well, did. Later, he called my wife, who brought my daughter over. I held her and cried for what must have been three hours. That is something that stays with you.

—Captain Len Yokum

I can still remember the first one. The guy still had his glasses on. I've been on a lot of search and recoveries and a lot are alcohol related.

—Sergeant Duane Taylor

I picked up a drowned child about nine years old, the age of my child at the time. Those kinds of things stick with you.

—Captain Alan Bankston

One that I remember is when two teenage boys in a paddleboat drowned in Lake Pontchartrain. We didn't find the last one's body for nine days. It was swollen, sunburned, and blistered. It was not a pretty sight. What I remember most was the fifteen or so family members of the boy that showed up at the boat launch every day and waited all day.

—Captain Stephen McManus

What stuck most in my career was trying to revive a four-year-old boy drowned on Toledo. We worked on him for over an hour. But he didn't make it. I can still see that little feller laying there.

—Senior Agent Ronnie Robertson

One that I remember was an eighteen-year-old that drowned in a bar [borrow] pit in Minorca. His family had a house on stilts on the riverside. Five kids from eighteen to their early twenties were in an overloaded boat. It took on water over the stern and he panicked and was the only one that drowned. We hooked him through a belt loop in only an hour. He looked like he was asleep. I still remember the family all standing on the bank waiting.

—Lieutenant Russ Kiser

A drowning that I really remember is when we recovered the body of a guy in Old River in Catahoula Parish. He fell out of a boat while white perch fishing. His hand was still clenched around a red Bic cigarette lighter.

—Senior Agent Charlie Ferrington

13

OUTLAWS

Day One: The Shining

"Hi, I'm Bobby Buatt," says the man as he sticks out a hand the size of a catcher's mitt. A look at the bone crusher makes me hesitant to extend my hand in return. Then I look at his face and the huge grin he wears convinces me that I'll get my limb back intact.

Lieutenant Bobby Buatt is a big man, not fat, just big. And his personality is bigger than his frame. He enters your presence with the unstoppable momentum of an ocean-going cargo ship.

Today Buatt is planning to patrol Acadiana, focusing on Vermilion and Acadia Parishes. Two other game wardens who work under his supervision, Senior Agents Derek Logan and Lonnie Campbell, will also be patrolling the area in their own trucks.

As we leave Intracoastal City heading toward Kaplan, the January day starts out unseasonably warm, but a cold front is predicted to blow through the area during the day. Deer and duck seasons have just closed, so hunting activity will likely be light even though it's a Saturday. He expects to check some rabbit hunters and says the possibility of someone illegally shooting geese from a public road always exists.

As we head north in his big Dodge 4x4 pickup, Buatt talks about his interest in becoming a wildlife agent stemming from when he was a little boy. His love of the outdoors started with his father, who, he says, "lived to take me and my little brother hunting and fishing."

He goes on, "In high school in Crowley, I had no time for sports. I was always in the outdoors environment. Dad is eighty-three years old now and he still hunts and fishes."

After high school Buatt did a stint in college at the University of Louisiana in Lafayette, but didn't graduate. While working as a truck mechanic, a game warden friend, Jimmy Jukes, helped him break into law enforcement, first with the Acadia Parish Sheriff's Office Reserves, then in the Crowley Police Department.

After two years, Jukes called and asked him if he wanted to be a game warden, as a position was opening. His response was an enthusiastic "yes." So, at twenty-eight years old he applied and was accepted.

Now at forty-six, with eighteen years of wildlife law enforcement experience and with three marriages and three divorces under his belt, he's a seasoned veteran. "In my early years as a game warden, I probably sacrificed some family time because I was so enthusiastic about the job," he says.

We are cruising through heavy-duty farming country, primarily cattle pastures and rice fields. Many of the rice fields are flooded and studded with the necks of crawfish traps sticking out of the water, all perfectly aligned.

Logan, who seems to have a nose for activity, raises Buatt on the radio to report a mass of geese rising from a field between Kaplan and Crowley. Someone may have shot into the feeding flock. The two men coordinate their positions on the radio to encircle the area. They search, find no hunters, and then go their separate ways.

The warm weather in the midst of a cold winter has hatched "bucket fishermen" like mayflies. Standing, sitting in lawn chairs, and yes, on five-gallon buckets, they occupy almost every culvert and many canal banks between. Buatt checks them as he passes by.

His demeanor is always the same. He jumps out of his truck like he hasn't seen a person for days, smiles broadly, sticks out a hand to shake, and says, "Hi, I'm Bobby Buatt."

At a rural crossroads, he stops briefly and rolls his truck window down to greet a farmer he knows. The farmer asks what he's doing. "Oh, you know, fighting crime and corruption," he replies with a toothy grin. As he drives off, he says to me by way of explanation, "I'm always trying to make more friends than enemies."

A prosperous pastoral landscape spreads before us as we move along— old and new houses, stately live oak trees, and rolling-fat cows grazing in bright green rye grass fields.

He stops and checks the licenses and catches of a few more bucket fishermen who are fishing in roadside canals and ditches. An open gate leading off the paved road catches his eye. "Hmm, I wonder why that gate is open," he says as he drives down the field road.

In a grown-over area he spies three parked pickup trucks. Nearby, wearing various amounts of hunter orange, are five rabbit hunters. Buatt greets them, shakes their hands, and checks their licenses. They have bagged one rabbit between them so far.

A portly man who identifies himself as the landowner becomes talkative, complaining bitterly about night hunting violations. Buatt asks him if he has reported the problems. The man replies that he has not. Buatt gives him instructions on how to report future violations.

Back in the truck, his sharp eyes catch something as he crosses a bridge over a small drainage ditch. A creamy liquid seems to be rising from the bottom and pluming down current.

Suspecting pollution, he carefully descends the steep bank and wades through the litter-strewn water. Picking up a metal rod from the debris, he probes the off-colored water and the water bottom where it seems to arise. He can identify no source and the water has no smell.

Gingerly wading back to the bridge, he stops to investigate a metal box that looks like a safe. Shaking his head, he explains, "People steal shit and dump it off bridges. I found a suicide victim like this once—a woman in her thirties that shot herself in the head."

Further down the road he spots two vehicles with out-of-state plates parked on private property near a crawfish pond pump. The passengers have a gentrified appearance out of place in the rural countryside.

The mysterious plume of milky water has no source that Bobby Buatt can identify.

Displaying cameras, they declare themselves to be birders. "It's not un-usual to see birders, photographers, and even artists with easels on the side of the road here," says Buatt. "Crawfish ponds attract a lot of birds."

The morning is passing peacefully and the talk turns to the elements of game warden work. "One of the most important things for a game war-den is having the element of surprise on our side. Sometimes we have to be sneaky. We often drive with no lights, blacked out.

"We are trying to catch night hunters, but we come up with all kinds of things. You'd be surprised what we find, including couples doing their thing. We are almost obligated to check every vehicle in that setting. We separate couples and ask the female if she is here of her own free will. You almost have to do that. I have heard of a sheriff's deputy who came across a rape that way.

"You have to be delicate. Sometimes we find married couples—ones mar-ried to other folks.

"We also find people doing drugs in the outdoors at night more often than you would think."

Buatt's discourse is interrupted by a radio call from an LDWF agent to let him know about a boat sunk in the Mermentau River. Buatt quickly turns the truck around and heads back to Intracoastal City to hitch up a boat. He juggles the radio and his cell phone in talking with two other agents to get more information and to possibly coordinate a search.

Then word comes over the radio that the Cameron Parish Sheriff's Of-fice has reported that the boat's occupants are safe and accounted for. "Now that's the kind of ending that I like to hear," says Buatt, grinning broadly.

Buatt then heads for a rendezvous with Derek Logan, who is sitting on four parked pickup trucks. Logan is scanning the surrounding fields and tree lines with his binoculars. He informs Buatt that he thinks the truck's occupants are rabbit hunters.

Logan uses the binoculars in his typically comical way, held vertically and looking only through the lower eyepiece, as one would look through a telescope. Soon he reports a bunch of hunters returning on foot and by ATV across a harvested cane field.

They are indeed rabbit hunters, ten of them, nine adults and a boy, with a modest bag of rabbits and a small pack of beagles. Buatt greets everyone in an enthusiastic but low-key way, like a gentle giant.

While the two game wardens are checking licenses and shotgun plugs, one of the hunters decides to run his ATV up homemade wooden ramp boards into the bed of his truck. One board snaps with the sound of a rifle

Buatt checks out a big swamp rabbit while Derek Logan monocularly uses his binoculars to check on more incoming hunters.

shot and the heavy ATV drops vertically to the ground and threatens to fall on the driver. Buatt and several hunters quickly spring to the driver's aid, and serious injury is avoided. All the rabbit hunters check out as legal.

As the two men are leaving the hunters, a loud gunshot rings from behind a nearby tree line. Buatt and Logan rev their trucks toward the area of the shot, their wheels slinging gravel everywhere.

They find two crawfish farmers trying to plug a leak in their pond levee. The men say that they shot into the air to scare away a flock of crawfish-eating birds. The bed of their pickup is half-full of sacks of crawfish.

While Buatt occupies them in conversation, Logan walks the pond's levees to make sure that the farmers didn't shoot at and kill a protected bird species rather than try to scare them off.

At 12:20 p.m. the front wall of a strong cold front hammers the four men with frigid mist. The temperature immediately begins to plummet.

The two shivering game wardens head for lunch at a local country store.

While eating, the pair talk about one of the fun things they do as game wardens, setting up in grass or brush right behind a duck blind. Buatt says that they will try to be set up behind the blind an hour before legal shooting time. If the hunters' camp is close to the blind, they will set up even earlier to avoid being seen. Lots of times this means getting out of bed at 2 a.m.

Logan, warming to the subject, says, "You've been sitting there freezing and shaking, then you hear a motor: They are coming. You aren't cold anymore."

Adds Buatt, "It makes up for all the times you set up and they don't hunt the blind that day."

"You ought to hear what hunters say in a duck blind," smirks Logan. "They talk about everything—everything!"

After lunch the two go separate ways. While heading north toward Rayne and Ebenezer, Buatt begins a tutorial on being a wildlife agent. "Some of the secrets to being a good game warden include knowing the area, knowing the people, and knowing the habits of the wildlife.

"Knowing the people is especially important because you can keep tabs on reputed violators. Knowing the people creates opportunities for them to interact with you. Game wardens are in a position of authority and leadership within the community. If people have a crisis, they can come to you."

He goes on, "To gain respect and trust, you must treat the people of the community with respect and trust. You must be nice to them. If you show respect and kindness, you get it back, even to some degree from violators.

"Get out of the truck with a happy smile, especially with kids. It sets the tone for a less intimidating encounter with a wildlife agent.

"People are interested in game wardens and their work."

As Buatt patrols the flatlands, he sees very few geese, something he comments on. "It concerns me. It's beginning to scare me. These rice fields ought to be loaded up with geese in January."

North of Rayne, rice fields extend endlessly into the horizon. The only real woods are along Bayou Plaquemine Brule, near Branch.

"We used to catch a lot of night rabbit hunters here. You don't see that much anymore. It's fun to ride in a blacked truck, right behind a truck with a fella in the bed shooting over the cab.

"They don't know you are there. When you turn on your headlights and the blue lights, the look on their face—the 'oh shit' look—is priceless. A picture like that is worth a thousand words."

The countryside is quiet; even the radio is strangely quiet. "This area," he says, "is more laid back than other areas of the state. Game wardens here have to work hard to make cases. Stuff doesn't just fall into our lap.

"Times have changed. The people that used to be career wildlife violators are older and have slowed down. Younger ones are more into dope or have gotten jobs to make something of themselves. Circumstances evolve."

Buatt makes a jog into Rayne to take a photograph for an accident report on the boat that had sunk earlier in the day at the Mermentau jetties. The boat's owner is still obviously shook up from his experience. Before leaving, Buatt explains to the man how to take quick action to salvage the outboard motor.

Near dark, it becomes drizzly and colder as Buatt's big, black, four-wheel-drive truck creeps through Midland and Mermentau. He sets up in an isolated spot near the Mermentau Cove area. The spot has a history of night hunting activity.

Buatt stands outside the truck, near a front fender, to see and hear better. It's a cold, misty, nasty night.

After an hour of seeing nothing, he gets back in the truck, cranks it up, and leaves.

Buatt slowly cruises the area's small rural roads, his head constantly pivoting on his shoulders, looking for anything out of the ordinary. On Highway 91, south of Gueydan, he spots something—a slow-moving vehicle in the distance on another road that intersects Highway 91.

He stops his truck, grabs his binoculars, and in the bitter cold climbs up onto the top of the wall of his truck bed to get a better look. "Oh yeah, we got us a night hunter!" His voice is filled with excitement and anticipatory relish.

The vehicle is moving slowly toward an intersection with Highway 91, stopping frequently. Pinpoints of light from the vehicle probe the blackness of the night, and periodically a bright flash of light from a Q-Beam shoots from the vehicle.

Buatt watches carefully from his perch, his big body standing like a black pillar against the starry night sky.

When the shiners' truck crosses the highway and keeps going, Buatt starts his truck and begins to drive toward the intersection. His vehicle lights are all out to keep from being seen.

The deep, wide canal on the right side of the highway reflects some starlight, but it is difficult to see anything else. Buatt seems to steer his vehicle more by instinct than by visual cues.

Finding the gravel road that the shiners are on without the aid of a light is difficult, but once on it Buatt pushes his blacked out truck hard to close the gap between the two vehicles. The gravel road is even harder to follow in the dark than was the paved highway, although it too is flanked by a wide canal.

Buatt gives the dangerous canal wide berth, over-compensating by riding off the opposite shoulder of the road. If he could follow the shiners' truck closely, navigating the blacked out vehicle would be simpler, but for unknown reasons the driver of the other truck repeatedly stops and walks several yards away from the truck with a small light. Buatt worries that the hunter will see his vehicle if he follows too closely.

Tension builds like static electricity as the two vehicles ghost down the remote road. The hunters shine the left side of the road steadily, but Buatt never sees or hears them shoot.

After what seems like an eternity, but is probably more like forty-five minutes, Buatt says, "I've got to take them; sooner or later he's going to see me when he gets out of his truck."

He guns his potent unit up to just a few feet behind the shiners' heavy-duty dually truck and flips on both his headlights and the blue lights on his light bar. The other truck's driver hits his brakes and throws his hands up in surprise.

Buatt launches from his truck like a rocket, holding his police flashlight high. He bellows, "State game warden; let me see your hands," while running to the offenders' truck. "State game warden; let me see your hands," he repeats. Two pairs of hands are tentatively extended from the windows of the truck.

Reaching the driver's side window, he shines his light into the eyes of the man. "Get out of the truck," he commands forcefully. How many people are in the truck—two? Both of you get out."

A steel-faced, middle-aged man emerges from the driver's side. Another man, a nineteen-year-old, steps out of the passenger's side door.

He tells them to step to the rear of their truck, into his truck's headlights. Buatt doesn't draw his sidearm, but is hyper-alert for any sign of trouble.

Buatt's public-friendly face and demeanor are gone. He wears a grim visage.

"Okay—you know what you were doing," he tells the two men. He reads them their Miranda warning. The younger man's eyes get wider, but the older hunter's stoic, blank face never twitches, never shows a sign of emotion.

"What were you doing?" asks Buatt.

"Nothing," is the older man's terse reply.

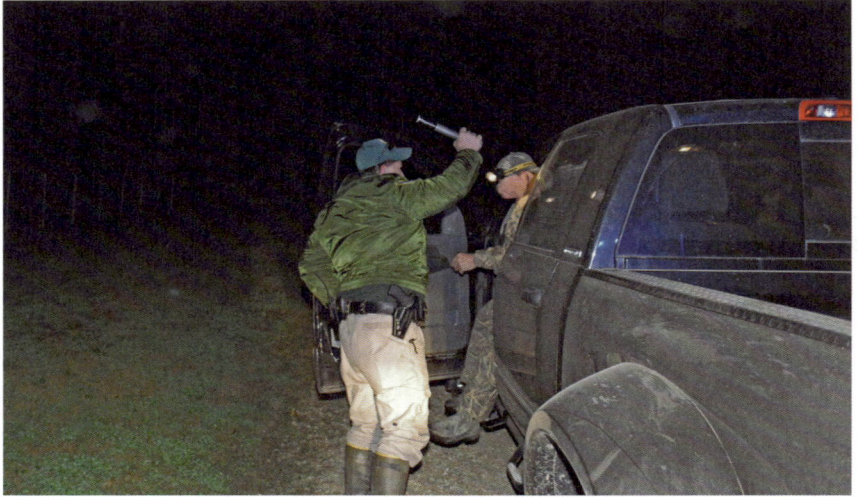

The night hunter steps from his truck into the beam of Buatt's flashlight.

"Don't hand me that," shoots back Buatt. "I've been doing this a long time. What were you doing?"

Again the older man speaks. "Looking for coons to come back to later with dogs," he replies impassively. It is obvious that the young man was coached not to speak.

Buatt directs the two to wait between the vehicles while he searches their truck. On the console between the front seats lay two loaded .22 caliber semi-automatic rifles. Two more unloaded .22 rifles are on the backseat. The men possess two 6-volt headlights and a 12-volt Q-Beam. Buatt keeps one eye on the men as he searches.

The game warden looks behind the rear seat and finds two 12-gauge shotguns loaded with T shot, "undoubtedly for road shooting geese," suspects Buatt. Under the driver's seat is a fully loaded 9 mm semi-automatic pistol. The inside of the truck is literally paved with hundreds of spent .22 shell cases. In the bed is a puddle of blood still fresh enough to be smeared.

Buatt returns to the two men standing in the cold wind. "Nobody is going to jail for this," he says. "Now don't lie to me. How this goes depends on how honest you are with me. You have two loaded rifles in the front. Do you normally just ride around with two loaded guns and headlights to shine with?"

"We were just looking for coons to come back to with dogs later," is the older man's reply. The young man remains silent.

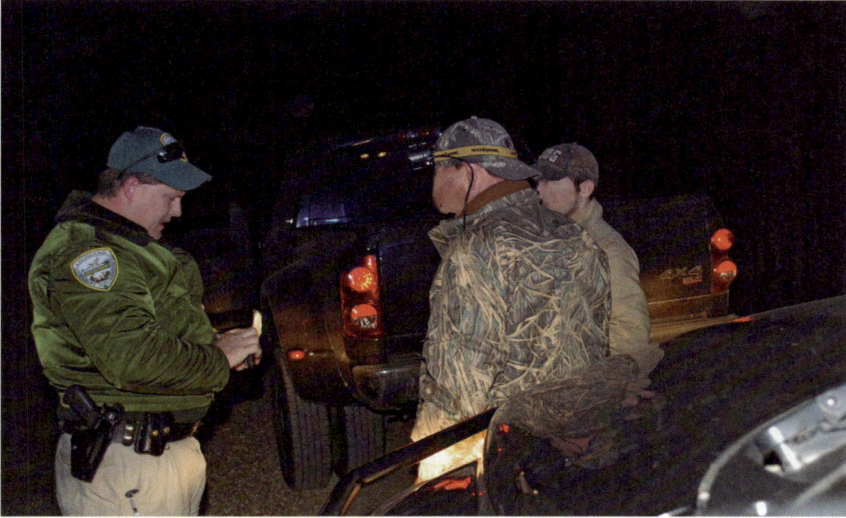

Close questioning of the two men reveals nothing. The older man sticks to the story that they are coon hunting. The younger man says nothing.

"I know better than that. Don't lie to me," says the exasperated Buatt.

Buatt calls for assistance from Derek Logan and Lonnie Campbell, then returns to the two men. "I've been watching and following you the whole time that you were shining, before you crossed the highway back there and all on this road.

"What did you shoot?" asks Buatt.

"Nothing," is the impassive man's reply, to which Buatt retorts, "Do you think I was born yesterday? That dog don't hunt with me."

Buatt then asks, "What about the blood in the truck?"

"Hog," is the stony reply.

Buatt seems to be losing patience. "I usually don't confiscate things, but I'm gonna take your guns for lying to me," he threatens.

"You came all the way from New Iberia to look for coons that you weren't going to shoot and you have two loaded guns. You expect me to believe that?" questions Buatt.

Buatt tells the older hunter that he is going to search his pockets. As he is reaching into the first one, he asks, "You don't have any drugs or other things in there you shouldn't have, do you?"

"Oh no," is the pious reply, "I don't drink, smoke, cuss, or go out; no sir." Buatt rolls his eyes ever so subtly. He finds nothing.

He tries the pair one more time with an accusation. "You were hunting rabbits."

The reply from the older man is as expected. "No, I wasn't hunting. I was looking for raccoons."

"That blood is fresh. Are you sure you aren't lying?" pushes Buatt.

"No," is the mumbled reply.

The game warden recognizes from the older man's answers that this isn't his first time hunting at night. He directs the older man to remain where he is and escorts the younger man to the rear of his patrol vehicle for questioning.

Buatt looks him in the eye and says, "Now tell me what you were doing. You don't want things to be worse on you than what they are. What were you doing?"

"Hunting coons," is the weak, mumbled reply.

"Look at me," says Buatt while pointing to his forehead. "Do I have 'stupid' written here? Now tell me the truth."

The young man partially caves in, admitting that they were hunting rabbits. "What about the blood?" asks Buatt.

"It is from a hog we killed yesterday," is his reply.

Buatt snorts, then shakes his head in disbelief of the latter answer and returns to the older man waiting between the vehicles in the cold, biting wind.

"Your partner gave you up," says Buatt. "Now what were you doing?"

"We were looking for coons to come back and hunt later," comes the rote reply. The man is unbreakable.

"Fine," said Buatt with finality; "you'll get a ticket for hunting raccoons illegally as well as your other citations."

As Buatt returns to his truck to begin writing tickets, Logan and Campbell arrive almost simultaneously. The two senior agents perform another search of the subjects' truck.

They unload the .22 rifles, then Campbell finds something Buatt missed, a clip of .30 caliber armor-piercing rounds. The rifle for the rounds is nowhere to be found in the truck. As they pore over the truck, Logan murmurs, "This isn't this guy's first rodeo."

There are plenty of tickets to write. Each of the two men receives tickets for hunting wild quadrupeds during illegal hours, hunting from a moving vehicle, and hunting from a public road, plus the bonus citation for hunting raccoons by illegal methods.

Buatt explains their citations to them and cuts them loose, saying, "Gentlemen, good night. Don't come back to Vermilion Parish and hunt like this again. I'll put you in jail next time."

The older man keeps his record intact. His eyes never focus on Buatt and his petrified face neither grimaces nor shows relief.

After the hunters leave, Campbell informs Buatt that the man just cited is a multiple and repeat offender. In his last night hunting encounter, he tried to outrun the game wardens and was caught only when he ran his truck off a dead-end road.

Day Two: The Posse

Early in the morning of the next day, Buatt expresses a suspicion that he may have missed something the night before when the shiner had exited his truck several times. Today he wants to return to the scene and see what he can find in daylight.

Before he returns there with his agents, they do some patrolling in goose country. Working today is Logan, as well as Sergeant Keith Delahoussaye. Campbell is off duty. Between Kaplan and Gueydan, south of Highway 14, the fields hold lots of geese, mostly white-fronted geese, locally called "specklebellies."

"This is migrating bird heaven," Buatt says gleefully while rubbing his hands together. "I love to eat specks better than anything. I love to cook specklebellies. My method is the best," he says without equivocation.

Buatt stops to check a pair of goose hunters tending a spread of shell decoys and wind socks. They are in compliance.

After leaving the hunters, Buatt fields a call from Delahoussaye that he is talking to a pair of hunters with license problems nearby. Buatt arrives to find a resident goose hunter who doesn't have any licenses. His hunting partner, a nonresident from Texas, seems to have no federal duck stamp.

The Texan, who seems to be both educated and monied, takes the approach that because of the money he is spending hunting in Louisiana he should be let off with a warning.

The argument goes nowhere. He receives a ticket for not having a federal duck stamp and his resident partner gets "the trifecta," as Buatt calls it: tickets for no basic hunting license, no state duck stamp, and no federal duck stamp.

Buatt makes a few more stops to check legal goose hunters and sac-a-lait fishermen. At each stop he is back to his old self, proffering a big hand with a smile and a self-introduction.

Keith Delahoussaye checks out the lone snow goose taken by two hunters.

Logan writes the nonresident goose hunter a "trifecta" hunting license citation.

Late in the morning, he rounds up Delahoussaye and Logan to return to the scene of the previous night's activities.

Things look a lot different by the light of day. The big canal on the right side of the road still looks big. But on the left side of the road, the side that we stayed on to avoid the canal, is a small but vicious ditch.

At one place where the shiners stopped, at least to the best of Buatt's recollection, both standing and downed roseau canes are speckled and smeared with dried blood. But the three game wardens can find no place with pooled blood, where it looks like game has been stashed.

The game wardens conclude from the way the blood is distributed and from the number of recently fired shotgun shells that daytime rabbit hunters had produced the blood evidence they found. The other stops yield nothing. If last night's bad boy had stashed game, he had returned and removed it.

The game wardens part company and Buatt heads toward home. Yesterday had been a long day.

14

THE TWIN PILLARS

I get my first daytime look at Senior Agent Jared McIver and Sergeant Mike Kelley in the parking lot in front of the Region 1 LDWF Enforcement Office. I had spent the night with them and Sergeant Patrick Staggs two nights before, set up on a deer decoy in northern Webster Parish. But since we were blacked out the entire time, I never got a clear look at their faces.

At thirty-two, McIver is the younger of the pair. Of medium height, with a muscular, sculpted body, he doesn't have a hair out of place. In fact, he doesn't have any hair; his scalp is shaved. With his ramrod-straight posture he resembles an elite military paratrooper. But when he is relaxed, he has a chink in his armor, an absolutely huge grin set off by big dimples in his cheeks. McIver has seven years on the job and a police officer background.

At forty-six years old, the avuncular Mike Kelley, with his grizzled-gray hair, neatly trimmed moustache, and friendly face, looks just like what your neighborhood barber is supposed to look like. But behind the unassuming face resides twenty-four years of experience and the confidence and good judgment that come with time.

It rapidly becomes obvious that the two men enjoy working together. They believe that working as a pair rather than alone offers several advantages. Many times a hunter in the woods can hear a game warden stop at his truck. If he is illegal, he just won't come out until he hears the game warden drive off.

The game wardens say that they often beat this game by having one of them stay at the hunter's vehicle while the other drives off. The subjects will often come out in a hurry immediately after the truck leaves. "They are shocked when one of us steps out from behind a bush after they come out," says McIver.

Another advantage in working together is in going into a hunting camp, considered to be one of the most dangerous situations for a lone game warden. "There is always a lot of drinking going on in camps, and one game warden can't watch what is going on behind his back," explains Kelley.

They add that by working as a team and having such different styles, they can also do the "good cop/bad cop" routine. "Guess who's the bad cop?" asks Kelley. McIver just grins.

Others have noticed the symbiotic relationship between the two. "Those guys just feed off each other," says a chuckling Roy Schufft, a lieutenant in the other district of the same enforcement region.

The two men exhibit what seem to be the twin pillars that wildlife and fisheries enforcement seems to be built on. McIver exhibits the élan and boundless energy of the younger officers. Kelley shows the wisdom and judgment (not to be confused with passiveness) of the experienced field officers who are senior in years. They may be the proverbial young bull and old bull.

Both officers' cell phones seem to ring constantly, especially McIver's. His is hard to miss. It rings with the theme song of the *Andy Griffith Show.* "I just love *Andy Griffith,*" exhales McIver passionately. The calls are all from complainants. "That's how Mike and I operate," explains McIver. "We give out tons of business cards and people call us. It gets a little burdensome at times, but we make a lot of cases."

"Most of our cases come from complaints," Kelley says, backing up McIver. Both men monitor their cell phones 24/7.

This call is from a reliable citizen who says that he is tired of having dogs drag deer heads into his yard from a neighbor who he suspects has been killing far too many deer. After listening patiently and asking a few questions, McIver asks the complainant to call them immediately the next time the subject hangs a deer in his yard for cleaning, and gives him Kelley's cell phone number as well.

After he hangs up, McIver explains that the subject of the complaint has been on their radar screens for some time now for killing too many deer. Repeated complaints against him have been lodged, some from coworkers. But he has been tough to catch.

He hunts in a securely fenced area that is not open to the general public and he gets a warning every time that the game wardens approach. It's going to take long and patient work with the newly instituted tagging system to make a case on the man. "He hunts just for the kill; he loves to kill things," says Kelley.

Ten minutes later McIver's phone rings again. This one is from a woman

Jared McIver listens to a man so irate and loud that he can't hold the phone near his ear. Both McIver and his partner, Mike Kelley, encourage the public to call them on their cell phones with concerns and complaints.

working at a construction site. She is calling about a sick fox, possibly one with rabies. They turn the truck around and head toward the small town of Dixie Inn to check on the fox. At the construction site, the woman office worker guides the two game wardens to where the fox is lying in the open, with hard hat-wearing construction workers stepping all around the ailing animal.

The gray fox is beautiful in its prime winter fur coat. The hapless creature is alive, but severely distressed. It is too sluggish to run from humans and excess saliva is copiously dripping from its mouth. After observing it for a few minutes, the officers decide that it must be removed from the worksite. Kelley pins its head with one foot and picks it up by its tail. The weak animal barely protests.

After securing it in the bed of the truck, they continue their patrol. Kelley asks McIver if he has heard anything about having passed his DRE (Drug Recognition Expert) test. McIver, it turns out, is the LDWF Enforcement Division's foremost illegal drug expert.

Probably opposite from what most people would expect, illegal drug use in the outdoors is a major and growing problem. Kelley says, "When I

Kelley (l) and McIver (r) deliberate on what to do with an obviously sick gray fox at a construction site.

started this job, if you found marijuana on someone in the outdoors, it was a once in every other year thing. Now it's monthly."

McIver pulls some figures off the top of his head. One in ten vehicles on any road will have illegal drugs in it. The average DWI violator drives inebriated eighty days a year.

McIver explains that not only has the amount of drugs in circulation increased, but the kinds of illegal drugs have changed. They have moved away from plant-based drugs like marijuana to laboratory-created chemical drugs and prescription drugs. Pain killers and methamphetamines are now common. "We are catching more people with crystal-meth than with marijuana," says McIver matter-of-factly.

McIver's experience with drugs began as a sheriff's deputy, when he attended Drug School. He showed an aptitude and was appointed as a field sobriety instructor while with the sheriff's office. When he was attending the LDWF academy, they learned that he was an instructor. After a couple of years he was called upon to teach at the academy he graduated from.

LDWF then gave him the opportunity to attend DRE training by the Louisiana State Police. DRE-trained people, says McIver, are trained to recognize signs of drug impairment beyond alcohol. "The training can be used when field sobriety testing shows impairment but the subject blows low in blood alcohol content."

"There are only 4,500 DREs in the world," he says proudly.

McIver did indeed pass the final test and has become LDWF's first Drug Recognition Expert.

The two men stop at several deer hunting camps, looking for signs of freshly cleaned deer, but find nothing and no one at the camps. They stop to lend assistance to two sixteen-year-old boys with a small pickup truck stuck in the bottom of the road's ditch. One boy's grandfather is present, but he is having difficulty pulling them out because his towrope is too short.

Kelley signals McIver to pull the pickup truck out of the soft ditch.

The game wardens unlimber a longer rope from their truck and have the vehicle back on the blacktop in short order. They receive profuse thanks from the grandfather and sheepish thanks from the youths and are soon back on patrol.

The rural countryside near the Arkansas line is beautiful, mixed pine and hardwood forest, but with little agriculture. Modest houses are strewn liberally over the landscape. The two men stop at a road intersection to examine two deboned deer carcasses that a hunter with little pride has dumped, half on and half off the road.

What they are looking for is a tag left on one of carcasses by the litterer. "We get a lot of complaints about that kind of stuff from nonhunters," drawls the soft-spoken Kelley. "They don't like to see that."

Further down the road, they spot a truck parked well back from the highway, several hundreds yards across a pasture. There are no gates, so the men assume that the hunter had to go from a house set next to the pasture. McIver drops off Kelley with his portable radio to cross the pasture and wait out the hunter, while he hides the truck and waits.

Soon, Kelley calls to say that the hunter has finished hunting and has

Kelley examines deer carcasses that have been thoughtlessly discarded in a highway intersection ditch.

come out, but didn't have his hunting license with him. He asks McIver to meet the two of them at the house they saw earlier. After a brief search of his house, the hunter, who smells strongly of alcohol, meets the two wardens outside with his license.

But things are not in order. He claims to have killed no deer, but a tag is missing from the license. In a rambling, confused way he explains that he had removed the tag to pick up a deer from a deer processor. A friend, he claims, had killed the deer in Arkansas and given to him. He has not called in to LDWF the use of the tag, which is a violation. The deer is almost completely eaten already, the man adds.

Although the two wardens suspect more is going on than meets the eye,

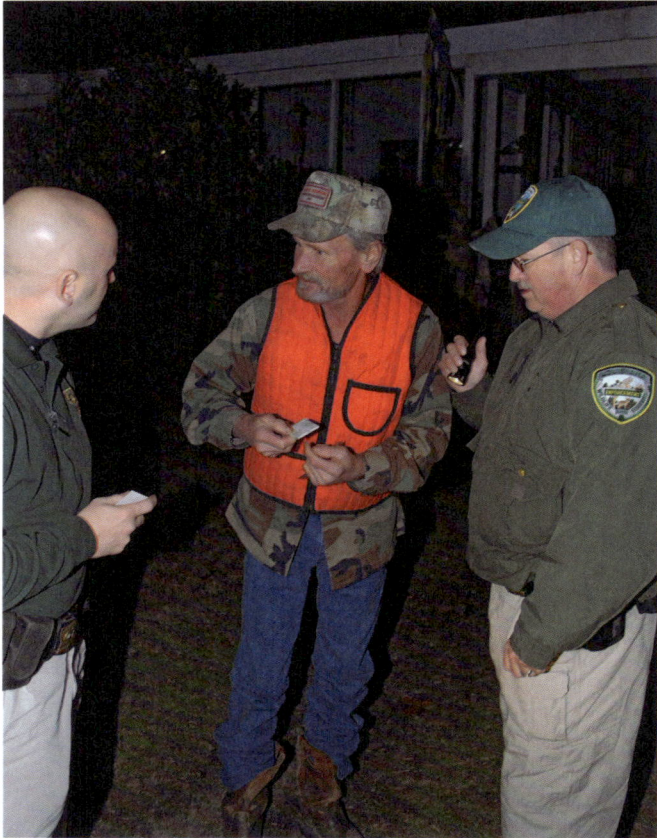

The grateful hunter thanks the two wardens for not writing him a hard ticket.

they have no proof of further wrongdoing and simply write him a warning ticket for improperly using a tag. The grateful man thanks them for not writing a ticket that would have cost him money, and adds that he hunts not for sport, but to feed himself.

The pair receive yet another telephone complaint, this one about late shooting from behind the complainant's house. After they arrive at the site, the complainant guides them to where he heard the shooting, but nothing more is to be heard or seen.

At 8:30 p.m., they pull their big truck up on the shoulder of the parish road and McIver gets out to stretch his legs. He hears the sound of mud grip tires growling on the road from behind the vehicle. As the truck passes him, McIver sees, by the light of his truck's headlights, blood running from the other pickup's bed onto the rear bumper

When the truck pulls into a convenience store lot, the game wardens pull in right behind him. A bag holding the rib cages and internal organs of two freshly cleaned deer is in the bed of the pickup. The wardens engage the driver, a man in his forties, in conversation.

Standing over the remains of the two deer, the man admits that he and his twelve-year-old son, the passenger in the truck, have taken two does today. Turning to the boy, the wardens ask the youngster if he has had a good season. The loquacious boy volunteers exactly how many deer both he and his father have taken.

The numbers don't add up to what the man's tags show he has taken. He has only used two antlered and one antlerless tag on the year. Realizing that his son has given him up, the man immediately caves in, "I'll tell you the truth, because you'll find out anyway. This is my fourth antlerless deer this year."

Kelley and McIver write citations to him for possession of and taking of over the limit of deer and for a tagging violation, then release him.

15

THE UGLY SIDE

"I do like writing littering tickets," admits Senior Agent Byron Cammack. "I get a great deal of satisfaction from writing tickets for littering. It's our land that is being trashed. I still remember that old television commercial with the Indian crying over litter."

The thirty-nine-year-old Cammack is something of a local legend among game wardens in central Louisiana. In 2008 he won both the annual Keep Louisiana Beautiful Award and the LDWF award for writing the most littering citations.

But the well-liked Cammack is known for more than excelling at a part of game warden work that most agents take very seriously. He is the only person to have gone through the challenging LDWF Training Academy twice. How that happened is an interesting story in itself.

Growing up in the small town of Effie in Avoyelles Parish, where he still lives, he spent a lot of time with the local game warden's sons. "I thought it was the coolest job ever," he grins. "My family wanted me to be a doctor or a dentist, but I wanted to do outdoor work." He decided to be a game warden even before he entered college and received a B.A. in criminal justice.

He applied for a job as a game warden as soon as he graduated from college, but there weren't any openings in the parish he applied for. So, he worked for the Louisiana Fire Marshall's office for two years.

Cammack applied again, expressing a willingness to take a job anywhere, was hired, and went through the training academy the first time.

Then in 1999 he and his wife, Dana, who had long had an interest in religious missionary work, accepted jobs in the Dominican Republic in the West Indies. There, they were house parents in a multidenominational mission, working with high-potential, under-achieving teenagers, kids who had gotten into trouble.

He describes their positions as "high stress," which was compounded by the death of their second-born son when he was seven months old.

They returned to Louisiana and worked for the Louisiana Baptist Children's Home. For a little more than a year they coordinated the renovation of the Cheatham House in Baton Rouge. The facility was used to house children in need of foster care.

But the Dominican Republic called to them and they returned for four more years, during which Cammack was chaplin of Esuela Caribe. During their time there, two more sons were born to them.

Cammack still has strong ties to the country, which he describes as "awesome, a beautiful place, with great people." He will still talk a person's ear off about the abundant tropical fruits produced on the island.

In 2005, Hurricane Katrina caused "a heartache to be back in Louisiana." He says, "I wished that I was there to help." That, plus the desire to have their children be around their grandparents, brought them back home.

He called the Louisiana Department of Wildlife and Fisheries and was told that it was unusual for them to rehire people who had left. But rehire him they did, under the provision that he pass through the academy again.

"It was easier the second time," he volunteers. "I was mentally prepared."

Today, I am riding with Cammack on focused "litter patrol," something that agents often do in the slow time of February and March between deer and turkey seasons. He adds that most agents also make litter cases throughout the rest of the year, as time permits and as a byproduct of other work.

As the sun dawns softly over the rolling pine-clad landscape of southern Rapides Parish, I get a good look at the game warden. He is slender, of medium height and build, with casually brushed hair. Two huge dimples in his cheeks set off a grin that could have been cast straight out of *The Little Rascals*.

He says that he plans to make a big circle through southern Rapides Parish, focusing on what he calls gross litter—garbage bag-size stuff and larger. There isn't much you can do to find the identity of those who throw Styrofoam cups, cans, and bottles out of their vehicles.

But he says that he will look in the small plastic shopping bags provided by stores. Sometimes these contain meth lab material, and if the buyer used a card for the purchase some indication of the individual's identity may be obtained.

I ask him how bad litter is in Rapides Parish. "Whoa—ugh," he reflexively responds, "Rapides is pretty bad. The parish doesn't provide rural garbage pickup, so people have to hire contractors or dispose of their garbage on their own. That may be part of the problem.

Byron Cammack holds his litter-fighting tools, a rubber glove for one hand and his digital camera.

"Of course, Avoyelles has parish-wide pickup, but they are nastier than Rapides."

Cammack is on a roll. "I don't understand why littering isn't a big issue. Everywhere you look along the road, there is trash." He points right and left, and indeed, the small road's ditches are liberally flecked in white. "They pick up litter on big roads, but not on small ones."

What Cammack will do is search bags of garbage in an attempt to find anything with the litterer's name and address on it.

Louisiana law makes it seem like a slam dunk. Louisiana revised Statute 30:2531.1 prohibits depositing refuse on other people's property, etc. It includes this: *(2) When litter disposed in violation of this Section is discovered to contain any article or articles, including but not limited to letters, bills, publications, or other writings, which display the name of a person or in any other manner indicate that the article belongs or belonged to such person, there shall be an inference that such person has violated this Section.*

You find someone's name and address in the garbage, go write them a ticket, and you got them. But I will find out that it's not that simple.

Cammack pulls off the road near a full black trash bag. He takes a photograph of the scene to document where the garbage is in relation to the road. He explains, "I need to do that because their first excuse is always that the bag fell off the garbage truck. They can't use that excuse if the bag is thirty feet off the road like this one is. A bag of garbage can fall off a truck, but it will be in the ditch near the road."

He puts a plastic glove on one hand to dig in the bag. "Oh wow, a needle, I gotta be careful." He digs and digs, finding nothing. "I don't know if he was smart or lucky. There's nothing to I.D. him," Cammack mutters.

Then, at the bottom of the bag, he exclaims, "Oh, oh—look here. An auto insurance card—got him! That's enough for that dude."

Cammack uses his gloved hand to rummage through the garbage, looking for anything with a name or address on it.

Cammack photographs the insurance card against the backdrop of the garbage and takes careful field notes on the location and type of garbage. Then, as a last touch, he removes his rubber glove and places it on top of the garbage as a sign to the next game warden that this garbage has been searched.

"Now, I might go right away to write the ticket if the person lives close like this one, or I may write it later," he says. This person does indeed live close, the first house up the road, less than a half a mile away.

No one is home.

As Cammack looks for more litter, he explains that one litterer can have a big impact. "I know of a guy who buys one beer on the way home from work every day. He throws the can in the ditch right before his driveway. There are fifty Natural Light cans on the left side of the highway right before his driveway at any time. I ain't caught him yet."

Cammack stops at a messy spot with a couple of garbage bags mixed with a bunch of shopping bags along a small road. One of the bags has partially broken open and the remains of a bunch of cleaned largemouth bass have spilled out. Mixed with the fish is a prescription medicine sheet with a clear name and address from Oakdale. He follows his usual routine in documenting the litter.

On the way to the address, Cammack searches several more garbage bags but doesn't find any clues. No one is home at the Oakdale address either.

Rural Rapides Parish is beautiful—except for litter. It is a seemingly endless pine forest, flecked with small homesteads. Little agriculture is evident, except for commercial plant nurseries. Nearby Forest Hill is the self-proclaimed nursery capital of Louisiana.

Cammack narrates as he drives. "Most folks here work out of the area, some in Alexandria, some offshore in the oilfields, and a lot do plant turnarounds. A lot of the parish is in Kisatchie National Forest. We'll work there later today because a lot of people dump in the national forest."

Cammack says that he loves what he does as a game warden. "I like the potential to do something good. I love meeting people. I like to teach hunter safety classes.

"I like talking to people who do things I like to do. I love being outside and I love the variety of things to do that come with the changing seasons."

As an example of the variety available in the work, Cammack says that he has been participating in a radio show out of a station in Alexandria called *Instruments of Peace*. Officers from a several different of law enforcement agencies appear on the show.

One of the worst things about the job, he chuckles, is getting a subpoena to appear in court the day before the case is heard and it's on one of your days off.

He brings the truck to a stop at a cluster of household appliances unceremoniously dumped on a lane off the remote small road. "He shakes his head as he says, "Both Rapides and Avoyelles parishes have services to come and pick up people's old appliances, but some folks would rather load an appliance up in their truck and haul it off to dump it along a road."

As he looks over the mess, he nudges a plastic bottle with one boot, "This is going to be here for many years."

Cammack cruises through the community of Hineston and what passes for the town of Otis, always on the lookout for "fresh garbage."

He stops at a small creek that would be picturesque if it didn't have dozens of cruddy plastic shopping bags hanging from what seem to be every other low-hanging limb. He sighs audibly and gets back in his truck.

"You should hear the excuses I get when I confront people about their garbage," he says. "The most common is that it must have fallen off the garbage truck. That's a textbook excuse.

"Fresh garbage" will cause Cammack to stop his truck sharply.

"You would be surprised how many times I also hear, 'Someone must have picked up my garbage to steal my identity.' Some claim that their mail got mixed up when they moved and that others have thrown their mail away.

"Less than half the people that I talk to admit to dumping their garbage, and that's probably being generous. The funny thing is that sometimes I almost hate to write up the ones that fess up. I just want to tell them to go pick it up.

"The ones that lie to you, those are the ones you really want to write up."

Near Otis, Cammack drives up an absolutely filthy logging road. At least two dozen boned out deer carcasses decorate the site, along with an assortment of household appliances, bedsteads, and general household garbage and refuse.

Search as he might, Cammack finds nothing to identify the dumpers. "That's the way it goes," Cammack explains. "I might search ten trash bags to get four or five I.D.s. And that will only result in one or two tickets."

Cammack swings by the residences of the two dumpers identified earlier in the day. Still no one is home.

Next stop is the Cleco Lake Boat Ramp. A riot of dewberry vines is in full bloom, but it's hard to enjoy them. The vines around the parking area are utterly despoiled. Not just the typical Louisiana boat ramp trash of Styrofoam earthworm boxes and empty cigarette packs and beverage containers is to be found here, but also egg cartons, refrigerator trays, body lotion bottles, and paint cans.

"Look at this!" says Cammack, standing with his hands spread in disgust. "Do you think any place in California looks like this?"

He goes on, "Remember how I told you about people's patterns showing how much one person can make a mess? Look at this." He fishes eleven shopping bags out of the vines. Each contains either three or four Natural Light beer cans in it. Each can is bent exactly the same way and each bag is tied tightly shut.

"Boy, would I love to catch this guy. He could be caught."

Leaving the scene of the garbage carnage, Cammack swings through Boyce on his way to Kisatchie National Forest. He's out of the hills here and in the Red River bottomlands. It's greener here. The eye-popping green winter wheat is shin high, and on fallow lands winter weeds are in full growth. The roadsides are a tangled profusion of purple-flowered vetch. In town the redbud trees are in their glory.

Kisatchie National Forest holds some of the worst dump sites of the day.

Shortly after entering Kisatchie, Cammack pulls the nose of his truck into a lane of waste that is beyond belief. Heaps of shingles, dozens of sheets of rusted roofing tin, a kitchen sink, heating and air conditioning equipment, automobile tires, mattresses, metal barrels, tangled snarls of hog wire fencing, two bathroom toilets, and bag after bag of household garbage are some of the delights that greet our eyes. When looking at this it strains the imagination to believe that human beings are "The Thinking Ape."

Cammack, with his working hand gloved, resolutely searches through several garbage bags that contain mostly used disposable diapers. "Um hum—look here." He brandishes a card with a complete name and address from Boyce.

Before he leaves, he flips open the doors and looks inside the half-dozen or so refrigerators and freezers lying scattered about like bleached corpses. "Every once in a while," he explains, "someone throws some of their trash in the fridge or freezer before they discard it. It's hard to make appliance cases, so I always look in them."

Another stop, also in the Kisatchie National Forest, quickly disabuses any thought in my mind that the trashing of public lands that all of us own is confined to a single anomalous spot. The only difference between this spot and the previous one is that this one holds a lot more appliances and the refuse is spread over a wider area.

Here, Cammack hits a jackpot of magazines addressed to a male, a sergeant either in the military or in law enforcement, in Boyce. A hundred yards further into the debris, he finds more magazines, some addressed to the same person and others addressed to a female at the same address. Ironically, hers are *Better Homes and Gardens* magazines.

The magazines are fresh, too—this month's and last month's. The people are still likely to reside at the same address. Cammack punches the address into his GPS and heads out. With all these fresh magazines, it seems Cammack can't miss now.

The rural location has few houses and none of their addresses match the one on the magazine labels. Cammack cruises the mail boxes and home sites three times, then stops to ask for help from one of the residents.

They have never heard of the people Cammack asks about. Neither do people at the next two stops. But to add to the confusion, a woman at the

Cammack finds multiple magazines from the current month, all labeled with the same address.

last residence goes in her house and retrieves a package addressed to the same man. UPS dropped the package off on her doorstep and she doesn't know what to do with it.

It's a Gordian knot. As hard as it is to let this one go, Cammack gives up and heads into the heart of the small town to find the person on the card that was in the bag with the soiled diapers.

When Cammack pulls up to the trailer, he finds a rather sullen man in his twenties emerging. Cammack confronts him respectfully with the evidence, but he disavows any knowledge of the garbage. His name doesn't match the name on the card.

He tells Cammack that he and his wife rented the trailer four months ago, then adds, "Me and her been fighting. There's been other men with her and other women for me. I don't know. Maybe one of them dumped the garbage." They do have an infant he admits, still in diapers.

Cammack takes the man's personal information and gets the name and address of his landlady, whom he proceeds to visit at her place of business, a children's nursery.

She says that the woman whose name Cammack gave her was indeed renting the trailer from her until four months ago, but that she has no children. Then she tells Cammack that the woman still works for her at the daycare center, although she is off work today.

Cammack thanks her and drives away. He says, "I'll need to think about this and come back to talk to them again. Is the dumper the couple who have an infant and live in the trailer and who perhaps threw the previous tenant's mail in the trash? Or is the dumper the previous tenant whose name and address are on the card and who works in a daycare center? Both are exposed to used diapers."

As he nears the end of his shift he decides to return to the addresses of the first two dumpers to see if anyone is home yet. Nix at the first site. No one is there.

But at the second site, the one from the envelope mixed with the fish offal, an SUV is parked in the garage. A woman in her early thirties answers Cammack's knock. Cammack asks for the man whose name is on the envelope. Her husband, she says, is returning later tonight from working out of town.

With some concern at the sight of Cammack's uniform, she asks what Cammack wants with him. He replies that he wants to talk to him about some bass. She replies that her husband hasn't fished in months and that they haven't cleaned or eaten any fish during that time. Cammack thanks her and leaves.

Another puzzle! Unless she is astute enough to have quickly figured out that the game warden had found some identification in the bag of fish waste, why would she lie?

"I'll be back," Cammack says as he fixes his blue-gray eyes on me.

After a few minutes of silence, he speaks up apologetically. "This is very common in litter patrol. You work all day, go to three or four addresses and not write a ticket. But when I write a ticket, I sure do get satisfaction."

16

CHANGING TIMES

Sergeant Keith Delahoussaye is no spring chicken. In fact, in Vermilion Parish he might just be the cock of the walk. At fifty-four years old, with twenty-three years in the Louisiana Department of Wildlife and Fisheries, he's been around long enough to compare the old days in the department to the present.

As an avid hunter and fisherman, he has also seen the changes that have crept over the face of hunting and fishing in southwestern Louisiana. Some of them are good, but others have him concerned.

With a strong jaw and brown eyes set in a heavily tanned, character-etched face, Delahoussaye is the image of what most people would imagine a professional fur trapper should look like.

His erect posture and his six-foot, one-inch frame disguise his 220 pounds well. He has no paunch. Only his thinning, silver-flecked hair provide a hint of his true age.

Delahoussaye speaks with a slight Cajun accent, but calls his surname "Cajun all the way." Although Vermilion Parish is peopled with many with Midwestern roots, Cajuns are still the ethnic backbone of the parish.

"Fanatical" may describe his attachment to the outdoors better than "avid." He describes himself as a "big-time fisherman," and he enjoys chasing speckled trout and snapper. But his secret love, he says, is fishing for sac-a-lait (crappie), probably because they taste so good.

He loves hunting as well, and "will hunt anything," as he describes it, but is more into duck and dove hunting. He makes room in his schedule, however, to go to Texas annually to hunt for axis deer, primarily because they are such excellent table fare.

"I love to eat," he says passionately. "I was traveling through West Virginia recently and they served me white gravy," he says as if insulted. "I couldn't believe it. Of course, a Coonass will eat anything. It wasn't bad; but I wouldn't cook it.

"I couldn't imagine living anywhere else than here. I've talked to my wife about retiring to some place like Arkansas, where we wouldn't have to worry about hurricanes. She says, 'No.' She wouldn't leave away from our daughter. People here like the outdoors, food, music, and family."

This love of the outdoors has intertwined Delahoussaye's family history with the Louisiana Department of Wildlife and Fisheries. His father worked for the department's Fur and Refuge Division on Marsh Island Wildlife Refuge. Delahoussaye himself has worked for the department for nearly two and a half decades.

His son-in-law, Byron Doré, was poised to follow him into both the department and the profession. But, in a tragedy for both the family and the

Keith Delahoussaye says that he can't imagine living anywhere other than Louisiana.

department, Doré died in a weekend boating accident in 2008 while still in training at the LDWF Enforcement Academy.

Today, Delahoussaye is set to make the grand tour of Vermilion Parish, starting in Intracoastal City, which is near the Intracoastal Waterway. If everything goes well, he plans to work his way from there up to the Kaplan-Gueydan area and then swing back south toward Freshwater City and the Pecan Island area.

He expects to check a lot of "bucket fishermen" fishing from canal banks and some goose and rabbit hunters as well. Duck and deer seasons are over.

The first areas Delahoussaye patrols are pastorally beautiful. It's low, flat country, interspersed with even lower swampy areas. Most of it is good pasture though, with fat, contented-looking cows. The pastures are rimmed with lots and lots of mature live oak trees stretching their muscular limbs over green palmettos.

In spite of being beautiful now, Delahoussaye explains, this area took six feet of storm surge from Hurricane Rita in 2005, followed by almost as much from Hurricane Ike in 2008.

Quickly, rangeland gives way to vast tracts of rice fields. With his characteristic cheery opening line, "How ya doing, guys?" he begins checking the first of the dozens of bank fishermen he will check today fishing in the canals around the rice fields. The older bucket fishermen especially get a kick out of being called "gentlemen."

By the time he reaches Mouton Cove, the lay of the land no longer looks like the rest of Louisiana, where modern roads follow old irregular Indian and settler trails. Here all the roads are laid out at right angles to each other, following the Midwestern range and township survey pattern.

Besides the constant supply of old-timers fishing off their buckets and folding chairs to check, there is precious little other activity.

The flooded rice fields are flecked with crawfish traps. Few geese are in the area. Most of the birds Delahoussaye glasses with his binoculars are glossy ibis, white ibis (locally called bec croche), and seagulls.

He keeps moving north toward Kaplan, hoping to find some geese. For where there are geese, there are goose hunters, and where there are goose hunters, there are always a few that will take a shot at geese from a public road.

But "drive-by shooters," as Delahoussaye calls them, are not as common as they once were. In fact, he says in the last ten to twelve years wildlife violations in Vermilion Parish have declined in general.

He speculates on the reasons. "We don't have as many people who hunt now as we used to. Hunting is dying. Also, it seems that we have less game, too, probably because of changed farming practices."

After a moment of silent thought, he adds, "A new breed of people is coming up now, even though there are still pockets of market hunting. People have more of a conservative [conservation] ethic.

"And it could be because we have more agents, with better equipment, fines are higher, and violators' guns can be seized. When I started, if you had a compass on a boat you were lucky and the radios we had didn't hardly work."

Delahoussaye grimaces as he remembers that game wardens' boats were so underpowered that almost all the violators could outrun them. He adds incredulously that game wardens even had to furnish their own weapons. "As you can imagine, some had a lot better weapons than others."

He dug deeper into his memory bank. "When I started, there was a six-week POST [Police Officer Standards and Training] course, then they strapped a gun on you and sent you out. Now the training in the academy is six months long and a lot better.

"Also, now, we go to in-service training every year to get advanced training on routine stuff, as well as training on new equipment like GPS. And we have to annually requalify in firearms proficiency, first aid, and use of an Intoxilyzer."

I ask him about pay. "Hewph," he exhales forcefully. "It's triple what it was twenty years ago. Of course, our roles have expanded now. For example, we are first responders when natural disasters occur. But better pay, along with better training and hiring better people, has improved morale, too.

"The way the public sees us now also helps morale. Since Hurricanes Katrina and Rita, they seem to respect us a lot more. They know that we do more than write tickets. People on the road wave to us rather than turn their noses up.

"This results in more cooperation from people who don't want others outlawing. They are more aware and have a better understanding of what is needed to have something for their grandkids and great grandkids. The majority of our cases come from complaints, especially during hunting season."

On a rural road through rice fields still abandoned since Hurricane Rita, Delahoussaye sees two trucks with dog kennels in their beds pulled off the road. "Rabbit hunters, I'll bet. Let's check," he says.

After tromping four hundred yards up an abandoned overgrown field road, Delahoussaye stops in the shade of live oak trees to get a visual fix on the hunters. Seeing them a half a mile away, he calls another game warden in the area with his portable radio, Senior Agent Derek Logan, and asks him to walk in from the opposite direction.

Delahoussaye demonstrates his cardiovascular fitness by relentlessly striding across the abandoned field through thigh-deep needlegrass. The strong southerly wind whipping the grass carries to him the sound of beagles yodeling dolefully and one of the hunters' encouraging whistles to the hounds.

Three men and a young boy, who can't help but admire every few minutes the swamp rabbit he is toting, make up the hunting party. Delahoussaye and Logan quickly check the four hunters' licenses and shotgun plugs and leave them to their pursuit.

A half a mile down the road, Delahoussaye stops to check on three bank fishermen sitting on the shoulder of the road in collapsible chairs. The trio has nine baited lines cast in every direction in the drainage ditch.

"Hello gentlemen, you doing any good?" he greets them.

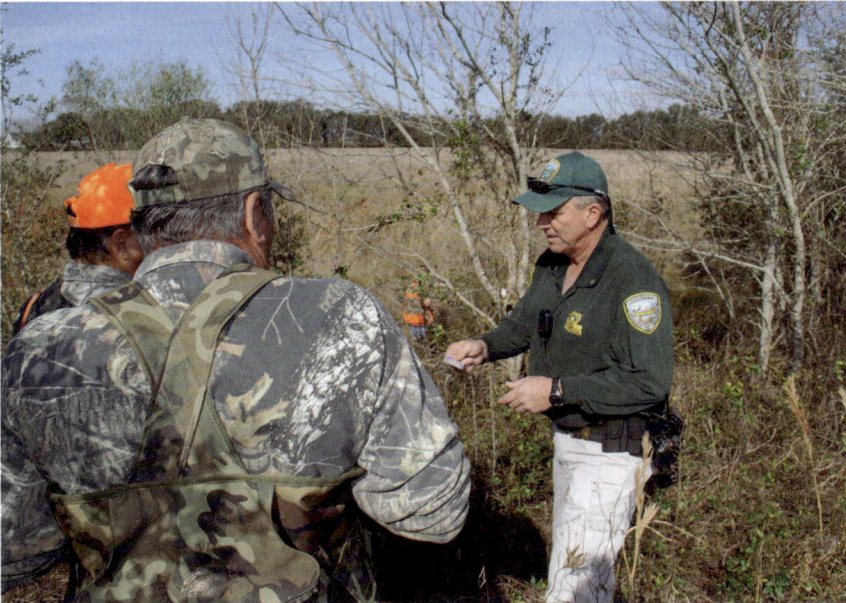

Delahoussaye quickly checks the rabbit hunters' licenses amid the sound of excited beagles hot on a rabbit's trail.

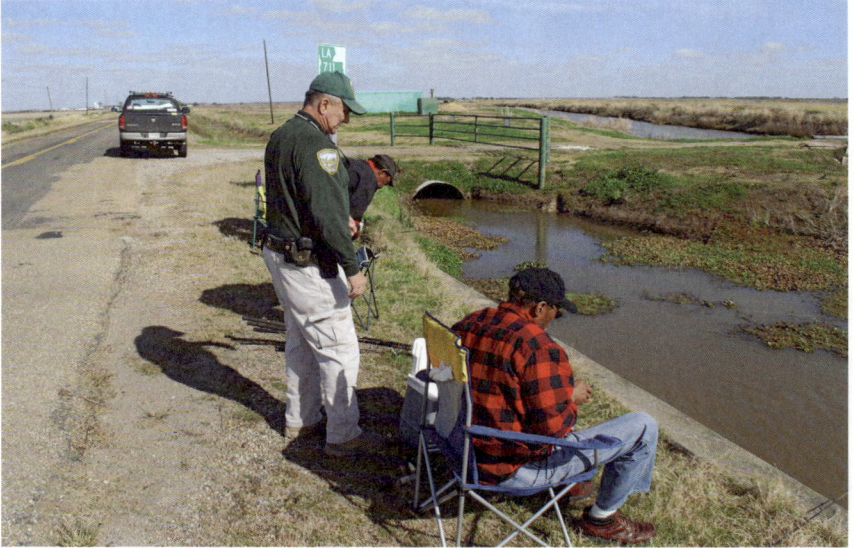

Delahoussaye's usual greeting of "Hello, gentlemen" produces good-natured chuckles from the many bucket fishermen he checks.

"One bass, one bream, and a red tail," is the reply. On hearing the latter, Delahoussaye's ears perk up and he asks permission to look in their ice chest, which is in the rear of their vehicle.

"Um, um, um," the officer grunts as he lays eyes on the obviously undersized redfish gasping in the ice chest. Delahoussaye informs the men that the fish is too small to keep and directs them to return it to the water immediately, then issues a warning ticket to the man who caught the fish.

As he drives away, Delahoussaye explains that he wrote a warning rather than a hard ticket, which would carry a fine, because it was only one fish, it was "fairly close" to the size limit, the fish was still alive and could be released, and because he believed the man when he claimed ignorance.

The area of Vermilion Parish we are patrolling looks more like the Great Plains than Louisiana. The wide-open fields are flecked with square, Midwestern-style farmhouses. Towns are identifiable in the distance by their tall grain elevators and exposed water towers.

Every so often, Delahoussaye uses his binoculars to view fields holding flocks of white-fronted geese, locally called specklebellies. "This is where we get problems," he explains. "People see these geese and shoot from a road into a flock. That's illegal, plus, because the geese are so densely packed to-gether, they kill more than their limit."

Today, there are a lot of geese, but everyone is behaving, so Delahoussaye turns the truck south. After we cross the Intracoastal Waterway heading to-ward Pecan Island, evidence of hurricane damage from Rita and Ike begins to pile up. Once-productive rice fields lie fallow and brown as a result of salt deposits from the storms' surges.

The further south we go on Highway 82, the worse it gets. South of Schoo-ner Bayou, agriculture gives way completely to land managed for hunting. Even pastureland has been abandoned to nature.

Enormous windrows of woody debris snake across the hurricane-damaged landscape, lodged against snarly and snaggy—but still alive—live oak trees. Other kinds of trees are simply represented as broken-off snags, six to ten feet tall.

The scene on Front Ridge, a chenier closer to the Gulf, is one of utter dev-astation. One empty house slab after another lines the road. The battered remains of the few houses that are visible are washed hundreds of yards into the marsh. Mounds of debris are everywhere. "A lot of people moved away after Rita," Delahoussaye says sadly, "and more after Ike. It may never be the same."

At Exxon Landing he checks a pair of fishermen who have just loaded their boat on its trailer. Amid the gray destruction around them, they hap-pily show their catch, a ten-fish limit of black drum, two redfish, and a hefty blue catfish.

On Highway 82 west of Pecan Island, Delahoussaye checks several an-glers. In the summer, he says, the ditch along the highway will be "solid peo-ple" on a weekend. They are hard to catch doing something wrong though, he explains, because along the straight road they can see the game wardens coming and will dump their illegal fish back into the water. "Cell phones hurt us plenty, too, yeah," he adds.

Game wardens have to work smart, he says with a grin. Sometimes we bring in agents from another area, dress them in plain clothes, and let them mix with the fishermen. "That's when it really gets good," he says gleefully.

"We have a lot of trouble with people disobeying fishing rules and leaving litter at some of the weirs here, where crabbing and cast-netting for shrimp is good. A while back we put a game warden in plain clothes and in an un-marked boat at one of them, where he fished with the rest of the people.

"He called on his cell phone as people left and told us what they had

Delahoussaye checks two anglers who have caught their limits of black drum and a nice-sized blue catfish.

done. I just sat at the boat landing and wrote them tickets for what they had done back at the weir. They couldn't figure out how we got the information. Some thought that we had a hidden camera or that someone was hiding in the marsh." Delahoussaye obviously enjoys remembering the episode.

When we finally work our way back north to Kaplan, the sight of normalcy again is welcome. As the patrol winds down, Delahoussaye returns to the subject of changing times.

"Judges have become very helpful to fish and wildlife enforcement agents.

When someone tries to talk their way out of a ticket, I've seen a judge say, "This man does law enforcement for a living. He says you did this—now prove that you didn't.

"Of course, most game wardens work to have credibility with judges. They recognize credibility in individual game wardens. Good game wardens can't write weak cases and they can't lie. Doing your homework goes a long way."

After driving in silence for a while, he offers his final thoughts. "In twenty-three years, I've never drawn my personal sidearm. Part of it is that I've been lucky. But part of it is that I treat people like I want to be treated. But you never know.

"You have to be unique to be a game warden, you have to be able to communicate with the public and you have to be able to take a lot from the public. But it's nice to be paid good and like your job."

17

THE CIRCUS

It's 5:30 a.m. Senior Agent Joe Arnaud is tying his shoes. His gun belt is on the table of the Lafourche Parish home that he shares with his wife, Lori, who is a sergeant with the Jefferson Parish Sheriff's Office. It's a law-and-order household.

When he unfolds, he's a big guy, six-foot, one-inch, 220 pounds. He sports a closely cropped military-style haircut. The only thing that keeps him from being intimidating is the smile of innocence that he uses a lot. But the smile masks a strong drive. He was recognized as the Game Warden of the Year at the 2008 Louisiana Wildlife Agents Association convention. He wrote an incredible 1,247 tickets that year. "I was lucky," he says modestly. "That was an exceptional year."

He must be lucky a lot. He has been with LDWF for six years and has been number one in the count on tickets issued by an individual in five of those years, something he attributes to working in a "target-rich environment."

For ten years before becoming a game warden Arnaud was a deputy with the Jefferson Parish Sheriff's Office. "One day," he says, "Lori and I were getting ready to go to work and I said, 'You know, I don't feel like going to work.' She looked at me and said that maybe I needed to start looking for another job."

Things catalyzed when the two of them passed a Louisiana Wildlife Agents Association booth at the Louisiana Sportsmen's Show. Joe liked to fish and hunt and he liked law enforcement. Lori suggested that it might be the job for him. "Where else will people pay you and give you top-flight equipment to be in the outdoors?" he asks.

Today he says we are going to Lake Boeuf, a very shallow, medium-sized freshwater lake plunked down in northern Lafourche Parish like a Rorschach ink blot. The lake supports so much aquatic plant growth that it can seem more like marsh than lake. But that plant growth attracts a modest number of ducks and a huge number of plant-eating American coots.

While classified as waterfowl, coots are not ducks, but rather members
of the rail family. Die-hard duck hunters often scorn them because they are
reluctant to fly. Invariably called "poule d'eaus" throughout south Louisiana, coots have chicken-like beaks and oversized lobed feet, rather than the
webbed feet of a duck.

Many Louisiana wild game chefs love to eat poule d'eaus, mostly in the
enshrined form of poule d'eau gumbos. Lake Boeuf is famous for its poule
d'eau hunting, as well as well as for "running poule d'eaus," a form of hunting not allowed under federal or state law.

Running poule d'eaus is simply chasing up the reluctant-to-fly birds with
motorized boats so that hunters in blinds or even hunters in the moving
boat can shoot them when they finally do take flight. It's been going on in
Lake Boeuf since the internal combustion engine was invented and is still
an institution, in spite of the dedicated work of two generations of game
wardens.

As Arnaud silently passes the Theriot Canal Boat Launch off Highway
308, a glance shows a large, solid mass of tail lights on vehicles waiting to
launch their boats for the morning's hunt on the lake. Arnaud is traveling
to a very remote private boat launch to put his boat in the water.

"Our trucks are so noticeable and cell phone technology allows people
to be able to alert each other so quickly that we have to be careful where
we launch. They call us the boogeyman," he says with humor in his voice,
adding, "I'm lucky enough today to be able to work out of uniform and in
an unmarked boat. Still, I have to have the boat repainted a different color
every couple of years because they get to recognizing it."

When he arrives at his turn off the highway, he douses his truck lights,
even though it is still dark. And like the boogeyman, he slowly and quietly navigates down a small lane packed with houses on either side. He
breaks out into cane fields and continues to travel the slimy track in four-
wheel drive through a spooky-looking willow swamp to a rudimentary boat
launch on Halpin Canal, part of the drainage system of Lafourche Parish.

It is a simple process to ready the venerable fourteen-foot Kirk's fiberglass mudboat for the day's work. Proudly, he notes that he found the rig in
bad shape in an LDWF scrap heap and rehabilitated it.

In no time, the peppy little boat is skimming the canals toward the
lake, passing from cypress and willow swamps through floating freshwater
marshes, locally called "flotant," before breaking into the open lake.

As we skim the clear water and profusion of aquatic plants, we put to
flight hundreds of coots. I find myself looking down the barrels of numer-

ous guns that seem to be directly pointed at us, but are really firing at the coots skittering into the air fifteen feet on either side of the boat. It's a scary sight and the small boat offers no place to hide. Arnaud, perched on his high seat like a king on a throne, is nonchalant.

Everywhere I look there are blinds of every description and coots, lots and lots of coots. Arnaud crosses the lake to where he wants to be and pulls the boat into an unused blind. I assume we will be in surveillance a while before moving out, so I take my life jacket off for comfort.

Shots are going off everywhere around us. It sounds like we are in the middle of a giant popcorn popper. Less than five minutes after we enter the blind, Arnaud says matter-of-factly, "There are our first ones; let's go get them." He had logged every shot on his field tablet that two young men had made from a moving boat not three hundred feet from the blind we are in.

He zooms up to them. "Gentlemen, Wildlife and Fisheries. Keep your guns pointed in a safe direction." The young hunters look nervous. Arnaud calms them with easy-going small talk, then explains what they did wrong and that he is going to write them tickets. "You can keep your guns and keep hunting, but I gotta take your birds." After he writes the tickets, he explains that until the case is settled they cannot sell or alter their guns in any way, then he explains their court date to them.

Joe Arnaud explains to the two young men what they did wrong before he issues any citations.

He is crisp, professional, and leaves no room for excuses or arguments. But his small talk actually keeps them smiling while they are getting their tickets.

As he writes the tickets, Arnaud takes notes on another illegal shooter. He doesn't have to go back into hiding in a blind, just straight to the next poule d'eau runner. The routine is repeated, almost word for word.

While he is writing the ticket, I sit there gape-mouthed. A constant crescendo of gunshots from what seem like hundreds of blinds hangs in the air. Boats are buzzing everywhere. Some are picking up downed birds, some are leaving the lake, some are just entering the lake, some are chasing and shooting coots, and others are rallying coots up from the water's surface for their hunting partners in blinds to shoot.

From this stop Arnaud moves into an unoccupied blind, but only for a moment. A boat that he watched rally birds while he wrote the last tickets continues without pause.

Out of the blind he goes. He pulls up to the boat with its single operator. "Wildlife and Fisheries. We got a problem." He explains to the hunter what he did wrong and tells him that he had been watching him for twenty-four minutes. He asks for the hunter's weapon and some identification, clips the driver's license the hunter produced to his ticket book, and directs the unprotesting man to pick up the birds around his partners' blind.

He goes to the blind and explains to the two shooters that their partner who is doing the rallying is in the wrong, but that they are benefiting and will also receive tickets. He asks them to point their weapons in a safe direction and hand them to him, along with their I.D.s.

He verbally admires their shotguns and makes small talk to put them at ease while he checks the weapons for plugs and makes sure that they aren't using lead shot. As he does the entire morning, he calls everyone "gentlemen" or "sir."

Keeping the weapons and I.D.s, he backs away from the blind to write the tickets. Arnaud explains that this is something he does as a routine. He patrols alone a lot and is often outnumbered by the people in the blind. "I don't want to be jumped while my head is down writing a ticket," he explains.

When he returns to the blind to explain the tickets and return the shotguns to the three young men, one of them grins and says, "That must be a pretty cool job, sitting back in the lake and watching people mess up. You must have thought, 'Look at those dumb-asses.'" Arnaud chuckles.

He stops several more boats—always the same story. In most cases, the boat operator is not wearing his kill lanyard and the occupants are not wearing life jackets. For these, Arnaud explains the new law that requires operators of boats under sixteen feet in length that are powered by motors with a tiller handle to wear their kill lanyards and have all occupants in life jackets. Then he issues them warning tickets, as well as any "hard tickets." Warning tickets, which can only be issued on the first offense and only for certain violations, carry no monetary penalty.

And so the morning goes. It seems that there is always a boat in sight running poule d'eaus, usually with Arnaud sitting exposed, completely in the open. He keeps writing tickets and seizing their kill and is accumulating a hefty stack of birds on his stern deck.

He begins trying to run down a rallier in a particularly fast boat. Several times the masked man looks directly back at Arnaud on his stern, but ignores the game warden and just keeps running in circles to chase up more birds. Arnaud keeps trying to get an angle on the boat to cut it off, but at just the last minute the other operator cuts the boat the other way. Round and round they go.

Finally the officer succeeds at cutting across the inside of a circle and getting head-on to the boat, forcing him to shut down. "I ain't got no gun," the man aggressively barks after pulling down his face mask.

Arnaud manages to maneuver his slower boat into position to meet the rallying hunter's boat head-on.

"I didn't tell you what I was stopping you for," Arnaud replies, adding, "I've been watching you for twenty minutes rallying birds for your friends in the blind to shoot. Let's go to the blind." The man glares at Arnaud.

Arnaud follows the boat as it leads him to a blind occupied by another boat and three hunters, clearly not the blind that his boat was in and not the blind that his partners are in. Arnaud shouts, "Is this the blind that you picked up birds for?"

With a sneer the man replies, "You tell me—you say that you have been watching me for twenty minutes."

Arnaud's voice hardens, "Okay, if that is the way you want to play it." The man waits a moment, probably calculating whether he can win this one, then puts his motor in gear and points it toward another blind. Arnaud quietly says, "This is our butt hole for the day."

At the blind, the drill is the same. Arnaud explains what they did wrong in detail and makes sure that they understand the charges. He asks them to count the birds out loud as they toss them on the growing heap in his stern.

From the corner of his eye, he catches them throwing a brown bird onto the pile of dark slate-gray coots. "Wait a minute. Who killed the helldiver—

The stern of the game warden's boat holds a growing heap of confiscated coots.

the plongeur?" he chuckles, using the Cajun French name for the bird. "Y'all are from Cut Off; y'all should know better."

No one admits to killing the bird, so Arnaud says, "This is the way it works. If no one claims the bird, everyone will get a ticket for killing a protected species." The boat driver resignedly says that he will claim it.

Backing away from the three hunters, Arnaud pauses and glances at me. "This is a day on Lake Boeuf."

If so many violations weren't involved, it would almost be comical.

It is 10 a.m. and Arnaud's morning shift is ending, so he pilots the boat out of the lake back into the entrance to the canal. When he reaches Halpin Canal, he diverges from the route back to his truck to motor by the Lake Boeuf Wildlife Management Area.

As he moves leisurely up the canal, another mudboat approaches slowly from the opposite direction. Arnaud decides to check it. When the two boats touch, the driver of the other boat and Arnaud recognize each other.

"Nice mess," comments Arnaud, admiring their two-man limit of poule d'eaus laid out neatly on the bow of the boat.

"Thanks, buddy," replies the fifty-two-year-old driver nervously.

Arnaud checks their licenses and weapons. Everything checks out. He respectfully addresses him with "mister" in front of his name during the entire encounter.

The driver becomes anxious to go after Arnaud asks him how he is doing with what they talked about last year. The hunter's face is flushed and his eyes are bloodshot.

"Have you been drinking?" asks Arnaud gently.

"A couple," he replies.

"Now what's the deal that we made last time?" asks Arnaud.

"Can't you just let me go, buddy?" is the driver's questioning reply. "I'm in good shape."

"No, you're not; no you're not," repeats Arnaud. "Now, how many have you really had?"

"Maybe four, buddy," he answers haltingly.

"No, you've had more than four. Now, how many beers have you really had, six, eight maybe?"

"Maybe about six, buddy," he replies. The man is obviously nervous.

"You know we had a deal," says Arnaud. "We need to take a ride."

The man begins to plead, "Aw c'mon buddy; can't you just let me go?"

"I can't," replies Arnaud, "it's a safety issue. Are you buzzing?"

"Yeah, I'm buzzin', buddy, but look—I'm fine," is the reply.

Arnaud removes a pen from his pocket and does a horizontal gaze nystagmus test on both the driver and his passenger, who has been sitting utterly quiet throughout the whole exchange. "You are both buzzing pretty good," Arnaud says firmly.

"Let's go out on the bank. I need to test you some more," he gently directs, still addressing him as mister. The man complies, while really intensifying his pleading. On the bank he tromps his feet and flaps his arms a couple of times while begging to be let go, the whole time referring to Arnaud as "buddy."

Arnaud persists and does another horizontal gaze nystagmus test. He decides not to conduct the rest of the field sobriety test on the muddy, sloping bank as he fears that the man, whose body is weaving, will fall into the canal and injure himself. "We're going to have to take a ride," Arnaud says, ignoring the man's piteous pleading.

He asks the passenger if he knows someone he can call to come out and get him and the boat, since he has also had too much to drink to operate the boat. The man says that he does and makes the call. After Arnaud is satisfied that the passenger will get help, he assists the driver into his heavily laden boat and proceeds slowly down the canal.

The whole way in the man pleads with Arnaud, even trying to make him feel guilty for taking him in. "I just wanna go home and play with my grandchildren. I was just having a good time."

Arnaud changes the subject. "You don't have any of that other stuff on you? Like last time."

"Nah, nah, buddy," he answers and momentarily stops begging.

After Arnaud puts the boat on the trailer, he handcuffs the subject. "I'm cuffing you in front. You will be more comfortable and you haven't been giving me any trouble." He helps him into the truck and fastens his seat belt.

Arnaud keeps trying to diffuse the tension by chatting about other subjects, but stays professionally respectful the entire time. They talk about hunting and cooking. The hunter brings up his family problems. He mentions, without thinking, that after cooking some sausage in the blind this morning that he drank some wine as well as beer.

Then he starts trying to appeal to Arnaud's sympathy again. "I should have went deer hunting this morning instead. This won't help me at all. It won't help me at all," he repeats. "I was going to go deer hunting this weekend."

Arnaud replies that he can still go, "We'll get you done."

"Yeah, and I'll be real happy," the man sarcastically replies.

Arnaud constantly tries to defuse hostility by changing the subject—talking about other stuff. But the man won't let him. "I am fine, buddy, I really am," is his repeated refrain, to which Arnaud replies, "If you blow under .08, I'll cut you loose. I promise."

"I guess you just can't pass a good time no more," he sighs.

Arnaud replies, "You can pass a good time; you just can't drive."

"Huh!" The man is unimpressed.

At the Lafourche Parish Sheriff's Office in Lockport, Arnaud walks the subject through the rest of the field sobriety test, which he fails miserably, staggering multiple times and almost falling down. He then verbally walks him through the process of using the Breathalyzer.

When the man blows, Arnaud pushes him, "Blow hard. Blow harder." The machine reads .059. Arnaud immediately tears the paperwork up and throws it away, declaring, "You are free to go."

The relieved man shakes Arnaud's hand and says, "I told you I was okay, buddy," and walks out.

Arnaud mutters, "He blew shallow on me, but I had to be fair. I couldn't do more because a defense attorney would question another test."

Before Arnaud can relax, however, he has a lot of confiscated coots to properly dispose of. He calls a local resident who routinely volunteers to clean and distribute confiscated wildlife to disadvantaged elderly people. The man promptly turns up and takes the sack of birds off Arnaud's hands.

Three p.m. finds Arnaud back in his truck. "I like a split shift," he explains as he drives, "because there is less downtime. It is more productive during hunting season. I am out there when the hunters are."

Between sips on a Lo-Carb Monster Energy drink, he chats. "I enjoy the rush of catching someone night hunting after I spend many nights watching fields. It's worth the unproductive hours. I guess I'm an adrenaline junkie. Look at my wife's and my motorcycles—Kawasaki crotch rockets."

He stops and checks three anglers fishing from the old Bayou Des Allemands bridge. One has fifteen undersized catfish. Arnaud warns him that the recreational limit on undersized catfish is twenty-five. He then shows him how to measure catfish by using the diameter of the opening of the plastic bucket that the man has been sitting on.

He rides by the Theriot Canal Boat Launch to Lake Boeuf and sees a "good many" vehicles there, so he turns back to get his boat and trailer to go back into the lake. As he is launching the boat, his portable radio crackles to life with a call about a boat that has sunk in Lake Boeuf with three adults and a child in it. Arnaud replies that he is at the launch to the lake now and will respond immediately. He asks if the people have a cell phone and what their number is.

Immediately after he launches the boat, a Lafourche Parish sheriff's deputy arrives with a small boat and outboard motor. After briefly conferring with the deputy, Josh Avet, Arnaud runs down the canal at full speed and into the lake, alternately clipping over clumps of vegetation and open water. It feels like we are flying low.

He stops the boat and scans the water.

He has been given bad directions. Nothing is to be seen, so he calls the subjects. They give him more directions. They aren't at that spot either. He has to call twice more to zero in on them.

When he spies them in the slanting rays of the evening sun, he sees two adult men standing in their sunken boat in the shallow waters of the lake. One is holding a four-year-old boy on his shoulder to keep the water's chill from him.

The men hand the boy and their shotguns to Arnaud, and then direct him to a blind to pick up the third adult, a fifteen-year-old girl. Arnaud takes off his shirt and drapes it over the wet child to help keep him warm.

The two men are standing on their sunken boat, holding the wet boy and their shotguns out of the water.

As he approaches the blind that the girl is in, he hears her weeping loudly and sees that she is clutching her cell phone like a lifeline. Arnaud helps her into the boat and returns to the two men.

Shortly after he returns, Avet arrives, followed by three people in a larger boat that the two men have called to help them float the sunken boat. The five men declare that they have enough people to raise the boat and Arnaud returns to patrol.

He sees that more hunters are returning to the lake for the evening shoot, so he pulls up next to a blind to see if anyone will shoot after sunset, the end of legal hunting hours.

Everything is peaceful and serene. Coots in flocks of hundreds have survived the morning's mauling and are peacefully pecking away at vegetation. The only sound is their contented "kuk, kuk, kuk." Nothing indicates the mayhem that took place this morning.

An occasional shot here and there turns into a peppering of shots as the end of legal shooting hours nears. The setting sun infuses the slate-gray clouds scattered over the blue sky with a soft peach hue.

He waits. Most people quit shooting, but some don't. He gets out his note tablet and begins recording the shots from a nearby blind. On the seventh

In contrast to the bedlam that prevailed in the morning, Lake Boeuf is beautiful and serene in the afternoon.

shot, he runs over to the blind. "Wildlife and Fisheries. Okay guys, here's it. You shot seven times after legal hours after sunset and you are going to get citations." One hunter loudly protests that the end of legal shooting time used to be later.

Arnaud asks for their guns and then checks their licenses. He backs the boat away from the blind a bit to write the tickets. It's almost completely dark, but shots continue to ring from another spot.

Arnaud can't take it anymore, tells the two hunters that they can begin picking up their decoys, and that he will return shortly. He keeps their licenses and shotguns. He runs to the scene of the shots and finds two eighteen-year-olds in a mudboat. He informs them that they have shot late, to which one responds, "Oh, sorry."

Arnaud directs them to follow him back to the location of the other blind. He finishes writing the tickets for the first two men while the two hapless youngsters wait disconsolately in the dark for their turn to get tickets.

With all his tickets written, Arnaud idles his boat across the lake, enjoying the unseasonable warmth of the night air.

"This is the greatest job on the face of the earth," he proclaims. "It really is."

18

THE OYSTER IS THEIR WORLD

Day One: Riding the Circuit

Thirty-two-year-old Senior Agent Mike Garrity would never make it as an undercover agent. He has "police officer" stamped all over him. Six feet tall, with a strongly built body, his demeanor and mannerisms are those one would associate with a peace officer. The face seems chiseled out of ruddy granite and his looks are coupled with an intimidating stentorian voice and speaking style.

His regular partner, soft-spoken Sergeant Bryan Marie, seems to be constructed of different timber, at least externally. Almost a head shorter than Garrity, with a sun-darkened olive complexion, his cheeky face is broadened even more by a smile that never seems to disappear. The mustachioed face, which would be at home on a chubby man's body, is instead perched on a lean and fit athletic frame.

The two men make up what is known within the LDWF Enforcement Division as the Oyster Strike Force. The strike force was created at the behest of the oyster industry and is dedicated almost exclusively to policing the oyster fishery. Funding for its special mission is provided by the proceeds from the sales of oyster harvester's licenses and oyster tags.

They are an oddity within the Enforcement Division in that the two men always work together, rather than in rotating shifts like other wildlife agents, and because they work the entire coast, from the Texas state line to the Mississippi state line, and even occasionally beyond on interstate violations.

The two men came to the Oyster Strike Force by different paths. Marie, now forty-three years old, was in the oyster business in Terrebonne Parish, as was his father. He grins as he says that when he got to the shucking house in the morning he started each day by eating a pint of raw oysters. Marie so loves oysters that he eats them competitively, having come in second twice

Although Mike Garrity and Bryan Marie will write tickets for other violations that they come across, their primary duty is to police the oyster industry.

and third once in the Acme Oyster House raw oyster eating contest. "My record is seventy-two oysters in sixty seconds," he states proudly.

His interest in being a game warden, he says, stems from his father having been one. "I was used to him being in uniform and I looked up at him; I guess it's in the blood." After spending eight years as a parish game warden in both St. Mary and Terrebonne parishes, he transferred to the Oyster Strike Force in 2001.

Garrity, on the other hand, has no special affinity for oysters. He doesn't eat them raw and is casual about eating them cooked. His interest has always been in law enforcement. "I always hunted and fished, and with my interest in law enforcement this job gave me a chance to be on the water and in the woods." In his time off, he still pursues wing-shooting and angling for trout and redfish with a passion that is apparently even greater than Marie's.

Reared in Slidell, Garrity spent six years as a game warden in St. Bernard Parish, where his family hailed from before moving to St. Tammany Parish. Shortly after Hurricane Katrina in 2005, Garrity transferred to the strike force.

Today, our destination is St. Bernard Parish, which, along with Plaquemines Parish, is described as "the heart of the oyster industry in Louisiana" by Marie. The forty-minute truck ride to the boat launch gives the two men a chance to explain what the Oyster Strike Force does.

Says Marie, without inhaling a breath, "We enforce laws on the theft of oysters from private leases, sanitary code violations, the fishing of oysters in polluted waters, license fraud by nonresident fishermen, the taking of oysters from unleased areas that are not seed grounds or reservations, the taking of oysters from closed seed grounds and reservations, and the harvest of undersized sack oysters from seed grounds and reservations, as well as working with other law enforcement agencies on the presence of drugs and illegal aliens on oyster boats."

A lot of their work involves enforcing laws that apply thousands of invisible boundary lines that demarcate the state's 7,915 oyster leases, sixteen seed grounds and reservations, and the innumerable areas closed to harvest because they are unleased or are polluted. The job is technically challenging, as Garrity recognizes. "I couldn't have done this a year or two out of the academy.

"A lot of our patrols are complaint-oriented. We spend a lot of time on cases where someone is stealing oysters from a private lease or on cases where someone is out there hurting the others in the industry," adds Garrity.

Marie adds that in several ways their work is very different than most other game warden work, where someone who takes fish or game illegally is not directly injuring another person. "Whenever we catch someone fishing in polluted waters, it is one of the only things that the Louisiana Department of Wildlife and Fisheries does that protects human health. Plus, when we catch someone stealing oysters, it is one of the only times that a violation handled by the department has an identifiable human victim."

In spite of the seriousness of some oyster violations, Marie maintains that since they deal with many of the same people within the business over and over again, it pays to treat people with respect. "If you do that," he says, "they will trust you and help you with information. With that you can concentrate on complaints and cut down on patrol time. We try to make our stops as quickly as possible, so that we don't interrupt their work too much."

Marie goes on to explain that the only way to do the job of patrolling the maze of invisible lines with any efficiency is by doing computer work before they ever get in the field. The two agents explain what they must do to be ready for fieldwork.

When they get a complaint about a particular oyster lease, they obtain the shot points for the lease from the grid system map that the LDWF Survey Section sends to them electronically. Then, using either of two computer programs, MicroStation or GeoMedia, they convert the shot points to latitude and longitude readings.

A GPS receiver is plugged into the computer and, using another program called MapSource, the shot points are transferred to the GPS as waypoints. The process for a small, basic lease involves ten to twelve shot points and takes an hour to an hour and a half to complete.

While the boundary lines for seed grounds and seed reservations have been mapped in the agents' computers for some time, the boundaries for all the private leases of the state, with their many thousands of shot points, are far too much to have done in advance.

In addition, a single GPS receiver does not have the memory capacity to hold all the waypoints for all the leases and boundary lines. So, for any particular day on the water, the agents download from their computers to their GPS units the data that they need for that day. Every day is different.

Compounding the work is the fact that four times each year the boundary lines between polluted waters and those waters safe for molluscan shellfish harvest are reviewed, changed, and redrawn.

With massive underkill, Marie observes, "Being prepared before we go on the water is the key to our success."

Grinning, Garrity notes that he and Marie are just a pair of "closet computer geeks." But he notes that they also carry a roll of paper maps on the water with them.

There is a reason for their intense reliance on technology and accuracy, says Garrity. "Defense attorneys will eat you up if you don't know the technical parts of this job. We have to be accurate. Our GPS units must constantly be checked against known sites."

They launch today at a secluded private launch north of Shell Beach, rather than in Shell Beach itself. They explain that they don't want to launch in an area where commercial fishermen are likely to see them. "That's the disadvantage of cell phones," says Marie. "If people see us, they might call their buddies who are violating the law and warn them."

Our ride is impressive, a white seventeen-foot fiberglass Triton V-hull, powered by a huge black 225-horsepower outboard motor. It will do a legitimate fifty-eight miles per hour, something that I will rue during the next two miserably cold February days on the water. Today the wind is up and gusty from the north and the thermometer tells me that it is just over 40 degrees Fahrenheit.

Breaking into the open waters of Lake Borgne, the boat, piloted by Garrity, slices past the 1850s brick ruins of Fort Beauregard. They sit forlornly in the waters near the shore of the lake, protected from the relentless pounding of waves by a low barrier of rock riprap.

As soon as we hit the open lake waters, the wind and cold immediately begin probing for every tiny opening in our clothes. Ahead of us, on the horizon, several oyster boats are visible. The cold arctic air deceptively magnifies their sizes, and framed against the bright blue winter sky they look like big white anvils.

The lake is big, more like a sea than a lake, and the ride is long before the two men near the closest boat. They ignore the larger boat and zero in on the smaller one before recognizing that it is a crab boat and is allowed to be fishing where it is, although the area is closed to oyster harvesting.

It's cold. Every breath feels like an icicle sliding down my throat. The open boat offers no place to hide, so I just have to face it and take it.

On they speed over the choppy sea. Garrity pilots the boat and navigates by GPS and Marie backs him up with his handheld GPS. During the course of the day, Marie will most frequently make the call on whether a target vessel is working in waters that it has a right to be in or not, while Garrity concentrates on navigation.

Many oyster boats are working today, churning in tight circles and drag-

Oyster boats harvesting from a reef churn in tight circles while dragging a dredge on each side by a chain.

ging their long-toothed dredges over the crown of the reefs they are work-ing at the time. The periodic clanking of steel chains on metal as the dredges are retrieved to empty adds variety to the steady roar of each boat's diesel engine.

Marie calls most of the boats "okay" and the two men bypass them. They recognize almost every boat, and since they have already pulled license checks on them this short year and the boats are presently where they are supposed to be, they are deemed not worth checking.

A selection of boats is boarded and their licenses and log books are checked. The harvest of oysters is tightly regulated. To prevent bacteria from multiplying unchecked inside the shells of the living creatures after they are harvested, Louisiana law requires that oysters must be put under refrig-eration within a certain number of hours after harvest. For boats without functional mechanical refrigeration systems on board, the limit is thirty-six hours during this, the coldest time of the year.

Even bypassing many boats, the number they check is beginning to add up. When they decide to board a working boat, the sleek Triton, acting for

The game wardens' small, maneuverable boat approaches the stern of each slowly lumbering oyster lugger from one flank to allow Marie to board it.

Garrity confers with the Mexican captain of an oyster boat during a boarding.

all the world like a predatory lobo, swings behind and slightly to one side of the big, cumbersome, constantly circling vessel, very much the way a wolf attacks its larger, hoofed prey from a rear flank.

When Garrity gets the boat poised just right, Marie vaults gracefully up on the bigger boat and over its railing. Garrity may back the boat off and watch Marie and the vessel's captain, or he may flag the vessel to stop and board it to assist his partner.

The check done and both men back on board, the sleek craft streaks over the open water looking for its next lumbering prey animal. The day barely warms and the ride is rough. The Triton, in spite of actually being a good-riding rough water boat, is beating me to death.

Looking at me with an inscrutable grin, Garrity nonchalantly says, "At least you picked a nice day to come. Lake Borgne and Petit Pass are the roughest place on earth. My God, I used to be six feet, three inches when I took this job." I can't tell if he is serious or not.

Like most game wardens, Marie and Garrity splurge on eye protection, their mirrored lenses making them look like big blue-eyed bugs. Garrity wears Costa Del Mars and Marie sports Ocean Waves. Garrity says that if he forgets the glasses in his truck, he will break a patrol to go back and get them. Marie agrees vociferously, "Oh definitely, you will only work twelve hours on the water without sunglasses one time."

"One time is it," echoes Garrity, adding, "You'll have the headache from Hell."

As the patrol extends further out into Lake Borgne, the Mississippi coastline becomes clearly visible to the north. Looming on its shore are the ruins of the massive concrete parking structure of the Silver Slipper Casino, which was destroyed by Hurricane Katrina.

The boat chops a wide arc around Half Moon Island and heads southeast toward Karako Bay. Everywhere we go, we pass working oyster boats. Many are stopped by the two agents, but written tickets are few. The polyglot nature of the oyster fishery is evident in the faces and accents of the skippers of the boats—Isleños, Croatians, and Mexicans. It's like the United Nations.

The patrol boat courses through the fragmented islands of the Louisiana Marsh. It is slightly warmer here, but the respite from the wind is short-lived. The wind swings from the north to the northeast and then to the southwest. Its direction presages another arctic front expected to arrive during the night.

The Triton stabs the mouth of Bayou la Loutre, which snakes through the

In spite of the cold, the sun's glare on the open water forces both men to constantly wear protective eyewear.

unspoiled wetlands of the Louisiana Marsh. At first, the marsh is a solid, unbroken stand of oyster grass wearing its winter brown color. Gradually, small woody plants begin to appear on the bayou banks, and then, finally, a few weather-beaten live oaks appear.

Garrity hooks the boat sharply to the right out of Bayou la Loutre and follows his GPS route through Stump Lagoon and then through Pete's Lagoon. In all directions, the two-foot-tall brown oyster grass undulates in the wind.

When we reach Lake Borgne again, we have traveled twenty miles from where we entered Bayou la Loutre and we haven't seen another boat. The hand of man is light here. Very few of the ubiquitous oilfield structures, so common in many south Louisiana marshes, are to be seen. Even litter is noticeably missing.

A few more oyster dredgers are checked, and then the men begin the return leg of the patrol toward Shell Beach. Garrity eases up on the boat's throttle so that we can talk. They express pride in the work of their two-man Oyster Strike Force, although Marie expresses a big wish for two more members, so that a shift would always be on duty. He opines that the oyster industry is the biggest commercial fishery of St. Bernard and Plaquemines parishes.

Violations within the fishery are down though, says Garrity. "Ten years ago, on a day like today, we could have written a whole book of tickets, just for the taking of undersized oysters from the seed grounds."

"The court systems of the two parishes back us up a lot, too," explains Marie. "They take oyster violations very seriously, and a major violation can result in the mandatory installation of an electronic vessel monitoring system on an offender's boat, and they don't want to be tracked twenty-four hours a day."

"I am proud of our case production being so high," says Garrity without sounding like he is bragging. "Oyster enforcement involves a lot of paperwork and the cases are difficult. When I transferred here, I thought that I would miss working night hunters and ducks, but now I don't think that I could go back into that. I love the oyster industry and the people in it."

Marie stands silently for a while, then speaks up. "I hope that the oyster industry is here a hundred years from now, but if they don't come up with something—I don't know. The equipment has gotten so efficient. Oyster dredges now have dive plates that allow them to dredge up the mud, shells, and oysters—everything. They are taking the public reefs with them to their lease, leaving nothing but mud on the seed grounds."

It has been a long day. "I'm from the old school," explains Garrity. "The more ground you cover, the more likely you are to catch violators." And cover ground they did, Lake Borgne Seed Ground, Christmas Camp Seed Ground, Karako Seed Ground, Turkey Bayou Seed Reservation, and innumerable private leases.

Day Two: Cold Case

The reinforcing cold front that blew through during the night makes it seem like it is a lot colder than the ten-degree actual drop in temperature should have made it. Riding in the open boat rapidly becomes almost unbearable.

Today, Garrity and Marie have launched the boat in Delacroix for a run down Oak River to the oyster-rich waters of East Plaquemines Parish. They are set to investigate complaints of thefts from private oyster leases, as well as to check out the Bay Gardene Seed Ground.

Not a boat of any kind is to be seen on the water through the length of the Oak River, across Bay Lafourche, and in Bay Gardene. Wind speeds

Marie carries a strong emotional attachment to the future of the oyster industry in Louisiana.

seem to double and the temperature drops even more on the open waters of the bays. It seems as if thousands of razor blades are being launched at my face. My fingertips and my toes are beginning to ache, in spite of the high-tech clothing I am wearing.

Nothing! Everywhere the two men look, they find nothing in the way of human activity. Just miles and miles of open water and waving marsh grass. The most numerous living creatures are ducks. There isn't a moment in which the sky isn't speckled with the moving forms of waterfowl. But no oystermen are stirring today.

Not just the wind and temperature have made things difficult for oystermen, but the tide level is also a problem. In fact, it may be the biggest factor limiting their activity. The strong north wind, coupled with the low tides of the lunar cycle and the season, has exposed vast areas of normally submerged water bottoms as mudflats. With water levels this low, the water over many reefs is too shallow to float even shallow-drafted oyster boats.

Taking a different route back toward civilization by way of the Twin Pipelines, Garrity encounters several places where the water is so shallow that he has to jump the mudflats with the boat. Before he enters Four Horse Lake, even Garrity has difficulty with the cold and noses the boat against the bank to warm up a few minutes. I had long before lost feeling in my feet and fingertips, but I wasn't about to cry "uncle" and ask them to stop.

While we try to absorb what warmth we can from the feeble winter sun, Marie comments that tomorrow will be spent in court on oyster cases. "We seem to be in court almost every Thursday," he says. Because of the seriousness of the fines for the type of violations that they write, he explains, a higher percentage of their cases go to court than for other fish and wildlife cases.

Even so, most defendants plead out in court at the last minute before trial, he says. But the agents still have to be there in case one does go to trial. "In fact," he says, shaking his head, "last year I only had one case that went all the way through trial, and that was, of all things, a gross littering case."

The case was interesting, as the two explain it. They had received a complaint from the public about an oysterman who was rehabilitating his leased reef by replanting empty oyster shells on it that he bought from a famous New Orleans-area eatery. The oysterman was taking part in a federally funded oyster reef rehabilitation program and one of the stipulations for receiving funding from the program was that no violations of the law could occur during the effort.

The project sounded well and good, but the fly in the ointment was that the restaurant's employees threw much more into the piles than just oyster shells, including dozens and dozens of rubber gloves used in the shucking process and many used plastic gallon and half-gallon oyster containers. Other debris was also present, even empty tubes of caulk from repairing the restaurant.

The oysterman used his high-pressure deck hose to blow the debris-laden shells off the deck of his boat. The shells sank on his reef, but much of the debris floated. "It was the most debris I have seen in my career on the water," says Marie. "A still camera couldn't record its extent. I wish that we would have had a video camera."

The defendant took it to court because if he had pled guilty he would not only have had to pay a fine, but return all the money that he had collected from the government. But he was found guilty anyway. The fine was only $500, but he had to return $60,000 that he had already collected.

After "warming up," if that is the proper term for becoming less cold, Garrity jumps the boat up on plane and crosses the lake before entering Bayou Terre aux Boeufs. Amazingly, the exposed mudflats along the bayou's shores are strewn with hundreds of large tree stumps that are rotted off almost to the mud line.

Seldom seeing the light of day or human gaze, because they are normally hidden by water, the stumps are silent markers to the fact that this utterly treeless saltwater marsh was once a freshwater swamp.

Not having even seen a boat and with the weather conditions not likely to allow for much fishing activity, Garrity and Marie decide to abort the rest of the patrol and devote the remainder of their shift to their mound of paperwork.

Two hours later, feeling returns to my toes.

19

BODCAU'S BAD BOYS

As my truck thunders west on the wide I-20 super slab past the exit to the Bonnie and Clyde Ambush Museum, I am struck by the beauty of the rolling pine-clad hills of extreme northwestern Louisiana. The cool winter air being provided by a front oozing through the area from the northwest showcases every visual detail as clearly as if it is chiseled in ice. I am late for my meeting with Senior Agent Michael Dunn, but I have a hard time tearing my eyes from the "eye candy" around me.

Dunn graciously accepts my apology for being late and we hop into his three-quarter-ton Dodge Ram pickup truck. We are heading further northwest to Bayou Bodcau Wildlife Management Area to meet two other agents, Lieutenant Roy Schufft and Agent Joey Melton. The WMA gets a lot of use and abuse by a wide range of users over and above the normal WMA crowd of hunters. Off-road driving, using ATVs in disregard of established ATV trails, seems to be a particularly popular activity on the WMA.

Our route up Highway 528 through the edge of what is known geologically as the North Louisiana Salt Dome Basin takes us through some of the very oldest oilfields in Louisiana, predating even the oldest marshland oilfields of coastal Louisiana. Looking like vast fields of big, one-legged kicking grasshoppers with their heads glued to the ground, the closely spaced pump jacks labor tirelessly round the clock, just as they have since the 1920s.

My chauffeur is a youthful twenty-three years old and already has three years of experience as a game warden. His lieutenant tells me later that he and his coworkers used to kid Dunn about being too young to legally buy his own bullets right after he graduated from the academy. Growing up in DeSoto Parish, where he is now assigned, he spent all his time as a kid hunting and fishing. "That's all there was to do there," he grins. His father was a deputy sheriff in nearby Sabine Parish, so becoming a game warden was almost a natural act for Dunn.

Dark-haired and dark-eyed, Dunn describes his job with passion in his voice. "It's a job that you can make what you want; there are so many different things to do. Besides enforcing fish and wildlife laws, we have to rescue lost and stranded people." Most difficult is dealing with the families of drowning victims while they conduct search and recovery efforts to find the bodies. "You feel helpless. It's weird," he explains.

Best of all is not being cooped up in an office looking at the same four walls every day, he enthuses. "Our scenery always changes." He enjoys meeting people, too, he says. Some people hunt and fish to feed their families and others do it for the sport of being outdoors.

Bodcau WMA, our destination, is a huge 34,355-acre multi-use area owned by the U.S. Army Corps of Engineers and a private landowner. LDWF, under a cooperative agreement with the Corps, manages the area's wildlife and its habitat.

Shaped like a giant koi carp with an enlarged head that is undulating its way down into Louisiana from Arkansas, the area is essentially a huge flood control project constructed on Bayou Bodcau by the Corps in 1949. The area, with its 2.3 million-cubic-yard earthen dam, is often called a reservoir, but it holds no water except during periods of extreme flood. Heavily wooded, its habitats range from cypress swamps to bottomland hardwood forests with tongues of intruding upland pine forests. Several permanent lakes are found on the area as well.

Besides hunting, multiple other activities occur on this unique WMA, including picnicking, fishing, canoeing, bike riding, horseback riding, and camping at its first-class improved campground. Because of its proximity to Shreveport, it attracts a lot of people.

Dunn meets Schufft and Melton at the WMA headquarters and the two trucks immediately proceed down into the heart of the area. Along the way they stop and check every parked vehicle to be sure that it has a check-in permit displayed on the dash. While they are at it, the wardens look into each vehicle's window to try to figure out what its occupants are doing on the WMA. If it is a truck, the bed is checked for the presence of blood.

The three men park their trucks out of easy sight at a choke point on the gravel road coming out of the WMA and take turns stopping every vehicle entering or leaving the area, including, briefly, a gaggle of lycra-clad bicyclists who speak very little English. Between stops, I chat with the other two game wardens.

Agent Joey Melton is also young and has been a game warden for only a year and a half. He is twenty-nine years old, a big guy, with closely cropped blond hair and blue eyes. He wears a big guy's grin constantly and speaks

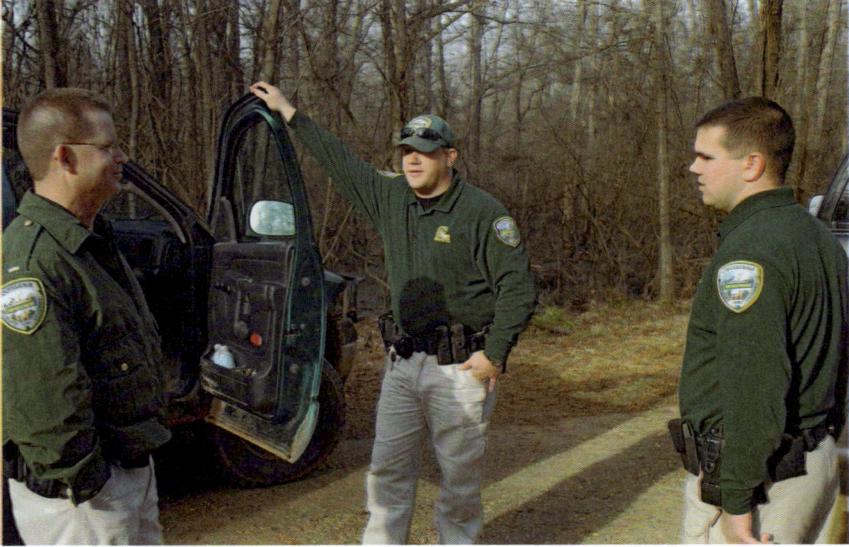

Roy Schufft (l), Joey Melton (c), and Michael Dunn (r) plan to spend much of the day patrolling Bodcau WMA.

with the gentlest of southern drawls. Assigned to DeSoto Parish with Dunn, he hails originally from Zwolle in Sabine Parish.

Similar to Dunn, he spent his youth fishing and hunting and comes from a law enforcement family. His mother worked in the parish sheriff's office and his father was a state trooper. His work as a game warden was preceded by four years in the U.S. Navy and a hitch as a state park ranger.

Lieutenant Roy Schufft, the two younger men's supervisor, has ten years in as a game warden. At fifty-seven, he bears the distinction of being the oldest person, at forty-seven, to make it through the rigors of the academy. Schufft had a twenty-six-year career in the U.S. Air Force before retiring at the rank of E-9 and pursuing what he had always wanted to do—be a game warden.

Slender, of medium height, and wearing glasses, Schufft carries himself with military bearing and seems utterly unflappable. He will tell anyone who will listen that a person couldn't ask for a better job. "You are independent. They give you everything that you want or need in equipment. I love it," he says with no room for argument.

The three wardens alternately stop vehicles and take turns ribbing each other. Although some of the vehicles hold hunters, most don't. Many just seem to be out for a drive on a pretty Saturday afternoon. With the pickings slim at this spot, the game wardens decide to kick around and see what else they can find. Their first destination is Ivan Lake, one of the lakes on the WMA. Rolling down the rutted red dirt roads, they found nary a soul, neither hunting nor on the lake. More slim pickings for the three lawmen.

With the evening's shadows getting longer, they depart for Wallace Lake on the opposite side of Shreveport. Situated on the Caddo-DeSoto parish border, the heavily wooded lake is used as a roosting site by a large number of wood ducks. The ducks typically do not come into their boudoir until after legal shooting hours. "Wallace Lake is usually good for a late shooter this time of year," says Schufft.

The wildlife agents can't launch their boat at their usual secluded spot because of floodwaters, so they have to time their arrival at the Wallace Lake Public Boat Ramp carefully. If they arrive there too early, their trucks parked in the lot will alert late shooters that arrive after them to their presence. If they get there too late, they will miss much of what shooting goes on, if any.

After the serene beauty of rural northwestern Louisiana, the trip across the ugly suburban sprawl of Shreveport is depressing. While navigating the urban traffic, Dunn explains that Wallace Lake is only one of several lakes in immediate proximity to the city. Others are Cross Lake, Cypress Lake, and Black Bayou Reservoir, all of which, according to Dunn, offer good fishing for "white perch," as crappie are called locally.

With just-right timing, the men reach the lake a few minutes before the end of legal shooting hours. As they launch the boat, several loud booms echo through the cypress trees from the shoreline just up from the launch. Schufft quietly slips through the brush along the shore to try to locate the source of the gunshots. Meanwhile, Dunn and Melton pull on leafy camouflage outerwear and idle the boat through the closely spaced cypress trees of the lake.

The two men pull up next to a cluster of trees and sit very quietly, listening for any sound. The only shooting heard is so far away as to be barely audible. Then they hear a thump, followed by voices. Peeking between the tree trunks and swaying Spanish moss, they make out the forms of two men in a boat.

But they don't look like hunters. The game wardens start their engine and idle to them, only to find two late-middle-aged men tending their yo-yos for white perch. Nothing else is kicking in the lake, so the two game wardens go back to the launch to meet Schufft, who was unsuccessful in locating the source of the shots.

"Well, sometimes you win and sometimes you don't," drawls Schufft philosophically.

After storing the boat, the men dine at a Chinese buffet in Shreveport. While eating, Schufft weighs in that their best option tonight will be to return to Bodcau WMA. "It might be slow, but if anyone is on the area after legal hours, they'll be up to no good." The two young men eat heartily, among much teasing. Finally, Schufft declares, "Let's go catch some bad guys," and out the door and into the darkness they go.

During the hour-long drive back to Bodcau, Schufft talks about what kind of person it takes to do game warden work. "The freedom in this job means that you have to have a strong motivation to do the job. You have to be a self-starter.

"Another important quality needed is to have strong moral values to put across the right image. A wildlife enforcement officer has to be very ethical. He has to do the right thing when no one is looking.

"The job takes some guts. There is no other way to put it. It takes courage

Wallace Lake is a shallow cypress tree–studded water body used by roosting wood ducks and duck hunters alike.

Dunn stands on the bow of the game wardens' boat in the failing light and listens for gunshots from hunters shooting late on a wood duck roost.

to go into the woods at night looking for someone that you know is armed with a gun. Of course, along with that, a person has to have good judgment. He has to know when to go in and when to back out.

"Finally, you need to be comfortable in the outdoors. It really helps to have an outdoors background. Someone with experience in hunting and fishing has a powerful advantage because they know how hunters and fishermen think." He adds that a lot of people who end up making it as a street policeman just can't make it as a game warden.

There are also some personality traits that don't lend themselves to successful work as an enforcement agent, he cautions. "People that can only function as a group or a team won't be happy here. Also, a person can't be too action-oriented. Game wardens spend a lot of time in surveillance, waiting for things to happen.

"We deal with people from all backgrounds. One of the biggest challenges is near the end of a twelve-hour shift when you have to be pleasant to people who aren't always pleasant to you.

"A big thing is to get a game warden to treat people the way that you would want to be treated. They [the people] are out recreating in the outdoors. It's easy to be gung-ho. We are not dealing with axe-murderers, for the most part."

As Schufft finishes his discourse, his truck, followed by Dunn and Melton's, plunges down the gravel road off of the huge Bodcau Dam and into the dense dark woods of the WMA. When they reach the spot where they plan to pull off the road into a semi-hidden nook, another big black Dodge with a Louisiana Department of Wildlife and Fisheries emblem on its doors is already there.

"That would be Lynn Presley," says Schufft casually. The two incoming trucks bracket Presley's, window to window, as the drivers of all law enforcement vehicles are prone to do. Down come the windows, and the first words out of Presley's mouth are, "Well, if it ain't the lieutenant and his two children." In the moonlight, the two younger agents grin good-naturedly.

Presley steps out of his truck briefly to stretch his legs, and by the bright moonlight I see a powerfully built, silver-maned and silver-mustachioed, late-middle-aged man. I later learn that the fifty-nine-year-old sergeant is a twenty-seven-year veteran of LDWF.

After he reenters his truck, the four men compare field notes on where they have been and what they expect of the rest of the night. Presley is nearer to the end of his shift than the other three men are. They are talking game warden talk mixed with some bantering, when suddenly all four tense up.

Vehicle lights are coming down the road. The lead vehicle of the two has a spotlight on, shining obliquely into the woods on the left side of the road—not a good sign. The men exchange hushed comments but never take their eyes off of the approaching vehicles' headlights.

Then, perhaps 150 yards before they reach the three hidden trucks, they stop. Their lights are still on and the engines are still running. Then shouting and screaming rend the air. The sounds aren't those of anger or terror, nor are they the sounds of drunken revelry. But none of the game wardens can hear distinctly what is being said.

In a tone much like one would use when siccing his dog on someone, Schufft says, "Okay, Joey, there they are for you." With that, the big guy, moving incredibly quickly without making any noise, runs through the woods to get nearer to the vehicles.

In the meantime, Presley has unlimbered his night vision scope and is aiming it through the trees at the two trucks. In what seems like twenty minutes, but what is more likely only three or four, the two trucks suddenly lurch forward and accelerate, gravel flying. Presley and Schufft throw themselves into their trucks and Dunn hides behind a tree, ready to jump out in front of the vehicles.

As Dunn steps forward out of his hiding spot, Presley executes a perfect blocking maneuver in front of the lead vehicle and Schufft pulls his Dodge Ram diagonally toward the second truck, with his headlights on bright to blind its operator. This isn't their first rodeo. Both game warden trucks have their blue lights flashing.

Dunn sprints to the driver's side window of the first truck and throws the bright beam of his flashlight into the eyes of the driver. Melton, barreling out the woods full bore, does the same to the driver of the second vehicle. All four men repeatedly scream "State Game Warden." It is bedlam to me!

The agents act like a well-rehearsed combat team. Each of the four seems to know intuitively what to do, without a single order being given by the lieutenant or sergeant.

The drivers asked to step from their vehicles, and a single passenger from each truck exits as well. The passenger in the front truck is a woman who seems sober as a judge and introduces herself as the mother of three beautiful, bright-eyed children riding in the back of the truck. Both drivers have obviously been drinking; how much is the question. Then there is the matter of the spotlight.

The drivers of the two trucks react to the blitz quite differently. The driver of the trailing truck is quiet and compliant. The driver of the front truck, obviously the alpha male of the group, is bold and talkative.

"Okay, what's going on here?" asks Schufft of the front truck driver.

He answers that they have been camping at the campsite, which is near the U.S. Army Corps of Engineers office, and that they decided that they just wanted to go for a ride. He repeats several times that he had been told

Schufft distracts the passenger of the second truck while Presley questions the driver of the vehicle.

by other game wardens that he didn't need a WMA check-in permit to camp at the campground.

Schufft asks him why he has a police spotlight mounted on the pillar between the windshield and the door.

"It was there when I bought the truck secondhand," is the reply.

"Why are you driving down a road in a Wildlife Management Area with it on," asks Schufft.

"My eyes are bad and the headlights on the truck are dim," he replies. The glib man has a fast answer for everything.

He brings up that he is a painter and is currently painting the new building being built for the game wardens' headquarters. Between each question, he reminds the game wardens about his work on their building.

As he talks, the other three game wardens search the trucks and make sure that the three now-distressed children in the bed of the truck are alright. A quick check reveals no weapons in either vehicle. But neither vehicle has the required check-in pass.

When asked if they have been drinking and how much, both give the stock answer: "A couple of beers." Both drivers are asked to perform the first step in the field sobriety test, the horizontal gaze nystagmus test, and both are determined to be on the borderline of inebriation.

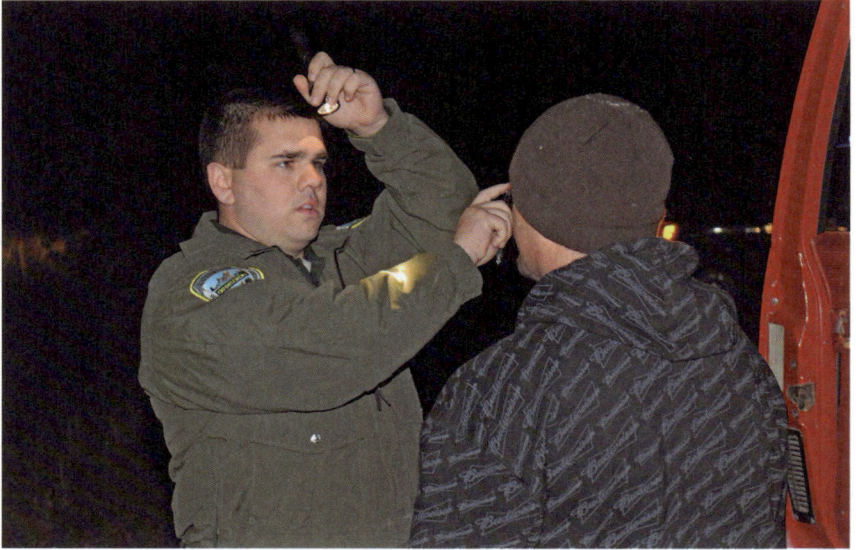

Dunn performs a horizontal gaze nystagmus test on the driver of the first vehicle.

After the game wardens confer briefly, they decide to write the drivers of both vehicles warning tickets for not having check-in permits and to write the driver of the front vehicle up for using a spotlight on a WMA. The two men are informed of the citations that they will receive.

As Dunn prepares to write the warning ticket to the front driver, he asks him if he has ever received a warning ticket for this violation before. He readily admits that he has indeed already received one warning ticket for not possessing a WMA permit. Dunn explains that this citation will now have to be a "hard ticket," since the law prohibits the issuance of repeat warnings to the same individual for the same violation.

"Well, let's just forget I said it," he instructs Dunn hopefully. Dunn says that even if he forgets it, the computer won't. "Aw man, you can't write me a ticket for being honest," he loudly protests. Dunn apologizes and keeps writing. "That's chicken shit!" the beer-emboldened man yells in Dunn's face. Dunn keeps writing.

Either feeling that he can control the rest of the encounter or that he can vent with impunity, the subject begins to violently protest the fact that he is also going to get a ticket for the spotlight.

"Let me explain something to you," booms the barrel-chested Presley.

"You have the right to remain silent. Anything you say can and will be used against you in a court of law. You have the right to have an attorney present during questioning. If you cannot afford an attorney, one will be appointed to you. Do you understand these rights?"

The subject instantaneously becomes meek and submissive. It becomes obvious again that Presley is no spring chicken in this line of work.

As the tickets are being written, Schufft is walking the scene, checking for anything that might have been missed. His observant eye catches something that he quickly wishes he had left overlooked. A head bobs in the small rear seat of the extended cab of the front truck. "What's this? Who are you?" he says as he opens the vehicle's door.

A bedraggled, almost emaciated face emerges. Sporting a week's worth of stubble surrounding a massive Fu Manchu moustache, and a mop of long, stringy hair, he is obviously far too drunk to even attempt to dismount from the vehicle. "I'm a licensed bounty hunter," he slurs. "You wanna see my knife?" Schufft doesn't reply.

The man tries to light a cigarette. The hand holding the lighter is waving wildly. He misses the end of the cigarette, nearly gets it lit in the middle, and then swings the lighter close to his face, singeing the hairs of his fuzzy whiskers.

"Hey," he pursues Schufft, "I tolja I was a licensed bounty hunter, huh? Ya wanna see my knife?" The slender lieutenant assures him that it is okay for him not to see his knife, and turns away. "Ya know, I'm a licensed bounty hunter," the man mutters again as he sinks back into the darkness of the rear seat and tries once more to light the now much beat-up and bent cigarette.

The drivers of the two trucks are instructed to leave the WMA and released. Presley, who has worked past the end of his shift, heads for home. In the remaining hour before midnight, the two trucks prowl the roads of the WMA. All is quiet on a cold 38-degree night.

20

LAND OF THE GREEN GOLD

"There is somebody doing something on the lake 365 days a year," states Sergeant Joe Dewil in a matter-of-fact voice, "no matter how bad the weather is."

Senior Agent Billy Joe "B. J." Shoemaker expands on Dewil's statement. "Toledo Bend Reservoir is a vacation spot. When people take off, they will fish"—the word "will" being heavily emphasized. "Their boats are too small; their boats are not right; there will be operator inexperience."

The two men, with twenty-four years as game wardens between them, are obviously correct. It is early March, and the weather is hostile and threatening to get worse. But before daylight, from Many, through Toledo Town, and on to the big 185,000-acre lake, the roads are a hive of activity.

A Bassmaster Open Circuit qualifying tournament is going on, and it seems like the whole bass boat-owning world has descended on the area. Shiny new heavy-duty pickup trucks and big SUVs pulling high-performance bass boats clog the roads. It is a pro-am tournament, meaning that each boat holds a professional fisherman and an amateur.

As daylight cracks, the two game wardens launch their twenty-two-foot Triton V-hull boat, powered by a big 225-horsepower Yamaha engine. They will be conducting a boating safety patrol in the central part of the sixty-five-mile-long lake. Two other game wardens will be working the northern end of the lake today, and another two will be on the south end. During boating safety patrols game wardens also actively check fishermen for compliance with fishing laws.

Joe Dewil is a powerfully built six-footer from nearby Florien. His demeanor and the neat, dark moustache planted on his big face scream law enforcement officer.

B. J. Shoemaker, on the other hand, looks like the boy next door from Marthaville, Louisiana, all grown up, which is what he is. His thin, closely cropped hair is prematurely grizzled gray, but his most noticeable features are a perpetual bashful grin set off by twinkling, mischievous eyes.

What both men share is a love of law enforcement work. Shoemaker calls the job "a dream," adding that if more people knew the rewards, more people would probably want to do it. He says that after a four-year hitch in the Marine Corps he looked closely at going to work as a state trooper, but applied for this job because it had more draw. "The people that we deal with appreciate what we do more than state troopers get appreciated."

Dewil wholeheartedly agrees. "This job is the best of worlds. We are outdoors a lot. Unlike with some other law enforcement jobs, the people that we deal with are not thugs. For the most part, they are good people. There is also a mystique about the game warden's job. Something different is always going on. We are not spending day in and day out stopping car traffic."

Dawn comes slowly under the misty, almost foggy conditions. It is dank and uncomfortable and even at this early hour the wind ahead of an oncoming cold front is huffing unceasingly.

Staying near the shoreline, they proceed down to Cypress Bend Park, the site of the bass tournament. An impressive site greets the eye. The cove is a maelstrom of metal flake madness. A steady stream of trucks is launching more bass boats into the sea of red, green, and white boat running lights.

With their huge engines snarling, the boats mill and churn, waiting for their release. What looks like utter chaos is actually well-organized and planned, according to Dewil.

After the last boat fires off without incident, the park's basin is eerily

The running lights of the churning mass of bass boats look like twinkling Christmas lights.

quiet. The only sound is the incessant wind sighing through the tall pine trees.

Taking their time in the roily water, the two men head north to begin their patrol. Talk drifts back to the challenges of the big reservoir. "You gotta respect the lake," says Dewil while eyeing the choppy waves on the open water. Shoemaker explains that a boater can be thirty minutes from the launch and a storm will come in and catch him exposed.

"Another problem," adds Dewil, "are tree stumps. When the reservoir was flooded a lot of trees were still standing, some in thirty to forty feet of water. Those trees have rotted off to where their ends are just below average water level. You can't see them, but you can hit them with your motor."

"A lot of our problems start when people just take off across the lake," says Shoemaker. "The lake looks innocent and open, but those stumps are just underwater."

As commercial fishing has declined because of economics, recreational fishing has become a big part of the local economy, the two explain. The lake is famous for its bass fishing, and people come from around the world to fish in it. Dewil ticks off South Africa, England, and Germany as being the homes of anglers he has recently checked. The southern end of the lake has more recreational boating and the northern end has more fishing activities.

The lake is also well known for its crappie fishing and has become a destination for snowbirds, northerners who winter in the south to avoid cold weather. While the reservoir was completed in 1966, recently the human population around the lake has exploded, says Dewil. "In the last sixteen years the number of people living around the lake has quadrupled. We have a lot of retirement homes, and a lot of people have built camps on the lake, especially since Hurricane Katrina."

In the very spot that we are now passing, a massive gray condo is perched on a steep, near cliff-like hill, like a Tibetan monastery. Yet, in spite of the development around the lake, most of its natural beauty remains.

Although the day's hazy weather does its best to paint everything a shade of gray, the scenery is beautiful. Ochre cliffs painted by iron ore deposits fringe segments of the shoreline. And everything seems cloaked in green trees, mostly pine.

I comment about the trees, to which Dewil replies, "This area has been called 'the land of the green gold' because of the value of the trees." Shoemaker explains that in spite of the contribution of the lake to the economy

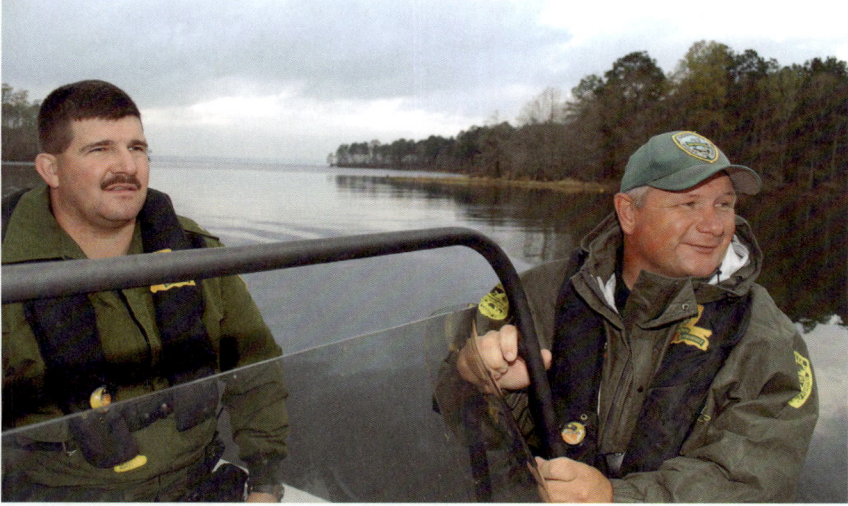

Joe Dewil (l) and B. J. Shoemaker begin their day's patrol in a cove protected from the wind.

of western Louisiana, timber harvesting is still the leading industry of the region.

Because of the strong winds, few boats are in the main body of the lake, so the game wardens hop from one cove to the next. Most of these coves are drowned creek beds deeply incised into the steep hills around the lake. There are a lot of boats to check, even in the poor weather.

The first angler checked doesn't seem happy to see the game wardens, but everything checks out. The next boat has two anglers, one of whom doesn't have a fishing license, personal identification, or boat registration papers. A quick point of sale (POS) check by cell phone with Dispatch confirms that the man has purchased a license and that the boat is properly registered.

In the next boat, the anglers have four bass in their live well. One is a spotted bass, which have no minimum size limit, but three are largemouths. All three are under the minimum size and therefore are illegal.

The game wardens pull their boat away from the anglers to discuss what to do. To the fishermen's obvious relief, they decide to issue warning citations rather than hard tickets. Afterward, Dewil takes a moment to teach them how to recognize the difference between the two species.

The officers check boat after boat. Most are legal; a few have problems, such as expired registrations or undersized largemouth bass. One boat has a passenger perched on the front pedestal seat as the boat is under way. The operator receives a stern lecture from Shoemaker about the danger of the illegal activity.

After they pull away, Shoemaker explains that one of the biggest challenges of the job is learning to speak tactfully to people who are doing stupid things.

The next boat holds two adult males, whom the game wardens speculate are participants in the Bassmaster tournament. They are moving hard with their troll motor from one side of the cove to the other. The man on the front, probably the professional bass fishermen, glares at them arrogantly, then turns his head and turns the boat away from them.

Shoemaker greets the backs of their heads and loudly asks if they have any fish. The fisherman in the rear desultorily turns his head, says "no fish," and then turns away. The fisherman on the bow never stops or turns his head.

"Shoemaker turns to me and says, "That's part of it, an example of learning to be tactful. They are probably legal because the tournament organizers check them for licenses and paperwork. But still. . . ."

As they move on, Dewil adds to Shoemaker's comments. "That is kind of typical of a pro angler—very arrogant. The ones that are even worse are the semi-pros, the ones who think that they should be pros."

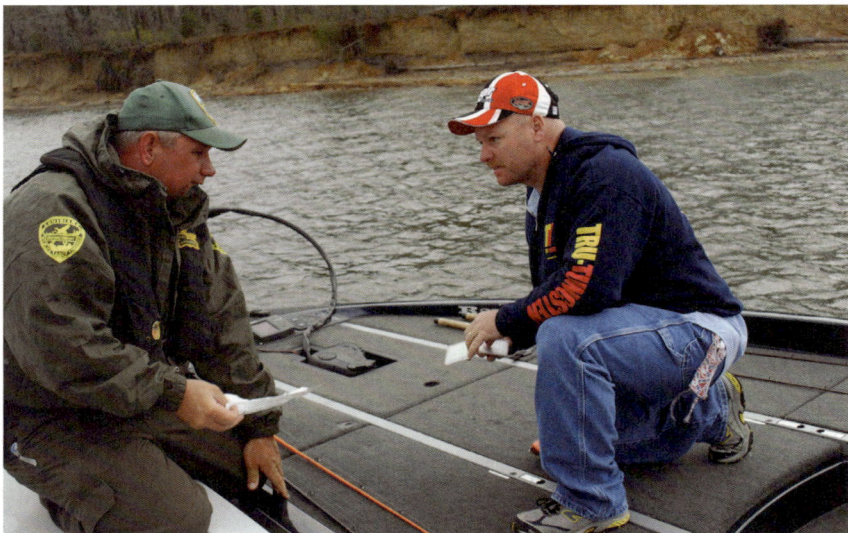

The friendly Shoemaker takes time to chat a little with most of the people he checks.

The day wears on and the game wardens seem to never stop. There is always someone to check. The two make a good team. Shoemaker has the slow, friendly southern drawl. Dewil comes across as the authoritarian.

Dewil uses his binoculars a lot. With them he can check out, long before they get to a boat, who is actively fishing and who is just riding. The glasses help him identify other potentially problematic activities early as well.

They find a lot of violations, most of them small. A boat with three women crappie fishermen has a registration sticker that expired in 2003. They get a warning ticket.

Another motorboat has three youngsters in it, none of which have attended the state-mandated boating safety class. Since they are very near their home, the game wardens direct them to use the troll motor to return directly to the dock. Their parents watch from the shore.

By 11 a.m. the wind on the open lake is really snorting, but the protected coves are flecked with boats. A stop of a boat with three middle-aged anglers produces panic in one of the men. He can't find his fishing license. He disassembles his more than full wallet and produces an expired Louisiana license, as well as licenses for New Mexico, Texas, and Arkansas. Shoemaker dryly observes, "Well, it's obvious that you don't mind buying fishing licenses."

A crappie angler shows off her catch, but still gets a warning ticket.

The angler, not to be defeated, looks in every nook in three tackle boxes, then takes everything out of his boat's compartments. Dewil gets on his cell phone and does a POS. "He has it," he declares to Shoemaker.

The angler is both relieved and frustrated. As the game wardens pull away, he begins searching the boat for the missing license again.

The next boat holds two anglers and fourteen fishing rods rigged and ready to go. "Got any fish?" asks Shoemaker of the casters. "Two" is their reply. Both are legal-sized bass. Never missing a chance for a little kidding, Shoemaker drawls with a huge grin, "Well, if you don't catch another one, it won't be 'cause you ain't got enough rod and reels." The men laugh heartily.

As the game wardens move from boat to boat, their craft constantly bangs and bumps over stumps in the creeks and coves. Next up is a party barge with two couples on it. They have run thirty miles up the lake from the area of the dam.

The game wardens express concern to them that they might not have enough gas to get back, pointing out that on the return trip they will be bucking a stiff headwind and running into the waves rather than with them. The operator of the boat is very casual, almost flippant, about the game wardens' expressed concerns. As he motors off, the two game wardens exchange knowing looks.

Three young men in an aluminum boat powered by an outboard with a tiller handle are stopped. None are wearing life jackets and the operator does not have his engine kill lanyard connected to him. The game wardens caution them about the new law requiring everyone in a tiller handle boat under sixteen feet long that is under way to wear life jackets and also requiring that the kill lanyard be attached to the operator.

The men admit that the ice chest in the boat is full of beer and nervously eye the empty can in the bottom of the boat. When the operator is asked how many he has had, he answers by saying that the empty on the floor is from yesterday. But he willingly submits to a horizontal gaze nystagmus test, which he passes.

After they leave, the game wardens chuckle about guilty looks, and how one can tell if someone is in violation just by their look. "Lots of times," says Shoemaker, "when I ask them if they got any fish, they will answer, 'I got a few,' and look down and refuse to make eye contact."

Dewil says his favorite is when they answer to the game warden that they have no fish and then the fish start splashing in the live well. "They get a real guilty look then."

So the patrol goes. Expired or forgotten fishing licenses and boat registrations, undersized largemouth bass, and missing life jackets seem to be routine. "This is pretty much what we do. It gets pretty monotonous in boating safety and fishing patrols," says Shoemaker.

"By July and August we are ready for hunting season," Dewil adds.

"Yeah, we are ready for a vacation then," grins Shoemaker.

In mid-afternoon, the men begin working their boat south, back to their launching point. As they leave the shelter of the coves, they feel the full brunt of the white-capped waves driven by a powerful thirty-mile-per-hour south-southwest wind.

Even taking their time, running directly into the wind is not easy. The boat is a deep V-hull and designed to handle rough water, but both men still have to stand in a semi-crouch to allow their leg joints to absorb the vigor-ous banging produced by pounding their way into the teeth of the wind.

The calm waters of the cove where they launched are welcome. When they turn the outboard motor off at the small pier, they hear the engine of another boat approaching. They turn and look. It's the party barge, whose occupants they had cautioned earlier in the day about their fuel supply.

"Hey," the driver shouts, "it looks like we're going to run out of gas. Can you help us?"

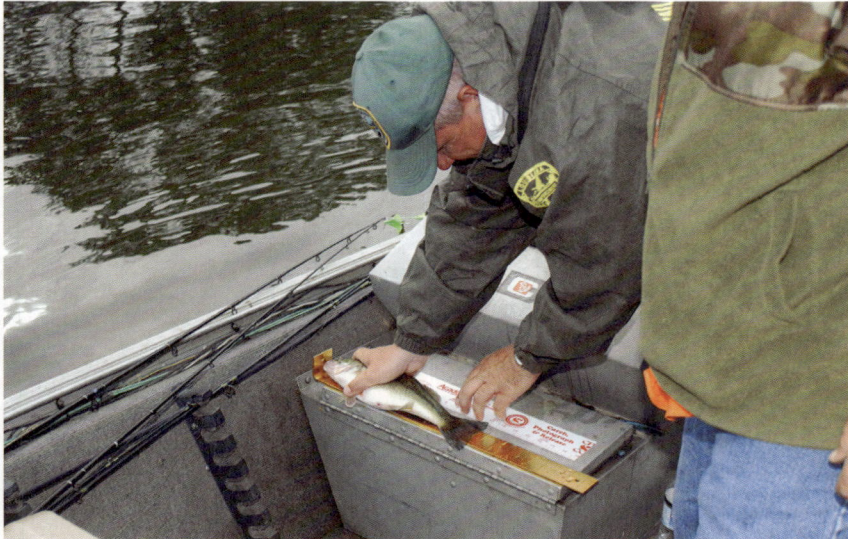

Shoemaker measures a largemouth bass for size limit compliance.

21

THE EDGE OF THE WORLD

It is a widely believed fable that before the first voyage of Christopher Columbus sailors feared long-distance sailing lest they fall off the edge of a flat earth. While learned men, and even semi-learned men, had believed that the earth was round since before 200 B.C., a trip to Venice, Louisiana, today still feels like a journey to the edge of the earth for many. The soft marshlands south of Venice are the last pieces of what passes for land in Louisiana. Beyond is only the void of the open Gulf of Mexico.

The wetlands below Venice are remote, subject to tempestuous and harsh weather conditions, and now largely depopulate, with the abandonment of Oysterville, Burrwood, Olga, Quarantine Station, and finally Pilottown and Port Eads. Most often heard among Louisiana sportsmen is the reference to the lower Mississippi River delta as being "the last frontier."

It's the last weekend of duck season, and a stubborn jet stream has been funneling frigid arctic air into south Louisiana for four days. Even in Venice, where the sharp edges of the Alberta Clipper are dulled by the surrounding warmer waters of the Gulf, the air has a bite to it. And as always in Venice, in all seasons, the smell of the water world that the area is part of perfumes each breath.

Today, Sergeant Scot Keller is accompanying Sergeant Adam Young to patrol the marshes south of Venice, paying special attention to duck hunting activity on Pass-a-Loutre Wildlife Management Area. Young explains that he has been receiving complaints of "double tripping," the illegal practice of harvesting two daily limits of waterfowl per day, one in the morning and one in the evening.

He is also concerned that other duck limit violations may be occurring. The limit on pintails is one per person per day, and the season is completely closed on canvasbacks this year. These just happen to be two of the most common ducks found at the mouth of the Mississippi River.

Although the skies are blue and the sun is blindingly bright, the long

Scot Keller (l) and Adam Young (r) are bundled up for the long, cold ride down the river from Venice.

ride down the river from Venice in the open twenty-one-foot boat, powered by a 225-horse outboard, is cold—like really cold. Tears well in my eyes and my nose begins to run.

In spite of every inhalation feeling like the icy air is snapping off in our lungs, we chat about how the two men became game wardens. Young, who is piloting the boat, says that his family had a camp on Rat's Nest Road in Slidell and that he hunted and fished all his life.

He remembers his imagination about the job getting sparked by being checked by a game warden. "What better job can you have? I kept it in the back of my mind when I went to college to study marine biology." Halfway through school, he decided that his goal was to become a game warden, so he changed his major to criminal justice and managed to snag a job as a student worker for the LDWF Enforcement Division.

He wanted to be assigned to Orleans Parish, his home parish, but there weren't any openings, so he took a position in Plaquemines Parish, which he now says that he wouldn't trade for anything. "I fell in love with Plaquemines. Working here is nonstop. There is always something to do," he says in a proprietary voice. "Plus, there is a still a real outlaw culture alive in the parish."

Slightly built and with the loose-jointed movements of a natural out-doorsman, Young wears a crooked, mischievous grin. Only thirty-one years old, and with only seven years under his belt, he walks with the swagger of self-confidence. Although he admits that the job has "odd hours," he says that he can't envision himself being behind a desk. "I actually feel like I am contributing here. To do this job, you have to want to do it. What you do is up to you."

But the best part of the job, he says, is the "extraordinary camaraderie" that he feels with his fellow game wardens in Region 8. Before Hurricane Katrina, eight agents lived very close to each other in St. Bernard Parish. We worked together and we fraternized together. "The friendships I formed are incredible," he says with emphasis, then sadly adds, "But we all lost everything in the storm and now we are scattered."

Keller, with his silver-flecked dark hair, at forty-one, is older than Young, and with thirteen years with the LDWF, has more experience. Originally from New Orleans, he is assigned to St. Bernard and has been living in Metairie since Hurricane Katrina. Slightly taller and bulkier than Young, he speaks with an "educated cadence," if such a thing exists. Some of that might be due to the B.A. in English literature that he holds from the University of New Orleans.

But Keller isn't an effete intellectual. His dad started taking him into the outdoors when he was five years old, and his fluid movements show him to be at home there. When he later discovered that there was an occupation that paid you to be on the water, it enticed him. That, coupled with an interest in law enforcement, took him to applying for a job as a game warden.

In his words, "The game warden's job is unique. It is not just reactive, but proactive. We seek out violations, not just respond to them." Like Young, what he likes best is the freedom of the job.

"You create your own destiny and you don't have a supervisor breathing down your neck. You are allowed to do your own job." He adds that being outdoors and having the best equipment and training available are big pluses, too.

He never does explain the degree in English Lit.

The banks of the river are lined with dense, seemingly endless walls of eight-foot-tall roseau cane. The giant reed-like grass canes are carrying the brown of winter interspersed with green, and they undulate nonstop in the brisk north wind.

Our first stop of the day comes when an expensive fiberglass sport fisher comes charging out of a smaller pass and turns downriver ahead of us. The sharp eyes of the game wardens immediately spy that the boat does not have a registration sticker affixed to the hull. In spite of the muscular Mercury OptiMax 225 hanging on the stern of their boat, the game wardens have trouble closing the gap.

The occupants of the other boat spot the wardens as they near and cut power, apologizing profusely. The owner of the boat explains that he has sent in his registration, but has not received his sticker yet. Young calls Dispatch to verify the story. Finding it to be true, they cut the men loose to hopefully chase tuna offshore.

The first WMA campground has several tents on it, but only one person is present, a man who has just paddled up with five blue catfish in his canoe. After identifying themselves, they ask the man if he has any game in possession at the camp. He replies that one of the boats tied off at the campsite has a drake pintail in it that one of the other hunters who is now out hunting had killed earlier.

They examine the bird and ask him for his WMA permit and licenses. He has the permit, but doesn't have a state or federal duck stamp. The two sergeants step off to one side and confer. They return to the man and explain that he could be written up for possession of waterfowl in the field without appropriate licenses and that the hunter who killed the bird and didn't tag it could be cited for failure to maintain possession. But they say that they are not going to issue any tickets because he was honest and they believe him.

Before leaving, the two agents split up and inspect each tent and all the ice chests in the campground. Satisfied, they admire the man's catfish catch, bid him good day, and leave.

The two men are obviously close friends. Keller, with a Sphinx-like smirk, baits Young constantly—about his equipment, about his boat operating skills, about everything. Young's reply is invariably the same: "Shut up," with an occasional "Shut up, Scot" thrown in for variety.

Keller later takes time to explain that this trip is kind of a treat since sergeants ordinarily work on different shifts. Much of their patrolling is also done alone. Only nighttime patrols on the water are done in pairs, because of the danger.

Young points the big aluminum boat in the direction of the main campground. When they get there, they find three tents. Two are pitched together and one is pitched separately. With no one at the campground, they take their time in searching ice chests and campsites. They find a large and a small plastic zipper-type bag with duck breasts in them and another quart-

The lone person at the first Pass-a-Loutre WMA campground is a fisherman. The waterfowl and hog hunters have not returned from their hunts yet.

size plastic bag of fish fillets. Three uncleaned ducks and several redfish are also in an ice chest.

A boat with three hunters pulls up as the game wardens are poking around the site, looking for ducks hidden in the marsh grass or for signs of canvasbacks having been cleaned. Fortunately for the hunters, it turns out that they had a lousy hunt and did not have a duck with them. Young searches their boat and all their equipment with the thoroughness of a ferret that has smelled a rat.

They check the hunters' licenses and permits, as well as the plugs in their shotguns. They are also on the alert for the possession of lead shot, which is prohibited for waterfowl hunting. They ask the men when they are planning to go home. The reply is "Today, maybe tomorrow."

With their agreement, Young empties the bags of duck breasts and begins to count them. He finds the breasts of thirty-one ducks, many of them from very large species. Coupled with the three whole ducks in another ice chest, that totals to thirty-four ducks in possession, only two ducks shy of the total multi-day field possession limit of thirty-six ducks for three men.

While Young searches the boat, Keller checks the hunters' shells to be sure that they are using nontoxic shot.

If they had made even a moderately successful hunt that day the men would have been in violation.

Again the two game wardens huddle. The two agree that they have no case now. The law clearly allows hunters to clean fish and game at a campsite and consume it. Only if they attempt to transport their cleaned harvest in unidentifiable condition can they be booked.

They also know that if confronted, the subjects will claim that they plan to eat everything today before they leave, a Sisyphean challenge that even six accomplished gourmands couldn't achieve. But the game wardens can't legally challenge their appetites.

The question before the two is whether to walk away whistling and try to catch them later on the water transporting their goodies out or whether to warn them now. With the hunters alerted by the presence of the game wardens, they may not leave until late at night or the next day—a long stakeout.

Young makes the call to warn them. As expected, the three piously plead that they are planning to eat everything. Keller again asks them when they are going to leave. They become evasive.

The two game wardens also warn them about transporting the fish fillets. The answer, as could be predicted, is that they brought them from their home freezer. Keller brooks none of that. He tells them that he is smart enough to know that bags of fish put in home freezers are almost always marked with a date and often with the species of fish in the bag. The men hang their heads like kids caught with their hands in a cookie jar.

Young gives them another warning that all the cleaned ducks and fish must be eaten before they leave. As a closer, he warns them against discarding the ducks and fish. "Wanton waste of fish and wildlife is a very serious offense," he tells the silent men.

After they idle away from the campground, Keller says, "We just didn't have a case; that's the way it goes."

Young adds, "It's not what you know, it's what you can prove."

"Pearls of wisdom; pearls of wisdom," mutters Keller ruefully as Young puts the boat up on plane.

"There is always this last campground," says Young hopefully as he nears it. He is shocked. It is deserted. Not a tent is present.

With that strikeout Young begins to probe the small passes and waterways through the high canes towering over their heads. "These are good places for illegal netters to stash their nets when they aren't using them," says Young. "I have found a bunch in this part of the delta." Some of the passages seem narrower than the boat and he has to power his way in.

You can't see around the next corner. It's a little spooky and reminds one of a mission on a Swift Boat in the Mekong Delta during the Vietnam War. Even the big, clunky boat the game wardens are using has a military feel about it.

Finding no gill nets and tiring of that game, Young and Keller go looking for other duck hunters. They begin finding waterfowlers who have finished their hunt. Boat after boat checks out as okay. An old man cagily tells the game wardens to be on the lookout for some South Carolina hunters.

Finally, at one boat, with three hunters and a ton of gear, they find an auxiliary mud boat with an expired registration. Also, one of the hunters can't produce a federal duck stamp. The game wardens agree to follow the men back to their camp, where the duck stamp is thought to be.

The camp is located on one of the few pieces of private property on this part of the delta and is called "Camp Canal." It has received its name for good reason. It is a solid row of closely spaced duck hunting camps. All heads at the camps turn in inquisitiveness and apprehension as the big game warden boat idles up the canal.

The small passes and waterways of the mouth of the Mississippi River are lined with dense walls of eight-foot rouseau cane.

While the hunter turns the camp inside out looking for his duck stamp, Young goes through the hunters' equipment and then their boats with a fine-toothed comb. Climbing out of the boat, he looks at me with a crooked little grin and says, "I love to dig."

Young doesn't quit searching yet. He picks through the high marsh grass surrounding the camp, looking for anything out of order.

Finally, the hunter gives up his search for the stamp and gracefully accepts his citations for failing to have a federal duck stamp and for operating a boat with an expired registration.

As they are idling down the canal to leave, a boat coming in towing a mud boat nears them. Immediately, Young whispers to Keller, "We got to check this boat thoroughly. It's registered in South Carolina. Young whips the boat through a U-turn and asks them how they have done. When they answer that they have a few birds, he informs them that he would like to check their licenses and suggests that they might want to proceed to their camp, which they do.

Keller immediately jumps into the towed mud boat and commences a search that Young would have been proud of. But Young isn't watching Keller; he is watching the behavior of the hunters in the boat.

At their camp, they check the hunters' kill, licenses, and whether their shotguns are plugged. Young gets permission to look in the ice chests stacked on the wharf in front of the camp while the men pull off their waders.

He finds a number of legally cleaned ducks with an identifying wing attached to each breastplate. But he also finds a large number of large, cleaned, deboned breasts. He counts them using the fingers of both hands several times and replaces them in their bags. When he asks the hunters what the breasts are from, they answer that the birds are coots. The breasts are far too large for coot breasts, but with a subtle sigh he accepts the answer.

After issuing a caution to them that they must consume the unidentifiable breasts and not transport them in, he joins Keller in the boat. They idle down the canal a final time and pull into the pass.

With the day winding down, Keller starts harassing Young again. "I'm not riding in this thing again unless you get it fixed." "Shut up." "The warning buzzer is always going off; it's embarrassing." "Shut up, Scot." "Look, the shifter for the engine doesn't work; it jiggles all around." "Shut up."

It goes on. "Adam, I need an ink pen. You got any?" "Got some in the front hatch," replies Young. "You got a lot of pens. Can I have some?" "No, buy your own and shut up," is Young's answer.

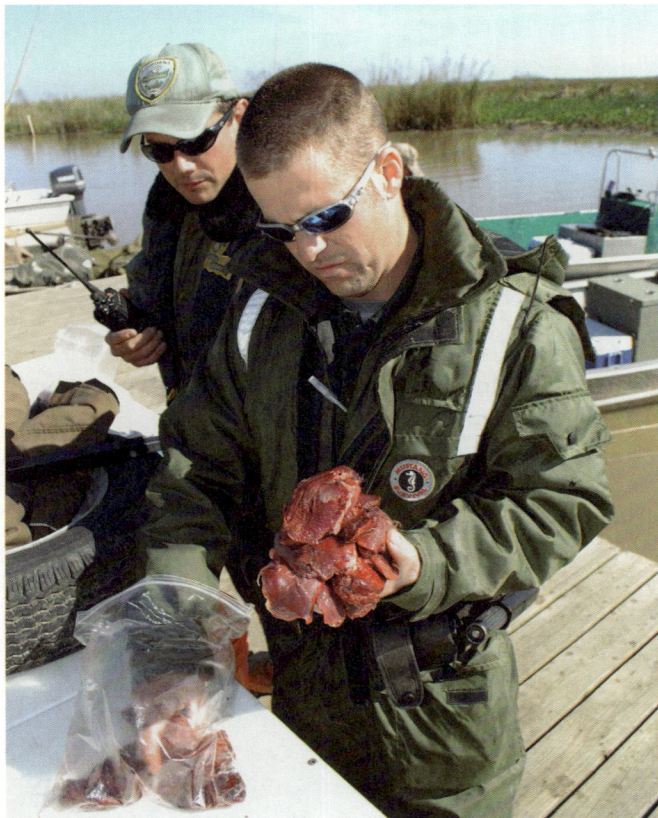

Young and Keller again have to count cleaned duck breasts at a camp-site.

Keller glances at me and explains, "When you are working twelve-hour shifts, you gotta amuse yourself somehow."

Trying to change the subject, Young repeats his earlier statement. "I love to dig," adding, "you ought to see me on a big double-rig shrimp boat."

"When you can get on," pipes in Keller.

Young groans audibly. "I didn't fall off getting on; I fell off getting off."

"You should have seen him—he looked just like a spider monkey hanging off that big tire bumper on the stern of that trawler," Keller cheerfully explains for my benefit.

Young grins good-naturedly and concentrates on his boat driving.

22

BRAKEDOWN

I called Sergeant Guy Adams the day before I was supposed to meet him. His reluctance to schedule the trip for today, a Tuesday, was apparent in his voice. I spot his truck parked next to the old railroad station, which is now the office of the Amite Police Department. I hop out of my truck and pull his passenger door open.

Holy Cow! Top Gun! I'm riding with Top Gun! Adams is the spitting image of the actor Tom Cruise in one of his short haircuts. The only give-away is eye color. Adams's are brown, Cruise's are green. I climb in the truck and we set out. He cautions me again that today is likely to be boring. Weekends are a lot busier, he explains. Little does he suspect what the evening holds.

As he heads northwest to check on deer hunting activity, Adams talks about his background. Although he now lives in Watson, in Livingston Parish, he originally hailed from Larose, in Lafourche Parish, where his grandfather was a game warden. He spent as much time as possible in the outdoors while growing up, hunting and fishing.

He first became attracted to the job when his best friend, Chuck Comeaux, who was a game warden in Lafourche Parish, took him out on a boat ride after he got a special agent's commission. On that very first ride, Comeaux had to chase a fleeing suspect. His thoughts, he says, were, "Man, this is cool." So, he applied for a game warden's job and left college before finishing his degree in criminal justice.

In his over thirteen years, he has moved around a good bit, something most game wardens don't do once they start work in an area. After three years in Lafourche Parish, he transferred to St. James Parish, where he stayed one year. Then he worked for two years with the Statewide Strike Force before finally settling down in Livingston Parish. He was trying to get closer to his girlfriend, he explains, as he flashes a grin.

Today, in northern Tangipahoa Parish, he will spend most of his time

Guy Adams expresses concerns that the weekday patrol will be uneventful.

slowly cruising through big blocks of timber company land looking for hunting activity. He plans to set up on a likely looking vehicle if he can find one and wait for the hunter to come out after dark, when he will check him for compliance. "I can't check someone for their license unless they are in the act of hunting," he explains.

"Deer hunters typically go in the woods at around 3:30 p.m. and hunt till dark," he goes on. "I like to let them get in their stands before setting up. If you show up too early and they see you, they will tag an untagged deer and otherwise behave different than if they don't know you are there." It's 3:45 p.m. now.

At some gated entrances to tracts of land, Adams fishes through an ob-scenely large wad of keys to find the right one. The keys, he explains, are given to them by the timber companies because they like having game war-dens patrol their lands. Not a soul is to be seen hunting.

Timber companies provide keys to game wardens because they want their presence on their properties.

As he putters up and down the timber company roads, he says that much of what a game warden schedules is based on weather. "If the night is clear and cold, the deer will be out and so will the night hunters. If it is hot or driving rain, the animals don't move."

He moves across the line into St. Helena Parish, the most rural of the Florida Parishes. The scenery is bucolic, with the landscape dotted with barns and sprinkled with beef cattle grazing contentedly on bright green rye grass fields. Mixed with the barns are modest houses and lots of churches. "Pretty land," Adams calls it.

On a small road, he finally passes a hunter's parked truck. "This is interesting," he says as he backs up. His game warden's eye misses no detail. "This guy is in law enforcement. He's got a jacket hanging in the window— probably for a reason. Let's find out why."

He radios LDWF Dispatch and requests a POS on the plates of the truck. While he waits for the reply, he looks over the vehicle and what he can see of its contents thoroughly. "I always look on the seats. If you see hunter orange there, chances are that he left it. A poorly kept up vehicle also attracts my attention," he says.

The call comes back that the owner of the truck has purchased all the licenses that he needs for deer hunting. He deems the truck not worth setting up on and moves on.

His next stop is at a deer camp. It is near dusk and everyone is in the woods hunting. Adams saunters into the skinning shed and checks out the board that records everyone's kills. "I see that one hunter here has two deer down for one day, a buck and a little bitty fifty-five-pound doe." The handwriting for the two entries is different, which raises Adams's suspicions that both deer may not have been validated. The law requires that all deer kills be validated by a telephone call within seventy-two hours of the kill.

He takes notes on the palm of his hand with an ink pen, something that a lot of game wardens seem to do, then returns to the truck to call Dispatch to make sure the kills were validated. They were. Everything is going too well. Maybe it is going to be an uneventful evening after all.

"A few people leave this job after they graduate from the academy because it's not what they expect," he explains. "It can be very boring at times. It's either boring or very exciting—balls to the wall."

He leaves the club and continues to poke around the pine plantations on small timber company roads. "Deer clubs vary," he says. "Some are shaky, like the one we just left. Others are self-policing and will even report their own members for violations. Those clubs feel that they have an interest in the resource and are not likely to shoot just anything or tolerate a violation."

He avoids traveling into the heart of the hunting leases, trying to be respectful of the hunters. "I would rather not check a hunter in his stand unless I know that he is unlicensed. A person works all year for two days a week in a stand. Hunting is expensive. I'm surprised if a person doesn't spend $5,000 a year to hunt. They buy corn, a four-wheeler [ATV], clothes, licenses, calls, gadgets, campers, and fuel. I would rather check them after they finish their hunt."

Adams pulls up behind an immaculate GMC Sierra pickup. "Now this is the kind of truck where you seldom find a violation. He moves on and checks out several more clubs. Nothing raises his suspicions, but he waits at one of them for a hunter to return from hunting. The surly hunter produces his licenses upon Adams's request. Again, everything is copacetic.

The first indication that the evening will be anything but ordinary is a call from Dispatch asking Adams if he knows anything about a tiger on the loose in the area he is working. He answers the call, looks at me, and rolls his eyes without saying a word.

Then, when he applies his brakes at a stop sign, a horrendous noise comes from the front end of the truck. It sounds as if the entire braking system has fallen apart and turned into gravel. In spite of being concerned, he continues his patrol, hoping that the sound will just go away.

It doesn't. It gets worse with each application of the brakes. Before setting up to watch for night hunters, Adams decides to duck into Greensburg for a basket of fried chicken livers. As bad as the brakes sounded before, they are worse when he stops at the diner.

Waiting for supper, he talks about job satisfaction. "If you like the outdoors, it don't get no better than this," he says. "I have a good boss and a flexible schedule and the pay is good. It has come a long ways since I started. Best of all is the freedom of the job. I like not having someone with a thumb over my head. Here, you are trusted to use your discretion."

As he munches on his livers, he says that the game wardens in his district have a good rapport with the sheriffs' offices in Tangipahoa, St. Helena, and Livingston. Especially Livingston, he emphasizes. "Livingston is getting so urbanized that you can't even shoot a gun at night without someone calling it in.

"Still," he goes on, "we only catch a fraction of the violations. Even with the sheriff's office cooperating, more times than not you get it handed to you.

"A game warden has to learn to live with that," he explains. "You have to treat it like a game. If you play a lot you will lose some. I don't take it personal. Ten years ago I might have, but not now."

As we leave the chicken place, the truck's front end utters the most gawdawful grinding scream. Just outside of Greensburg, warning indicators light up the truck's dash like a Christmas tree. It sounds mortally wounded. He calls his region captain, Len Yokum, for instructions and is told to bring the truck down to Hammond, in the lower part of Tangipahoa Parish, to swap it out for another.

He starts the thirty-four-mile run. Before he gets to I-55, Dispatch radios with a complaint about shots being fired in a rural area north of Albany. The laid-back Guy Adams disappears and his predatory alter ego comes to life. He wants to get there—fast.

Then the brakes fail entirely.

When he realizes that it is impossible for him to respond, he calls Senior Agent Buck Hampton, another game warden on duty in the immediate area, to get him to respond. The cell phone cuts out. He redials and starts talking. The cell phone cuts out again. "Some nights nothing works," he mutters as he redials.

After sending Hampton, he climbs the truck onto the interstate and heads south. "Hold on!" he directs, adding that if he encounters a traffic problem he will take to the ditch before endangering other drivers. Barreling down an interstate highway at night in a truck with no brakes is an interesting experience.

Before exiting from I-55 onto I-12, his cell phone rings. "Hampton got 'em!" he exclaims. Adams is excited and smells action. "We need to get there as soon as possible. He has detained three suspects and will need help in interrogating them separately." He adds that dealing with multiple armed violators in the dark is best done by more than one game warden.

As he swings onto I-12, he discovers that he can get something resembling brakes, enough to slow down the truck's momentum, by vigorously pumping the brake pedal. It isn't a long way to the replacement truck now.

When he gets there, Yokum has the driver's door swung open and ready to go. Grabbing a few essentials, Adams bounces from one truck to the other and takes off. The excitement in the air is palpable.

Realizing that he forgot his fuel card in the other truck, he calls Yokum on his cell phone. The captain decides to join in the action, as well as bring Adams' card. In the dark, the location is difficult to find from the directions he has gotten. He calls the complainant and gets better directions. Yokum catches up with Adams and the two appear on the scene at once.

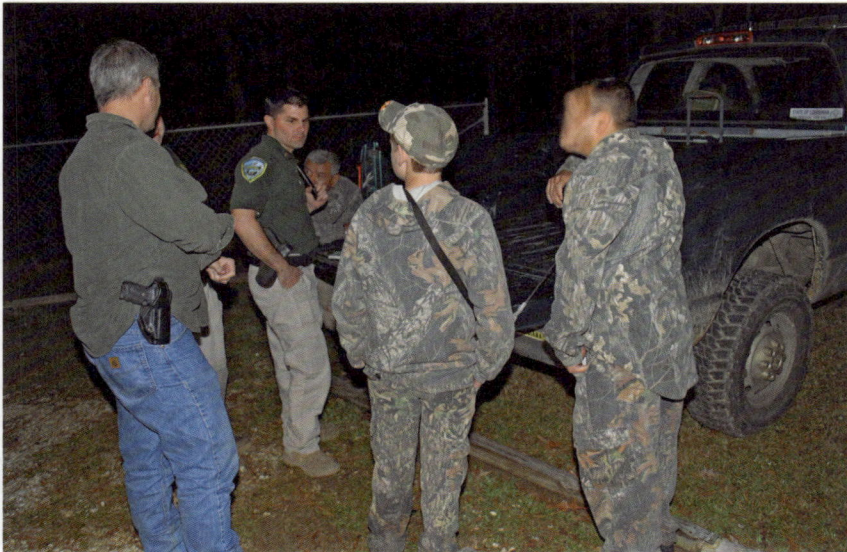

When Adams (c) and Len Yokum (l) arrive, Buck Hampton has the three night hunters detained.

Hampton has two adult males and a thirteen-year-old boy at the rear of his truck. He explains to Adams and Yokum that when he got there all three of the subjects were on an ATV searching in the woods for what they had shot. The middle-aged subject claimed that they had shot at a fox with the .270 caliber, scoped rifle now laying on the tailgate of Hampton's truck. He vigorously, and with a straight face, protested that the three were innocent of any wrongdoing.

Immediately the game wardens separate, each with a subject, and begin questioning them to hear if their stories hold any discrepancies. After questioning and huddling, Yokum and Adams go into the woods on foot with their flashlights while Hampton watches the subjects.

Ten minutes later a single light starts bobbing its way back to the four men. Yokum is holding the light and Adams has a freshly killed doe draped over his shoulders and an "I gotcha" grin on his face.

Yokum takes charge. "Here's the way it is. From this point on, anyone that lies to us is going to jail." The youngster's eyes open wide in alarm. Adams pipes up, "We aren't stupid. You don't shoot a fox with a .270 and then put three people on a four-wheeler to go get a ten-pound animal."

A pregnant silence follows. "What's the story?" asks Yokum. The middle-aged man confesses that he shot the deer. He says that the other two are

Adams emerges from the dark woods with a dead doe over his shoulders.

innocent. The older man is his father, here from Mexico to visit him. The youngster, he says, is the son of his best friend who died. "I am teaching him how to hunt."

The last statement is more than Yokum can bear. He verbally rips into the man for teaching the youngster to hunt illegally at night. The boy begins to sob, and while Adams and Hampton begin to write the ticket Yokum takes the youngster aside.

"Am I going to jail?" asks the distraught boy.

"No," Yokum replies. Then, in a comforting but firm voice he tells the

Yokum takes a moment to teach the sobbing thirteen-year-old boy a lesson in obeying the law.

boy that he should learn a lesson from this. "This is serious business and it's dangerous." He adds that lying to police officers really makes them angry. The youngster stops sobbing, but is still upset.

The thirty-seven-year-old is ticketed with hunting deer during illegal hours and contributing to the delinquency of a minor.

The deer is donated to feed other youngsters at the Lighthouse Ranch for Boys in Loranger.

23

WILD HOGS, UGLY DOGS, BIG KNIVES

As I cross over the Mississippi River bridge out of Concordia Parish in the darkness, an endless loop of images that I have seen that day plays through my mind—rough men carrying big knives, piles of dead hogs, young girls splattered with blood, mud-filled boots, and dogs—lots of dogs, some of them wearing armor.

My mind flashes back to meeting Senior Agent Frank Mason III before daylight in Ferriday. . . . I have no idea what to expect. As he steps out of his truck, I see that Mason, who answers to the nickname "Trey," is tall and lean at six feet, two inches and 185 pounds.

He is only twenty-five years old, but I see that he wears his hair cut on the long side. Most young game wardens seem partial to low-maintenance buzz cuts. His flashing brown eyes are as hard to miss in the overhead lights as his eagle-like nose. When he speaks to greet me, however, it is with an easy-going, almost gentle voice. Today, he says, he is scheduled to work during a managed hog hunt on Three Rivers Wildlife Management Area and the adjacent Red River WMA.

A Honda Rancher 420 ATV rides in the bed of his pickup, and the truck is pulling a trailer with a fifteen-foot aluminum flatboat powered by a twenty-five-horsepower Mercury outboard. He seems ready for anything. The boat, he explains, is to be used to check out a complaint about illegal net use.

He expects to spend most of the day, however, checking hog hunters for compliance with permit requirements and checking ATVs for proper tire size and proper use. On WMAs, ATVs may only be taken off ATV trails to retrieve downed animals and their riders must be weaponless.

This the second year that LDWF has sanctioned a two-week season in February on the two WMAs to reduce feral hog populations. "River country is overrun with hogs," he explains. "They tear up the land and damage deer habitat."

Mason makes small talk as he guides his truck down Highway 15 along the Mississippi River levee through Deer Park. "I grew up around game wardens and knew that it was the ultimate job. I wanted to make a living hunting and fishing. I just loved it so much I wanted to be around it all the time.

"I majored in criminal justice at the University of Louisiana–Monroe and got hired three and a half years ago. Right now, catching someone shooting a deer at night is as much fun as hunting for deer."

The huge Mississippi River levee is on the left, but the table-flat terrain on the right is heavily farmed row crop land broken by pieces of bottom-land hardwood forest.

"The economy of this parish is heavily oriented around farming," explains Mason. "The farmers do okay, but you would be surprised by the money that hunters bring into the economy. This is trophy deer country, and hunting leases cost $20 to $25 an acre.

"Lots of dollars also come in from hunters who hunt on the 70,000 acres of wildlife management areas and the 8,000-acre federal Bayou Cocodrie Wildlife Refuge. Hunting is a big industry here."

Inside the boundaries of the Red River WMA, Mason spots Lieutenant Russ Kiser on the levee checking a burly hog hunter. The man is accompanied by two rough-looking blotched and spotted Catahoula cur dogs and a scarred-up pit bulldog that looks like a walking sledgehammer.

It begins to drizzle. The two game wardens drive their trucks further into the WMA and stop at its headquarters building to check in with the WMA technicians.

They are followed into the building by a tall, angular, bearded hog hunter who is looking for a lost dog. He complains in disgust that besides losing this dog yesterday, the first day of the season, his best dog was cut up by a hog too badly to hunt today.

Over a cup of steaming coffee, I chat with the thirty-two-year-old Kiser, an eleven-year veteran and one of the youngest lieutenants in the state. Kiser is a medium-sized man, with a round, pink face, a shaved scalp, and a sweet, cherubic smile.

He explains that he was going to school at Northwestern State University to be a biologist when a job as a student worker at the local LDWF Enforcement office attracted him to law enforcement. He shifted his aspirations when he realized that a biologist might work ten years before seeing the results of his work. "With enforcement, you see the results immediately every day you work. Even if you don't write a ticket, if people see a game warden's truck it results in deterrence."

With a grin he adds, "This job is fun. You get paid to ride on four-wheelers; you get paid to ride in boats." Then, he quickly adds, "But it's not all fun and games. Today, I can be on a high after making a big case, then tomorrow I might get a call to recover a twelve-year-old who drowned in a borrow pit."

Kiser shifts his attention to Mason, his co-patroller today. It turns out that Mason has a pedigree in the LDWF Enforcement Division. He is a member of the well-known Tarver clan, which has contributed many family members to fish and wildlife enforcement. Mason's uncle was the noted Junior Tarver, who became captain of the region. Older cousin Joey Tarver and younger cousin LeRoy Tarver are currently active game wardens in the region. To top it off, another cousin, John Tarver, is a federal game warden.

"Trey's mother was a Tarver, so he doesn't carry the name. So we just call him 'Tarver Lite,'" Kiser says with his superficially innocent but mischievous smile.

The modest Mason admits to a certain amount of pride in belonging to the family.

Trey Mason comes from a whole family of Louisiana game wardens.

As soon as the rain stops, the two game wardens launch their small boat in a borrow pit, where a complainant has reported the presence of illegal nets, likely set for white perch.

Once in the location where the nets were reported, Kiser lowers a metal drag hook on the end of a rope and drags it slowly behind the boat, hoping to snag the hidden nets. As he searches, he notes several places near the waterline on trees where ropes, probably from the offending nets, had been cut.

After forty-five minutes of dragging fruitlessly for the nets, Kiser resignedly says, "They must've picked them up. I passed a truck on the way here that fit the description provided by the complainant. We probably missed them by hours."

As he slowly runs the boat back to where it was launched, his eyes scan the banks of the water body. "I hate that," he says with disgust while pointing at several discarded garbage bags. Like most game wardens, he is sensitive to litter.

After dropping the boat and trailer off at WMA headquarters, Mason

Russ Kiser drags the bottom of a borrow pit on the WMA in an attempt to locate an illegal net that has been reported to be in the spot.

heads south to check hog hunters, who seem to be everywhere. Several days of rain have left the earth slimy-soft. Ahead, a big, black hog, obviously disturbed by all the hunting activity, humps out of the woods and over the Mississippi River levee.

Mason and Kiser patrol separately in their trucks but maintain regular contact with each other. Mason stops and chats with three women tending a gaggle of children while sitting in lawn chairs on a utility trailer parked on the river levee.

To Mason's great amusement a pair of young boys, ages six and seven, importune him to take their mother to jail. Their grievance is that she insisted that the youngsters stay with her rather than run with the men in the woods hunting hogs with their dogs.

Mason checks two more family groups of hog hunters. In each group ten- or twelve-year-old kids and their mothers hunted as actively (and were as muddy and bloody) as the men.

Three Rivers WMA has just as much hunting activity as does Red River WMA. At the campground a group of nearly twenty people, hunters and their families, are eating breakfast in a compound of tents and travel trailers.

Dead hogs are everywhere in their camp—piled on trailers and strapped on ATVs. Smallish brindle curs and baleful bulldogs eye Mason as he checks the hunters' licenses and permits. Most of the men carry large, sheathed, wicked-looking variations of bowie knives that they use to stick the pigs (pig stickers) their dogs have caught.

One of the hunters questions Mason about why LDWF seems to want hogs exterminated on the WMAs. Mason replies that the department's biologists feel that they are severely overpopulated. "There are too many of them. They are a nuisance, even though they are good eating. The problem is that you don't get just one hog; you get the whole family. Deer hunters complain that hogs ruin their hunts."

The hog hunter listens quietly while Mason goes on. "They tear up the ground and damage the river levee. They kill vegetation and they compete with deer for food."

The young hog hunter ambles away without argument but shaking his head. He is obviously unconvinced.

Everywhere Mason goes it seems like dogs can be heard frantically baying, mixed with the echoes of their masters' whoops in the woods.

Mason stops at one group of men, women, and kids. They have bagged

The six- and seven-year-old boys finally get to go on a hunt later in the day.

a couple of hogs, but much of the party is still hunting. He notices that the group's ATV is missing and inquires as to whether it is being used right now to retrieve a downed hog or for hunting.

Mason backs his ATV off of his truck and runs to the general area of hunting activity. He quickly sees ATV tracks going into an overgrown open field.

He finds the fourteen-year-old operator with a loaded .22 caliber rifle.

Women and children hunt hogs alongside the men.

Dead hogs are piled up everywhere at the Red River WMA campground.

Mason uses his ATV to run down a hunter's suspected illegal off-trail use of a four-wheeler.

The boy readily admits that he is hunting. Mason directs him to unload the weapon and follow him back to the vehicles.

There, he warns the young man and his mother that what the youngster has done is a ticketable offense. She is obviously expecting a citation. When Mason leaves her with just a warning not to use the ATV off-trail for anything but retrieving downed animals, she profusely thanks him.

As he drives to his next stop, Mason explains why he let them go with a warning. "I tend to be lenient and the kid was only fourteen. But two things will upset me. One is when I am lenient and someone spits in my face. The other is being lied to."

And so the day goes. Mason jumps from group to group, with only an occasional lone hunter in the mix. Families, families, families, everywhere. Hog hunting seems to be a social activity that involves all ages and both genders.

Most notable are the dogs, a remarkable assemblage of Catahoula curs, blackmouth curs, brindle curs, and just general all-round curs of undecipherable lineage. Mixed with them are the catch dogs, the hammer-headed pit bull and bulldog crosses, some with varying amounts of Catahoula cur in them. All the catch dogs are girded in heavy leather or ballistic vests.

Many of the dogs carry wicked scars on their heads and bodies inflicted by the razor-sharp canine teeth, called "tushes" or "tusks," that both sexes of mature hogs sport.

The only distinguishing and uniform characteristic of the dogs is that most uninitiated people would consider them ugly—U.G.L.Y. Hog dogs truly are working dogs—exactly the opposite of their fat, glossy, and smug canine cousins pampered and babied by city folks.

As the day's shadows get longer, the hog hunters begin loading up to go home and Mason turns his truck north. On the ride he chats about his work.

"I'm big on drugs. They kill people from the inside. It changes who they are and demoralizes them. I blame much of the poverty I see on drugs.

"But I don't want to be a narc, trapped in a patrol car all the time, dealing with bad people. I love being outdoors, so I'm a game warden.

"I know I will be in law enforcement until the day I die—that's a fact. I have a passion for it. Just talking about it, I get pumped up. I want to see people get what they deserve."

He drives in silence for a while in the descending darkness before speaking up again. "My favorite thing to do is to catch night hunters. That feeling,

Hog dogs seem to come in all shapes and colors, but are always lean and agile.

when you see the shot. Wow! Amazing! I can't describe the feeling of excitement. I can't get to them quick enough.

"I shake all over. I can hardly breathe. I am so anxious to get to them. At the same time, my mind is going nine hundred different directions. Are they going to run from me? Are they going to shoot at me?"

He rides the rest of the way back to Ferriday in silence.

24

SPINNING YARNS

As I drive into Chalmette to meet the three game wardens I am going to spend the day with, a horrible sense of melancholy washes over me. I have been here several times since Hurricane Katrina blasted the communities of St. Bernard Parish into oblivion, but the feeling of dystopian loss and despair has never gripped me as it does now.

Almost three and a half years after the storm, the scene is still post-apocalyptic. What were once thriving middle-class suburban neighborhoods are now fields of concrete slabs, interspersed with the gutted shells of homes that have not yet been restored and punctuated with the occasional home or cluster of homes that optimistic owners have rehabilitated to pre-storm conditions.

Before Katrina decimated it, Chalmette had become the last intact community of refugees from the white working-class neighborhoods once located on the downtown side of Canal Street in New Orleans. In Chalmette, "Yat" was still spoken, and many of the old New Orleans customs that were part of making the city unique were preserved.

The Katrina-induced Chalmatian diaspora has strewn the culture in fragments across the face of southeastern Louisiana and southern Mississippi. The words of the Australian novelist Delia Falconer echo in my head, "We don't need to know the way home."

I turn my truck toward the corner of Paris Road and West Judge Perez Drive to meet Sergeant Scot Keller. Keller, a forty-one-year-old, thirteen-year LDWF law enforcement professional, introduces me to two younger agents, thirty-two-year-old Robert Cossé and thirty-year-old Jason Gernados. Both hold the rank of senior agent.

Gernados, who goes by the name of "Jay," was in his fifth year of college in pursuit of a degree in education when a game warden's slot opened up in St. Bernard Parish, right were he wanted to work. He says that he has never regretted the decision to leave school for the job in the eight years that he has been with LDWF. "There is never a day that I say I don't want to go to work." In his time off, he pursues fishing with a passion as great as the one he has for his work.

He is slender in build and his jet black hair, flashing brown eyes, and dark complexion give away his Filipino heritage through his paternal grandfather. Carrying a big, shy smile, he is remarkably quiet, never expressing his view until everybody else has spoken first.

That means Cossé always speaks first. A big guy with the massive sloping shoulders of a heavy-weight boxer, Cossé produces a constant stream of one-liners and pithy observations on whatever subject is being discussed. Everyone seems to enjoy his company, but Gernados seems to be especially amused by Cossé's loquaciousness. He scrutinizes the big guy closely, as if he wants to be sure not to miss the next humorous observation he makes.

Carrying the nickname "Boozie" since childhood in Plaquemines Parish, Cossé still lives there and carries a deep affection for the parish. He began his eight-year-old career as a game warden in an unusual fashion. The department was looking for someone with a master's license to operate its big, sixty-five-foot offshore enforcement boat.

Cossé had the license and the experience and accepted the job, patrolling offshore waters between the Texas and Mississippi state lines, looking for fisheries violations. He loved it, never getting tired of being on the water.

But in 2005 the decision was made to sell the expensive-to-operate patrol boat and Cossé moved into a regular game warden's job. Now married, the schedule of the job he now holds is probably better for a family man than the one he had on the offshore boat. Still, it's hard to miss the note of nostalgia in his voice when he reminisces about his days offshore.

The first order of business, announces Keller, is that he must donate an ice chest of drum, sheepshead, and redfish, which were seized from illegal recreational fishermen by game wardens the previous day.

The department has very strict procedures, with a detailed paper trail, for the disposal of illegally taken fish and wildlife that has been seized in conjunction with a case. Fisheries products seized from commercial fishing activities are sold and the proceeds held until the case is disposed. Other fish and wildlife must be donated to needy people or to recognized charitable groups.

Often this is more difficult than it sounds. The most needy people may be the least able or even the least willing to clean game and fish for preparation for the table. Today, Keller has people in mind that he knows are willing and able to clean fish. The recipients are an elderly brother and sister living

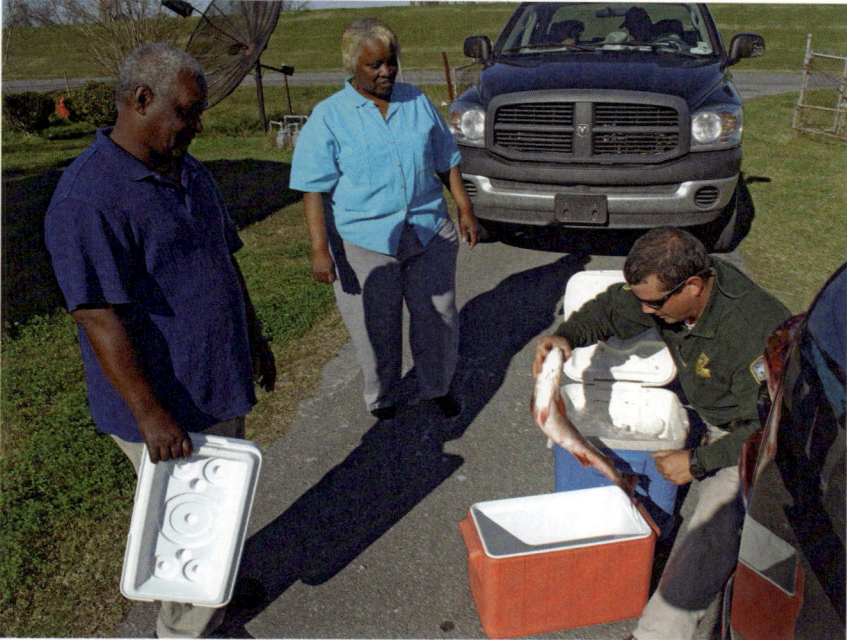

The first thing that the game wardens must do is donate to a needy family illegally taken fish which were seized the previous day.

in Braithwaite on a fixed income and caring for their ninety-three-year-old father. Keller is received at their home like Santa Claus.

That task done, he proceeds to rendezvous with Gernados and Cossé for a late lunch. It's unlikely that the agents will get a chance to eat again until after their shift ends at midnight. While they wait for their order, Keller explains, with commentary by Cossé, the structure of rank within the Enforcement Division of the Louisiana Department of Wildlife and Fisheries. By the time they finish, what seemed byzantine before is quite simple and understandable.

Each of the state's sixty-four parishes has two to five game wardens assigned to it. The agents carry the rank of cadet, agent, senior agent, or sergeant, with only one sergeant being allowed per parish. The rank of cadet is held by every agent for at least the first year, which is comprised of six months in the academy and six months of close work with an experienced game warden, called his field training officer or FTO.

If all goes well up to this stage, the cadet will be promoted to the rank of agent, which the individual will also hold for at least one year. The first two years of a game warden's career are considered to be a probationary period. Only then, if all goes well, does the individual move off of probation and become a senior agent.

Senior agent rank is often held for many years, as promotion to sergeant can call for some luck and flexibility as well as job proficiency. A senior agent working beneath a very young sergeant may not find an opening for promotion until the sergeant himself gets promoted or transfers elsewhere, unless he is willing to transfer to another parish or unit or is competitive enough to apply for an opening at the lieutenant level. Transferring is rare.

The staffs of two or three parishes are organized into a district, headed by a lieutenant. In turn, two to three districts are organized into a region, which is headed by a captain. While game wardens within a region will often work outside of their district, especially in response to a request for help from another district, it is at the district level where most game wardens work and patrol routinely.

The duties of lieutenants require them to divide their time between office work and field work. The position of captain is almost entirely administrative, and only occasionally do captains get to make forays into the field.

The nine regions of the state are divided into two groups, with each region reporting to a major. Both majors report to a lieutenant colonel, who, in turn, reports to the colonel, the highest rank within the agency.

After eating, the men tow two boats powered by surface drive mud motors to a primitive boat landing near White's Ditch in East Plaquemines Parish. Their intent is to patrol an area where they have received a complaint about illegal deer hunting by trespassers. When they top the levee, the sight that greets their eyes isn't pretty.

The launch is most accurately described as rubble embellished by debris that has been arranged and rearranged by hurricanes. The sight is made worse by an extraordinarily low tide, which exposes black mudflats and even more debris that is normally (and mercifully) hidden by water.

The canal (if the ditch can be dignified with the name) away from the levee holds only four to six inches of water and untold feet of stinking, sulfurous black mud that has been deposited in it successively by Hurricanes Katrina, Gustav, and Ike. The latter two storms ravaged the area within the last six months.

The area is, or at least was, a freshwater marsh. But the storms have burned the salt-susceptible freshwater vegetation to a mushy mess and deposited its remains high in the skeletons of the few willow and live oak trees

The freshwater marsh near Oak River has been decimated by three successive hurricanes.

of the area. Everywhere, everywhere, is just black mud, spotted with shocks of more resistant brown grasses or windrow piles of dead vegetation. The smell of the mud that the motors turn up as they churn down the canal is of rotten eggs.

All during the long run down the canal to Oak River, not a living thing moves. Not even blackbirds or nutria, those large, ubiquitous marsh rodents that can be found anywhere in south Louisiana, are present.

The three game wardens quickly find the hunting camp that they want to visit. They are greeted by four men and two boys. The men are watching football playoffs on TV and cooking. The boys are doing what boys do at camps—getting into everything.

The men give the three wardens an earful about the reported individual's nefarious activities. The wildlife agents listen sympathetically and, after looking at some hunting photos with the men, chug back into Oak River and proceed southeastward before stopping to confer.

"I sure would like to get this guy," says Keller, adding, "He's a known violator, but he has influence in the parish." Gernados is familiar with the man as well and comments that he has the reputation of having a bad temper. Cossé's comment is characteristic of his bluff and confident temperament,

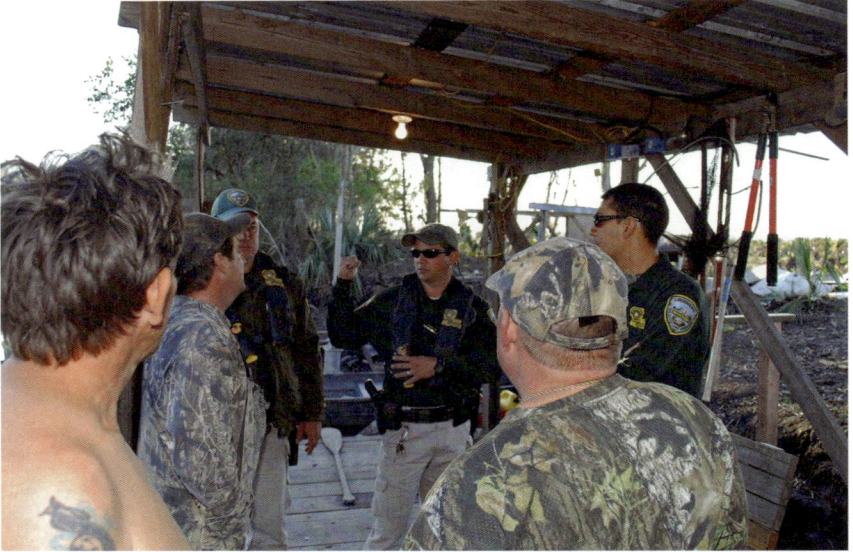

The three game wardens (left to right, Robert "Boozie" Cossé, Scot Keller, and Jason Gernados) listen sympathetically to the men's complaints about illegal hunting.

"We can jack him up." They discuss in general terms some possible strategies for catching the outlaw.

With daylight ebbing, the men decide to drift with the wind in Oak River with their boats side by side and listen for any after-hours shooting. Today is the last day of duck season.

It doesn't look like good duck country. This end of Oak River, unlike the parts of the river in the salt marshes, which are more resilient in the face of the saline storm surges of Gustav and Ike, is just as desolate-looking as the area the men came through earlier.

As they drift, they begin telling stories of interesting times on patrol. Cossé, a raconteur's raconteur, goes first.

"I was on patrol in the sixty-five-foot offshore patrol boat near Grand Isle. Some other agents in a smaller boat had stopped a king mackerel fisherman, but couldn't make contact with Dispatch to check on the rules to know if a federal violation had occurred. They had to run closer to shore to make contact.

"It turns out that it was a good license violation, so they contacted me and Ray Champagne on the big boat to be on the alert for the boat, an old shrimp boat converted to a king mackerel boat. We found the boat, boarded

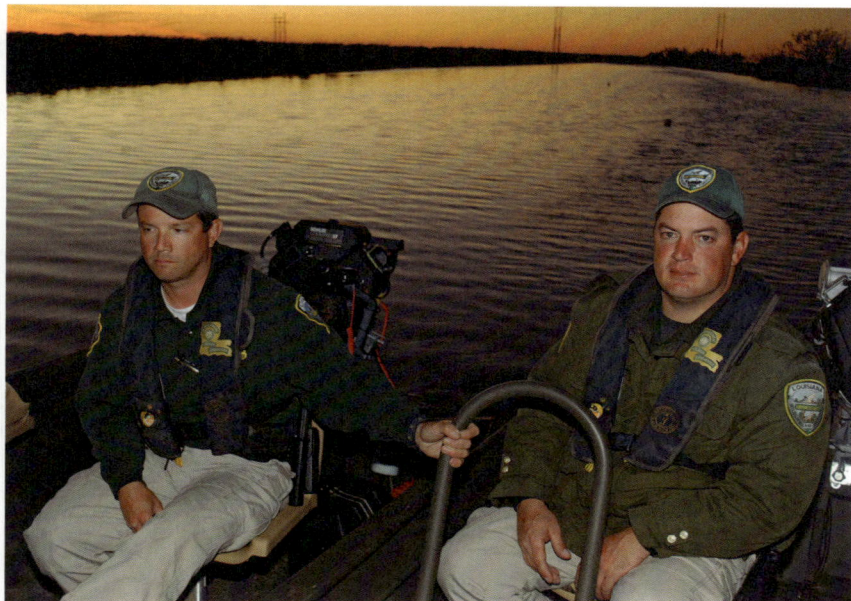

As the two boats drift down Oak River, Keller (l) and Cossé (r) listen for gunshots and begin to spin yarns.

it, and informed him that we were going to write him a citation. We told him that we were going to escort him in and that his catch would be seized. Neither of us stayed on the boat.

"While following the subject in, we noticed that he was starting to take fish out of his icebox. We told him to stop, and he said that he was just cleaning the icebox. The next thing you know, he was throwing them overboard.

"I got on the P.A. and told him to stop, but he wouldn't. I pushed in to get close enough to get my partner on the boat, but the skipper of the boat ran to the throttle and turned his boat into a hard circle and kept it there, running wide open. That boat could really turn in a hard radius.

"It was really hard to track him in that tight circle, running as fast as he was. Finally, Ray jumped on his boat and tackled him on the deck. He subdued and handcuffed him behind his back while the boat was still running in circles. When Ray went to the throttles, the subject jumped through his handcuffs so they were in front of him and went back to throwing fish overboard.

"Ray came out of the cabin and we placed him under arrest and cuffed him to a belly belt and put a life jacket over his head. After all that, the guy kept asking, 'Why are you doing this?' His two helpers on the boat sat there inert the whole time.

"We still had enough fish left to make the case. He paid a hell of a fine, from what I hear.

"I called Ray 'Jackie Chan' after that. He put a Hulk Hogan move on him."

Gernados, who has been listening to and watching Cossé in bemusement, says, "You gotta be a little silly to do this job."

Cossé responds, "You gotta be a little crazy to go into the woods after guys with guns."

"It's not the people with the guns," the way Keller sees it. "It's the toll on your body that comes from working in boats. You are constantly pounding. And the sun damage. . . . This job has different dangers than what road deputies are subjected to."

Cossé, as usual, has an answer. "Yeah, but that's one of the good things. You are constantly exposed to different kinds of activities."

Gernados brings up the scariest time he has had in his career.

"Mike Garrity and I were on the way back home from patrol in our truck. We passed over a little canal in St. Bernard Parish when I spotted a light up the canal. I suggested that we turn the truck around and listen for shots. We U-turned, hid the truck, and walked to the canal, which was bordered by woods. We began to hear shots spaced every few minutes apart. They were night hunting.

"It was pretty cold as we waited for them, hidden in the woods. They were hunting from pirogues and you could hear them talk as they got closer. When they got out of their pirogues, one of the hunters unloaded the magazine of his semi-automatic .22 caliber rifle by firing into the woods that we here hiding in.

"We hugged the biggest trees possible. I was scared, so scared. I could hear the bullets hitting all around us. They had rabbits and nutria, and we cited them for hunting after legal hours."

Not to be outdone, Cossé regales the men with a story of the funniest thing that has happened in his career.

"Me and Adam Young were working out of a truck, checking spots in Plaquemines Parish where people fish off the bank. We came over the levee by the pumping station in Home Place and noticed a vehicle, but couldn't see anybody. When we pulled close, I saw a guy up in the marsh waving his arms.

"We parked the truck and walked to the subject. He was stuck in the mud up to his waist, I mean really up to his waist. He was a slender male. Adam, joking around, says, 'You look like you are as much in trouble as a one-legged man in an ass-kicking contest.'

"The guy laughed and said, 'It's funny you say that, I really only have one leg.' Adam was so embarrassed. He apologized over and over again. The guy said, 'Man, I ain't worried about that; just get me outta this mud.'

"Adam couldn't budge him. He was really stuck. So I grabbed him and pulled. But he started yelling, 'Hold on, my leg is coming off.' He had a pros-thesis leg. We had to dig it out of the mud.

"When we got him out, the guy was so happy. 'God bless y'all. You saved my life,' he said. He was really stuck. If we hadn't come along, there is no telling how long he would have been there, at least overnight."

The sun slides over the horizon and the western sky lights up in a fiery orange color. The men decide to head back to the landing to put their boats into storage and stake out some possible night hunting spots.

Cossé, in particular, is interested in sitting on a spot in his truck further south, near East Pointe a la Hache, from where he has heard some gunshots. He lives on the west bank of the Mississippi River immediately across from the area.

When Cossé nears the spot, he douses the truck's lights and crosses over

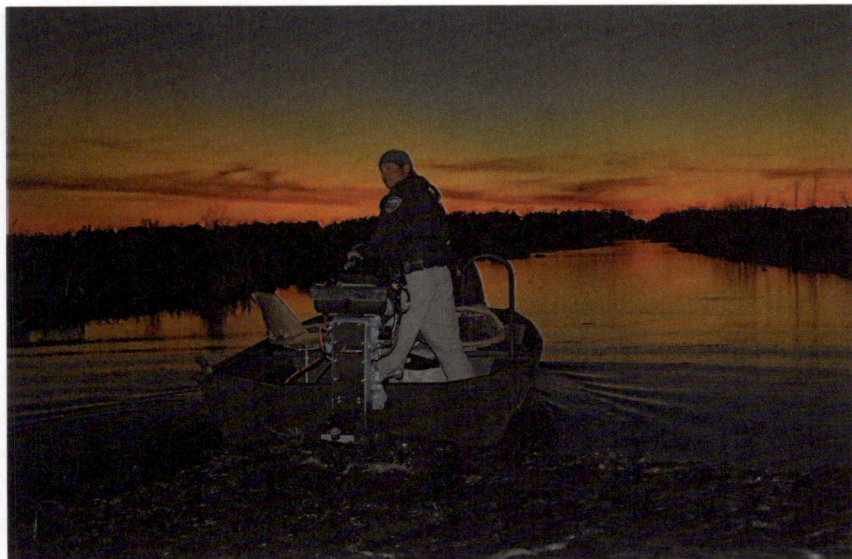

The brightly lit western sky signals the end of daylight.

the levee to the marsh and swamp side. He creeps along the base of the levee in the darkness until he finds a spot that he can hide the truck in, then backs into it.

He turns the engine off and rolls the windows down so that he can hear any shots. It's 7:40 p.m. Cossé will spend over three hours here sitting in the dark, as game wardens so often do, listening for the shot that will trigger him into action.

He passes the time in conversation. "Setting up on night hunters isn't so bad, unless you got mosquitoes; they will drive you crazy. Those are nights when you sit there with just tiny cracks in the windows." Tonight, there are no mosquitoes. It gets cold quickly.

"I like Plaquemines Parish," he muses. "It's hard to beat Venice. It's good for fishing; it's good for hunting. My family has lived here for generations. Dad is the captain of the Marine Division for the Plaquemines Parish Sheriff's Office."

Hearing some popping from the river side of the levee, Cossé eases his big frame out of the truck and slips up to the top of the levee so that he can hear and see better. When he returns, he confirms that the sounds are from someone firing off leftover holiday fireworks.

The night has its own beauty. Our side of the levee is enveloped in inky blackness. The lights of a busy working river reflect against low overhanging clouds on the other side. Periodically, the running lights of a grain vessel, container ship, or tanker float along over the top of the levee as the big ocean-going vessels ply up or down river.

Over it all, as if giving its quiet approval, hangs Venus, glittering like a diamond in the southwestern winter night's sky.

25

JUST ANOTHER DAY IN VENICE

Most game wardens are proud of the parish or area in which they work—the diversity of its natural resources, the people who use them, and the challenges that the people using the resources present. Sergeant Adam Young is no exception. He never seems to tire of talking about working in Plaquemines Parish. In his expressed view, it is one of the last places in Louisiana that still has a strong culture of living off of the land with no apologies to anyone.

Not tall, and slightly built, Young is an endless fount of enthusiasm. Today he is really wired up. He is going to meet his partner, Sergeant Villere Reggio III, in lower Plaquemines Parish to go on patrol in offshore federal waters. He glowingly describes snapper season and duck season as his favorite times of the year. Red snapper season has been open less than two weeks.

On the ride down Highway 23 from Belle Chasse, he explains that they will launch their big twenty-three-foot Boston Whaler in Venice and run out of Red Pass into West Bay and then further offshore from there. They expect to find plenty of double-rig offshore shrimp boats to check, as well as recreational and charter fishermen.

They plan to work offshore most of the day, then drop back to a choke point for boat traffic and intercept boats returning from the day's fishing. He is especially excited over the possibility of catching a particular charter captain, whom he stopped last week and ticketed for not having federal Reef Fish and Highly Migratory Species permits.

A reliable informant has told him that the charter captain has been bragging of having fooled the game warden by hiding fish that he had taken over the limit in the bean bag chairs that he carries for his customers to use in rough weather. Young hopes to intercept the same man, as he has information that he is still fishing without his permits. He wants to catch him twice in one week.

Even if he misses connecting with this charter boat, he expects the day to be productive. "The number of red snappers offshore this year is ridiculous," he says. "People are complaining that they can't catch mangrove snappers or groupers because red snappers grab the hook first."

He says that he and other game wardens have been making a lot of over-the-limit cases on red snappers, but very few are being made for undersized fish. "Everyone is catching solid twenty-five-inch fish."

The weather looks like it will cooperate, too. The forecast for today is for five- to ten-mile-per-hour winds from the southwest and seas of less than one foot. He tunes into the NOAA weather radio to see if anything has changed. It predicts seas of less than one foot out to twenty-two miles offshore. "I love it," he blurts after listening to the forecast. "Everybody is going to be out fishing."

The ride south from Belle Chasse is interesting. Under puffy cumulus clouds set against royal blue skies, Plaquemines Parish seems incredibly green. Cattle pastures give way to citrus groves until the road nears Port Sulphur. Below that point the destruction wrought by Hurricane Katrina becomes increasingly obvious.

The citrus groves are gone, and where houses were once nestled in live oak groves, mostly concrete slabs and a few gutted house shells can be seen among the skeletons of the dead trees. A few surviving trees are struggling mightily to put out new growth to replace what was stripped by the massive storm four years ago.

In spite of the presence of a few refurbished houses, most of the occupied residences are trailers. The crawl back to civilization will be slow.

After the two men meet, they pick up their boat from storage and head to the water world below Venice, a place that is truly more water than land. The boat is impressive, powered by twin three hundred-horsepower engines and a dazzling array of electronics. In addition to a GPS unit, the boat has radar, a satellite phone, and a forward-looking infrared (FLIR) unit.

At the marina, trucks and boat trailers are overflowing the big parking lot out onto the shoulder of the road. Young grins broadly, "This is a sign of a good day."

Reggio grins in reply. At five feet, eleven inches and 230 pounds, he is a bigger guy than Young and a lot less animated. Holding a B.S. in criminal justice with a minor in marine biology, he worked as a biologist with the department for nine years before transferring over to the Enforcement Division, where he has worked for the last five years.

Once out of the marina, Reggio scrambles the big boat up on a step and heads southwest out Little Red Pass. Lush green bullwhips, roseau canes, three-corner grass, and cattails whiz by as the boat skims the brown river water pouring down the pass.

In West Bay, the boat bangs head-on into modest groundswells driven by the southwest wind. The five-foot, six-inch Young stands in an athletic crouch beside the console, so that his knees absorb the jarring.

Without slowing, the boat passes the Green Monster, a huge oil and gas platform that houses a compressor station. The big platform is the anchor for dozens of small satellite well platforms, together known as the Sandy Point Rigs, one of the most famous speckled trout fishing spots in Louisiana.

The Green Monster sits squarely on the invisible line that divides federal and state waters. But the men have business further out and don't slow down here. Although the sky is clear and cornflower blue, the foghorns on the Sandy Point Rigs moan dolorously as the boat passes through the oilfield.

The officers cross a rip, the flotsam-filled, foamy dividing line between different water masses. Outside the rip, the water no longer shows the effects of muddy Mississippi River discharges. Instead, it's green and clear.

Beyond the rip, recreational fishing boats are tied at every oil and gas platform. The first boat they check is six and a half miles offshore. The agile Young does the boarding, while Reggio mans the controls. The two sport fishermen on the boat have one flounder between them and their first question of the wardens is where the fish are.

Four anglers are in the next boat. Again Young does the boarding, as he will the rest of the day. They are in the process of unhooking an undersized red snapper and a shark, both of which they release. They have several fish, one of which is a mangrove snapper that appears to be close to the legal minimum size. Young measures the fish, which makes the cut.

The game wardens bounce from boat to boat. Everyone is legal until they pull up to a boat with a surprised angler holding an obviously undersized grouper in one hand. He is legal at this stage. It isn't illegal to catch an undersized fish, just to retain one.

He releases the fish, but the concerned look on his face indicates that all may not be well. Young quickly boards the boat and immediately looks in the ice chest. He finds a good catch of mangrove snappers and red snappers. But he also finds a redfish and another undersized gag grouper.

Reggio holds the boat in standby mode while Young explains to the four anglers in the boat that redfish are illegal to possess in federal waters, even if they were legally caught in state waters on the way out. He issues a

Adam Young explains to the anglers that redfish may not be possessed in federal waters.

citation to one of the fishermen for the redfish and a warning for the under-sized grouper.

Back in the game wardens' boat, Young explains his reason for giving a hard ticket on the redfish and only issuing a warning for the undersized grouper. "We are not here to slam people on every little thing. We want to educate, too. But some things you can't ignore."

On the horizon, several large double-rig shrimp boats are working. After checking more recreational fishermen, the two wardens head in their direction. Boarding these big moving boats is going to be a lot different than hopping into a small, stationary but bobbing sport fishing boat.

Reggio powers their boat up to the stern of the first ninety-foot vessel, which dwarfs their boat in size. After waiting a moment to catch the right wave, he jams the bow of his boat into one of the huge bumper-tires slung from the stern of the shrimper.

Young climbs hand-over-hand up the big tire and over the rail. One can't help but think that this is the way pirates of old boarded large cargo vessels.

The working deck of the shrimp boat is deserted. He strides quickly to

Young prepares to clamber up the stern of the large offshore shrimp trawler.

the back door of the cabin, raps on it sharply, and sticks his head inside. You have to move quickly, he explains, because if they happen to see you coming, they could hide evidence.

The crew in the galley is startled by the sudden appearance of an armed man in uniform in their midst. Apparently they didn't see the game wardens' boat coming. Young has to ask for the captain several times, as the Vietnamese fishermen's English skills are weak and Young can't speak Vietnamese at all. The captain is catching some sleep in his bunk room.

After he is roused, Young patiently asks the sleepy-eyed man for the vessel's U.S. Coast Guard registration papers and the required federal shrimping permit. The crew members are constantly chattering in their native tongue, and because he doesn't know what they are saying, Young is careful to keep them in sight at all times. He is firm but almost deferentially courteous during the entire time in the cabin.

While the skipper is retrieving his paperwork, Young opens and quickly checks the galley refrigerator and freezer as well as all the cabinets in the floating kitchen. He later explains that it is not unusual for crewmen to take illegal fish from the freezer or refrigerator and hide them in the cabinets if they spot the game wardens early enough. Then he checks the forecastle.

The bewildered crewmen watch him with their mouths agape.

The shrimp boat captain and game warden review the state and federal license and registration paperwork necessary for the operation of the vessel.

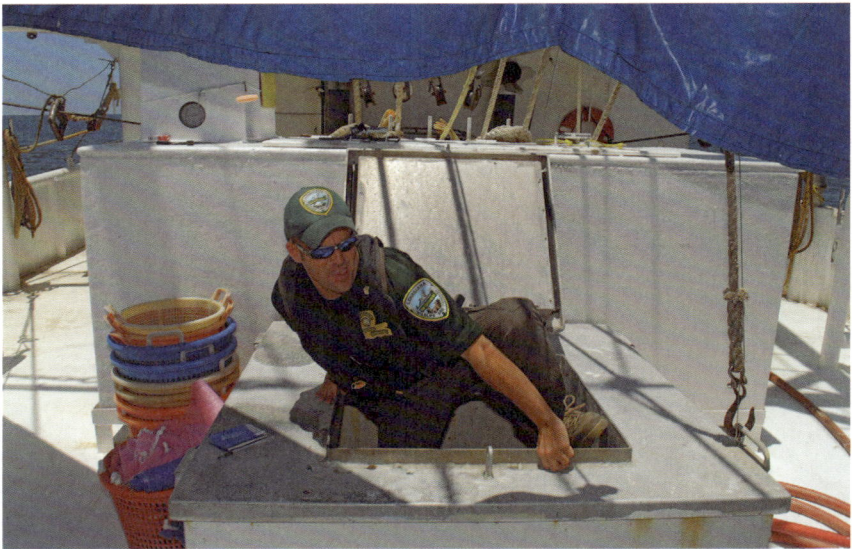

Young descends into the shrimp vessel's freezer hold.

All the paperwork checks out and Young informs the captain that he must check his catch, which is stored in a freezer hold. Before going in the hold, the game warden does a quick tap on his radio to make sure that it is where it is supposed to be. He is most vulnerable while he is in the bowels of the vessel.

After opening the deck hatch, he descends into the yawning hole. It is cold; the thermometer shows 20 degrees below zero. Hoar frost covers everything in the cavernous hold.

Mesh bags resembling onion sacks contain either shrimp or fish. The fish are all of species that are legal for the shrimpers to possess—flounders, cutlassfish, and kingfish, commonly called channel mullet.

His work done, he closes the hatch and exits the vessel as smoothly as he boarded it.

The boarding of the next shrimp vessel is a repeat of the first. The shrimp boat's huge diesel engine roars intimidatingly as Reggio closes in over the wheel wash produced by its big propeller.

Young again does the boarding. Here, he finds a paperwork problem. For some reason the captain, who is also the owner, has not renewed his federal shrimping permit. This could have consequences far greater than the ticket that Young issues to him. The permits are limited entry permits, and allowing their expiration may be grounds for nonrenewal.

The boarding routine is repeated over and again with each shrimp vessel that they stop. All the captains and crews are of Vietnamese extraction, and communications are challenging. During each boarding, Reggio is nervous until he gets his partner back. Much of the time Young is out of sight, either in the vessel's cabin or in the hold.

There are no more shrimp vessels nearby, so they change pace and go back to checking recreational fishermen. All are okay except for one boat. There, the four anglers have limited out on red snapper and cobia, and have two king mackerel and a mangrove snapper. But they also have two redfish.

The skipper, from Houma, is chagrined to the point of indignation that he will receive a citation for the redfish. He admits to retaining redfish in federal waters for years, somehow reasoning that repeatedly breaking the law should exempt him from its provisions. Young is polite but businesslike.

At 3 p.m., Reggio and Young return to Venice to set up in Tiger Pass and Grand Pass to check incoming boats. On the way in, Reggio stops to pick up a floating plastic bag that once held fifty pounds of salt. "These are engine-killers," he explains. Salt from these bags is commonly used on

After each boarding, Villere Reggio, who has been standing by with their boat, runs it to the stern to pick up Young.

shrimp boats, and apparently the wayward bag has blown off such a boat.

As Young predicted, there are plenty of boats to check. The game wardens ask the occupants of each boat that they stop to produce life jackets, unless they are wearing them. Registrations are also scrutinized and the boaters are asked if they have been fishing.

If so, they check their catches. Two things become obvious. First, the Venice area provides good fishing. Fish of every species imaginable are in the anglers' ice chests, from speckled trout to yellowfin tuna. Second, Venice is a fishing hub recognized by anglers from throughout the Gulf states. In the few hours left to them, the game wardens check fishermen from Texas, Mississippi, Alabama, and Florida. These are people in their own boats, not just riding with charter guides.

Charter guides do make up a large percentage of the Louisiana boats, though. Reggio comments that an increasingly common problem is people guiding in federal waters without having the required federal permits. The permits are under limited entry to control the charter boats' impact on the fishery. It seems that a growing number of budding offshore guides aren't deterred by the slim availability of permits. They just fish without them.

Grand Pass is a hornets' nest of boat traffic of all kinds—oilfield vessels and commercial fishing boats as well as recreational fishers. While Reggio is picking up Young from a boarding of a Mississippi family's fishing boat, one of the many passing boats (absolutely none of which slow down) creates a wake that catches the big Whaler wrong and throws its bow into the rear side of the other boat, leaving a scratch. It is superficial, but a scratch nonetheless.

Both the man and the woman in the boat flare up immediately. "You got a credit card?" the man barks.

"Look what you did. I can't believe what you did," the woman moans while glaring at the two men. "You hit our motor, too," she adds, although it seems obvious that no contact was made there.

The men do the best that they can to apologize and explain that the department will make good their damage. They write down telephone numbers for both the department's regional office and the Baton Rouge headquarters on a slip of paper and give it to them.

As they pull away from the patrol boat, the man and woman can be heard over the noise of their motor, off into the distance, grousing about the incident. In spite of the accident's being nearly unavoidable, the two game wardens are unhappy as well.

The next boat has an Alabama registration and four Alabama anglers who are happy about catching their limit of big red snappers. Young counts the fish once, then he counts them again. The numbers are the same—nine fish, one over the limit.

The man at the helm cheerfully takes responsibility. "I'm from Alabama and I can't count," he explains. One of the passengers laughs and adds, "I'm in lumber sales, but obviously I don't count the lumber tickets." The boat's driver accepts his ticket gracefully and they surrender their smallest snapper, which they identify as the last one caught, to the game wardens.

In Tiger Pass, Young's sharp eye catches a forty-foot shrimp trawler riding low in the water, but without shrimp trawls. "I wanna check that boat," he states assertively to Reggio, who obliges by attempting to push the bow of their boat up to the stern of the trawler.

The trawler makes a hard right-hand turn and the game wardens' boat loses contact with it before Young can get on board. Immediately, two Vietnamese men run out of the rear door of the trawler's cabin to a large ice chest on the rear deck. One man, who is later identified as the captain, flings open the lid of the ice chest and both men immediately start throwing great gobs of fish fillets overboard.

The alarmed Young sees armloads of evidence sinking in the murky river waters and screams at Reggio to close the gap. But it is difficult. The fishing boat is moving at a good clip and still turning right. Meanwhile, fish fillets are flying through the air.

When their boat finally begins to close in again, Young leaps across the gap between the two vessels, grabs the man, pushes him away from the ice chest, and then slams the lid shut. The other man backs up slightly. Then both men become aggressive.

First, the fortyish captain feints a move on Young. The game warden extends his arm palm outward toward the man and rests the web between the fingers and thumb of his other hand on his service weapon. "Get back," he screams.

With his attention focused on the captain, the other man, who looks to be in his sixties, makes a move toward Young. "Back up," Young shouts as he turns slightly to face him. These aren't kids. They are grown men and they know what they are doing.

Then the captain, with his chest puffed out like that of a strutting pigeon, attempts to close in again. Young catches the movement and warns him off. He switches his attention from man to man until they calm down.

Meanwhile, Reggio is helpless. If he cuts the power on his boat to go to Young's assistance, the trawler, which is still under power, will pull away immediately. If he leaves the controls of his boat while it is in gear to go to the bow to tie up to the shrimper, a very real possibility exists that the patrol boat may go out of control.

The fishing boat, which is now running bow-on toward a commercial seafood buyer, seems to be running way too fast to avoid a collision with the dock. Reggio, who can't see that a third person is in the wheelhouse of the boat, screams at Young that the vessel's helm is unattended and that a collision is likely.

At the last moment, the man running the trawler puts it in reverse and Reggio has to react to avoid damage to the boats. Meanwhile, Young checks the ice chest and, to his chagrin, finds that the two men succeeded in throwing every fillet overboard.

He begins to check the other ice chests on the deck. At each one, the boat's captain, wearing a fierce scowl on his face, attempts to reach in to interfere. Young pushes him aside each time and orders him to keep his hands where they can be seen. While Young searches, he keeps watching the older man out of one corner of his eye.

After the boat is secured to the dock, Reggio and Young remove its hatch covers. The bins in the hold are popping full of brilliant red vermilion snap-

The boat's holds are full of fish, including brilliantly colored vermilion snappers.

per and smaller, but still large numbers of, blue runners, as well as miscellaneous fish, such as cobias, little tunnys, lesser and greater amberjacks, almaco jacks, and sea chubs.

The two game wardens check the fisherman's licenses and permits. He has a federal reef fish permit, but no permit for red snapper. They strongly suspect that the fillets were from red snappers, which the fisherman is not supposed to possess in any form. Filleted fish, beyond meal-size portions, are illegal to possess on both recreational and commercial fishing boats because they are impossible to identify outside of a laboratory.

While Reggio oversees the off-loading of the fish to the dock to make sure that no prohibited species are present, Young begins to write the tickets. They will be for failure to keep saltwater fish intact and for intentional concealment or destruction of illegal fish.

The fisherman, who a short time ago was openly aggressive, now turns supplicating. "Please, please; just bait, just bait," he wails plaintively.

"No, no, no," Young answers firmly.

"First time, first time; please, please," keens the fisherman in strongly accented English. He has seated himself directly in front of Young so that he can look directly into his eyes.

"Do you think I am stupid?" asks Young. "The answer is the same—no, no, no." But Young does ask Reggio to radio Dispatch to check if the man has had prior charges.

Reggio tells Young that he has three priors, two of which were for federal fisheries violations. While the two wardens talk, the crimson stream of vermilion snappers continues as if the boat's holds have no bottom.

Only when the man is presented his tickets to sign does he become silent.

It's getting late in the day, but boats returning from fishing still clutter the passes. Since the men are on federal patrol, paid for by the National Oceanic and Atmospheric Administration's National Marine Fisheries Service, they focus on boats that they judge likely to have fished offshore. The size and hull design of a boat can indicate whether the boat is likely to be used offshore. So can the presence of the heavy-duty rods and reels used for offshore species.

The rod and reel thing doesn't always pan out though. In checking a boat with only medium-weight tackle aboard, they spy the tip of what can only be a tuna's tail sticking out from under the lid of a large icebox. The men proudly open the box to display a yellowfin tuna to the wardens. Incredibly, they subdued the big fish with freshwater bass fishing tackle.

Then Young asks them for their Highly Migratory Species Permit. The anglers look at each other with that "Huh?" look in their eyes. They don't have one. Young climbs back in the patrol boat to confer with Reggio. "We have to take their tuna. I don't think that there is anything we can do." Reggio agrees, then generously tells Young that he should be the one to tell them.

Young turns to the anglers and says, "There is no easy way to break this to you. You are going to receive a ticket and you will lose your tuna. You need an HMS Permit and it is your responsibility to get it."

Resignedly, one of the crestfallen anglers says, "We are trout fishermen and didn't know." Then they actually help Young transfer the creature's carcass from their boat into the game wardens' boat. Young provides the cordial men with the twenty-four-hour National Marine Fisheries Service hotline telephone number so that they can get a permit before they fish tomorrow.

On the way to find a facility to weigh the fish and store it until it can be picked up for donation to a charity, Young says, "Those were sure nice guys.

People almost always get mad when you have to take their tuna." The commercial dock they were at earlier in the day is now closed, but a marina agrees to weigh the fish and hold it for a day in their cooler. It tips the scales at 89.6 pounds.

The day is shot. It has been nonstop action in the blistering heat and both men will welcome the air conditioned refuge of their trucks' cabs.

Young sits pensively for a moment, sips on a bottle of water, and murmurs softly to himself, "Just another day in Venice."

Reggio prepares to off-load the confiscated yellowfin tuna for overnight storage.

26

THE LAST PATROL

For almost a year, I've had the privilege of riding with Louisiana game wardens all across the state. Now, I am lost in thought as my truck perks down Highway 56, paralleling Bayou Peitit Caillou. This will be my last patrol.

My feelings are deeply mixed. It is hard to believe that I won't spend another day on the water, another night in a truck staring out into the blackness over a green field. The shield-shaped shoulder patch has become my companion.

I know that I will miss the agents. They came in all shapes and sizes, but they were all highly trained professionals and they opened their world to me—a world that before this had existed only in my imagination. I know that I will also miss the outdoors people that they interact with, even the miscreants.

But on the other hand, I am eager to share my story with others, something that I can only do if I step out of the field and finish my writing. Still, I have a lump in my throat.

It is 12 noon on a beautiful day. Great big, white cumulus clouds float against a blue topaz sky. Yes, it's hot. Louisiana is always hot in late summer. But compared to the three-week stretch of 100-plus degree temperatures we experienced earlier in the summer, 92 degrees feels almost comfortable.

I am going to meet Sergeant Richard Purvis and Senior Agent Stephen Rhodes for a noon-to-midnight hitch. The weatherman has predicted a high probability of rain, but right now I can't see it happening.

The two thirty-nine-year-old men are waiting for me when I get there five minutes ahead of time. I had already interacted with Purvis a good bit, as he is serving his second term as president of the Louisiana Wildlife Agents Association. He is engagingly friendly, and speaks with a soft southern lilt rather than the more common Cajun brogue of Terrebonne Parish. Indeed, his family hails from Arkansas. His father brought them here when he went to work in the oilfields of coastal Louisiana.

He is fit and trim and looks taller than his five feet, ten and a half inches in height. His scalp is shaved as bare as a billiard ball. "Oh man, it's just convenient," is his explanation for his choice of hairstyle.

Rhodes is slightly taller, at an even six feet, and has a larger body frame. His neatly trimmed, almost black hair is short by "civilian" standards, but makes him look positively hirsute when the two men stand next to each other and take their caps off.

When Rhodes takes off his sunglasses and puts on his regular spectacles, his appearance changes. His hazel eyes burn with native intelligence. The eyes, accented by dark, full, bushy eyebrows, give him a scholarly appearance.

It doesn't take long for his quick wit to become apparent. After I go through the drill of explaining to the two men how to deal with having a photographer and writer in the boat with them, Rhodes, with an utterly straight face, informs me that he has an issue with my taking photographs of him.

"I don't like images made of me; they might steal my soul." I have to pause and look for a break in his granite-like demeanor to see if we have a problem. Finally, one corner of his mouth twitches and I realize that I have been had.

Richard Purvis (l) enjoys Stephen Rhodes's (r) wry sense of humor.

Instructions done, Purvis guides the patrol boat into the Houma Navigation Canal and immediately apologizes for our ride today. "My boat is in the shop with a steering problem," he explains. "Everyone's boat is broken; this boat is from the pool."

It looks fine to me and I tell him so. He looks at me and raises an eyebrow.

As the boat idles away from Cocodrie, Purvis explains the day's plans. Until near dark, they plan to focus on boating safety and sport fishing checks in the interior marshes. It's a Sunday, and while Sundays aren't as busy as Saturdays, there should be some recreational fishermen on the water.

Near dark, they will take the boat farther south, near the "inside-outside line," the demarcation between waters presently closed for shrimping (inside) and those that are still open to shrimpers (outside). Temptation is great to fudge the line and trawl in closed waters, which, according to Purvis, are loaded with big shrimp. The season will open soon, and some shrimpers are impatient.

"We've made some good closed season shrimping cases down there lately," he explains, adding, "But we don't want to go down there too early in the day. We don't want to be especially visible and advertise our presence right now."

Right out of the gates, the game wardens intercept a sport fisher. As the two boats near each other, Rhodes moves to the bow to stabilize them. Immediately, loud laughter breaks out. Their first stop of the day nets a boat with Lane Kincaid, a north Louisiana game warden, and his family out for a day on the water.

After some quick pleasantries, the two boats break off from each other and Purvis and Rhodes resume their patrol. A brisk, hot wind, strangely enough feeling almost dry rather than humid, is blowing from the south.

The next boat holds a couple fishing, with an absolutely cute-as-a-button four-year-old boy who is casting his rod and reel tenaciously. Purvis greets them openly, promising to be quick. As the game wardens' boat pulls next to his, the youngster eyes the wardens suspiciously before deciding to give Rhodes "five."

Life jackets and licenses are checked and Purvis steps into their boat to check the fish in their ice chest. As they pull away, both men wave to the boy, whose eyes never leave the game wardens.

They check two more boats, one of whom does not have enough life jack-

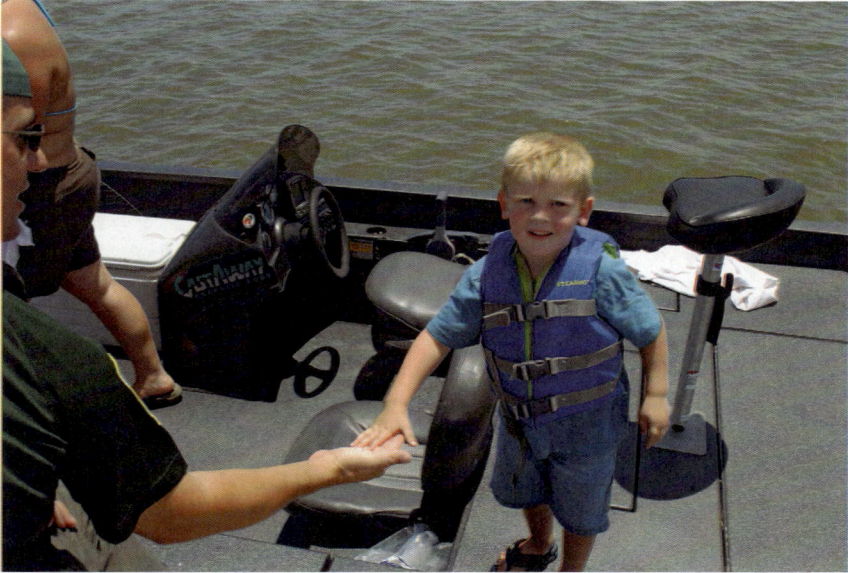

A young fisherman watches the two game wardens carefully.

ets. Purvis gives them a "loaner," explaining where it must be returned to and when. Rhodes writes a warning citation, which does not carry a fine.

Next, they stop at a camp and talk to the owners, who are loading their boats to go in. Then boat traffic and fishermen dry up. The two men comb the marsh: Bayou Sale, Bayou Colyell, Bayou Grand Caillou, Lake Hackberry, Treasure Bayou, Dog Lake, Bay de Mongles, and Four Island Bayou.

Nothing!

The closest thing to activity the two men can find is a capsized boat. Its bottom is encrusted with oysters, so it has been in this condition for some time. Nevertheless, its low profile, almost at water level, makes the derelict hull a serious hazard to boaters.

The two men repeatedly try to find some place to tie a towrope, but find nothing. Then they try to push it up to the bank with their boat, but it resists being moved. Since they can't move it and they have nothing to mark it with, they make a mental note to bring a drill with them next time to make holes in the hull so that attaching a towrope will be possible.

What the afternoon is missing in activity is made up for in beauty. The marsh is still wearing its summer coat of green. Rustic camps fleck the banks

Both men worry about leaving the capsized hull in place, but they have no way of moving it.

of tortuous bayous. Most of them sport a single rectangular-framed wharf net that is lowered into the water during shrimp season to catch shrimp and bait fish for sport fishing.

The ebbing tide has exposed flat after flat of gnarly clumps of oysters to view. Sea birds wheel and dive on schools of shrimp that speckled trout and other fish predators drive to the water's surface.

An envelope of peace surrounds us. The chatter of the wardens' communications radios faintly punctuates the zone created by the hum of the twin 150-horsepower outboard motors. With their baseball caps turned backward, the two wildlife agents look like predatory hawks as they face into the wind.

The only cloud on the day is, well, a cloud.

It is an ugly and ominous blue-gray color and it is dragging a sweeping gray broom of precipitation beneath it. But it's still far to the north, and doesn't seem a threat.

In late afternoon, Purvis powers the nose of the patrol boat up on the marsh vegetation on a lee shore. They will wait for darkness to mask their movement down through Pelican Lake and Bay Round. The plan is to work

Purvis's concerns about the patrol boat's reliability would prove well-founded.

the Whisky Pass and Caillou Boca area, looking for shrimpers who may try to open their season a little early.

They aren't there five minutes before Purvis grumps, "I wish darkness would fall; I'm not good at sitting. It's too bad there aren't more recreational fishermen out, but fishing has been slow and today the wind is really blowing."

While we wait, we talk about what took them into this line of work.

Purvis, with a wry grin, says, "There's nothing else to do in south Louisiana, so you might as well hunt and fish. And that is what I did when I was younger. Because I'm an outdoorsman, the thought of being a game warden always intrigued me."

He goes on, "Out of high school, I joined the army for four years and was a military policeman. When I got out I worked for a while in the Orleans Parish Sheriff's Office as a corrections officer. Law enforcement was the only job skill I had.

"So, because I had an interest in being a game warden, I applied, and got accepted on the first try." Sensing that he left himself vulnerable to a verbal jab by Rhodes and seeing Rhodes's mouth opening, he quickly adds, "They must have been scraping the bottom of the barrel."

Rhodes's path was more poignant. Coming out of high school, he says, he played around in college and didn't make it. Then he worked in the oilfields offshore until he realized that most of his coworkers there were missing fingers. Deciding that he wanted to keep all rather than some his phalanges, he worked his own way through college, getting a B.A. in government.

But the degree didn't result in an instant career. Rhodes worked as a handyman until he got married, and then a while after. Only when the couple decided to have children did Rhodes realize that being a handyman, however well-paid, was not good enough in the long run.

So, in his early thirties and still not settled in a career, he applied for and got a job as a juvenile parole officer. The day he took the job, he walked into his office and looked out the window at the Region 9 game wardens' office across the street.

Every day he watched the comings and goings at the game wardens' office. He says that he said to himself, "That's where I need to be. I love being in the outdoors."

The parole officer's job produced more than a few frustrations for him. He didn't feel that he was really helping people within the system that existed. He provides an example.

"I had a kid of about fourteen who had just been paroled. I explained to him that while he was on probation he had to stay away from negative influences and bad people. And he had to attend school regularly. I told him that he would be drug screened at least once every three months and that failure would get his probation revoked.

"He looked at me and just flat said, 'I can't stay away from drugs.' I didn't know what to say. I asked him, 'What do you mean you can't stay away from drugs?'

"He said, 'Every time I go home there's drugs all over the house. My mom is passed out on the couch and she's got it lying around everywhere.'

"I can't tell him not to go home; I don't have any place to send him. So I tell him that I will have to notify Child Welfare, and in the meantime to try to stay clear and off drugs.

"You get a sense of hopelessness.

"It's a common thing. Kids are broken at home—destroyed before we can get to them. The best we can do are Band-Aids. The recidivism rate is through the roof, 60 percent of what we dealt with. Then, once a kid comes back on the second bite, they have the system figured out. They know we can't do anything.

"Here, I can help people, plus I love being outside."

As Rhodes is talking he is keeping a wary eye on the bad weather looming to the north. Purvis, who is facing south, doesn't see it, so the discussion continues.

Purvis pipes up. "Once you do this for a while, you are ruined for anything else—too much fun. I guess I could do other things if I had to, but. . . .

"It's not so much a job; it's a lifestyle. The people that leave the job can't live the lifestyle."

"I agree 100 percent," says Rhodes. "The ones who go have a peripheral attachment to the outdoors. Making the outdoors your life is different than enjoying it as a hobby. Some people can't take extremes in weather, like twelve hours in the hot sun and . . ."

Purvis is excited and interrupts, "You got to go in where it is all thick and nasty if you are a good game warden. Some of the people we chase are career outlaws. They won't come out with their illegal take. You have to go get them."

"That's the ones I love to get!" interjects Rhodes.

"Oh yeah! Oh what!" says Purvis. His voice is bleeding as much passion as his laid-back demeanor can allow.

Neither of them has been watching the approaching weather in their excitement over talking about catching career outlaws.

They note that the old, hard-core outlaws are fading out. Most of what they see now are crimes of opportunity.

Both men agree that they enjoy boating safety work. Purvis says that it is the one thing that they can do that affects public safety. Rhodes notes that he loves all the personal contact in boating safety work.

Rhodes glances up at the weather and scowls. He calls a bolt of lighting to Purvis's attention. "Whoa, it's black as the ace of spades to the north," the concerned sergeant says. "I've been facing the wrong way."

As if on cue, both men's wives call on their cell phones to give them a severe weather alert. They decide to move to a more sheltered location in anticipation of the approaching storm. Purvis soon has both big motors humming, headed north toward the weather to keep it from cutting them off from more sheltered waters.

Then a warning buzzer sounds. Purvis slows the boat and says to Rhodes, "It's that right motor overheating again. He revs it in reverse and then puts it in forward. The buzzer stops.

Two minutes later, the left engine quits and the boat dramatically slows. Purvis looks at me with an "I told you so" look in his eyes. Try as he might, he can't get the engine restarted.

The remaining engine struggles to get the boat up on plane. Purvis sends Rhodes all the way to the boat's bow, but that isn't enough. So Rhodes brings a big cooler full of ice from the rear of the boat to the bow. With the ice chest and Rhodes in the bow and with Purvis standing in front of the console, the boat slowly crawls out of the hole and begins to plane off.

The priority now is no longer finding shelter in which to wait out the storm and then finishing the patrol. It is to get the badly crippled boat and its passengers back to Cocodrie. Then the remaining engine overheats again. Purvis has to slow down and repeat the whole procedure.

It's an agonizingly slow going and the black weather is drawing closer.

Twice more the engine overheats before the boat makes it to the safety of the landing. It is near dark. As they load the boat on its trailer, it starts to sprinkle rain. The men go to the Louisiana Universities Marine Consortium facility to check the weather forecast on a computer.

It doesn't look good. The outlook is for two hours of rain. The nearest replacement boat is in Houma, and it is small, too small to venture into coastal waters in bad weather. The men scrub the boat patrol.

We linger a while before leaving the shelter of the lab.

When we step outside, we find it raining pitchforks. A maelstrom of wind is tumbling garbage cans around Cocodrie. But it is time to go.

We shake hands and part ways.

No ceremony.

My journey is over.